Survival

GLOBAL POLITICS AND STRATEGY

Volume 62 Number 4 | August–September 2020

'Public debates in Israel over its Iran policies have largely disappeared. Once the Trump administration decided to withdraw from the JCPOA and apply maximum pressure, Israelis across the political and security establishments embraced American policies.'

Dalia Dassa Kaye and Shira Efron, Israel's Evolving Iran Policy, p. 20.

'Even with General Milley's remarkable apology, there have been mutterings of resentment among senior officers and veterans that he put himself in such a compromising position. Anticipating ambushes is, after all, something soldiers are trained for.'

Kori Schake, The Military and the Constitution Under Trump, pp. 35–6.

'Strategic partnership is based on two patently false expectations: on the US side, that Russia will accept American leadership, which it won't; and on Russia's side, that the United States will respect it as an equal, which it isn't.'

Thomas Graham and Dmitri Trenin, Towards a New Model for US–Russian Relations, p. 119.

T0003030

Survival
GLOBAL POLITICS AND STRATEGY
Volume 62 Number 4 | August–September 2020

Contents

Survival
GLOBAL POLITICS AND STRATEGY

The International Institute for Strategic Studies

2121 K Street, NW | Suite 801 | Washington DC 20037 | USA
Tel +1 202 659 1490   Fax +1 202 659 1499   E-mail survival@iiss.org   Web www.iiss.org

Arundel House | 6 Temple Place | London | WC2R 2PG | UK
Tel +44 (0)20 7379 7676   Fax +44 (0)20 7836 3108   E-mail iiss@iiss.org

14th Floor, GBCorp Tower | Bahrain Financial Harbour | Manama | Kingdom of Bahrain
Tel +973 1718 1155   Fax +973 1710 0155   E-mail iiss-middleeast@iiss.org

9 Raffles Place | #51-01 Republic Plaza | Singapore 048619
Tel +65 6499 0055   Fax +65 6499 0059   E-mail iiss-asia@iiss.org

Survival Online www.tandfonline.com/survival and www.iiss.org/publications/survival

Aims and Scope *Survival* is one of the world's leading forums for analysis and debate of international and strategic affairs. Shaped by its editors to be both timely and forward thinking, the journal encourages writers to challenge conventional wisdom and bring fresh, often controversial, perspectives to bear on the strategic issues of the moment. With a diverse range of authors, *Survival* aims to be scholarly in depth while vivid, well written and policy-relevant in approach. Through commentary, analytical articles, case studies, forums, review essays, reviews and letters to the editor, the journal promotes lively, critical debate on issues of international politics and strategy.

Editor **Dana Allin**
Managing Editor **Jonathan Stevenson**
Associate Editor **Carolyn West**
Assistant Editor **Jessica Watson**
Editorial Intern **Niklas Hintermayer**
Production and Cartography **John Buck, Kelly Verity**

Contributing Editors

Ian Bremmer	Bill Emmott	Erik Jones	'Funmi Olonisakin	Angela Stent
Rosa Brooks	Mark Fitzpatrick	Jeffrey Lewis	Thomas Rid	Ray Takeyh
David P. Calleo	John A. Gans, Jr	Hanns W. Maull	Teresita C. Schaffer	David C. Unger
Russell Crandall	John L. Harper	Jeffrey Mazo	Steven Simon	Lanxin Xiang
Toby Dodge				

Published for the IISS by
Routledge Journals, an imprint of Taylor & Francis, an Informa business.

About the IISS The IISS, a registered charity with offices in Washington, London, Manama and Singapore, is the world's leading authority on political–military conflict. It is the primary independent source of accurate, objective information on international strategic issues. Publications include *The Military Balance*, an annual reference work on each nation's defence capabilities; *Strategic Survey*, an annual review of world affairs; *Survival*, a bimonthly journal on international affairs; *Strategic Comments*, an online analysis of topical issues in international affairs; and the *Adelphi* series of books on issues of international security.

SUBMISSIONS

To submit an article, authors are advised to follow these guidelines:

- *Survival* articles are around 4,000–10,000 words long including endnotes. A word count should be included with a draft.
- All text, including endnotes, should be double-spaced with wide margins.
- Any tables or artwork should be supplied in separate files, ideally not embedded in the document or linked to text around it.
- All *Survival* articles are expected to include endnote references. These should be complete and include first and last names of authors, titles of articles (even from newspapers), place of publication, publisher, exact publication dates, volume and issue number (if from a journal) and page numbers. Web sources should include complete URLs and DOIs if available.
- A summary of up to 150 words should be included with the article. The summary should state the main argument clearly and concisely, not simply say what the article is about.

- A short author's biography of one or two lines should also be included. This information will appear at the foot of the first page of the article.

Please note that *Survival* has a strict policy of listing multiple authors in alphabetical order.

Submissions should be made by email, in Microsoft Word format, to survival@iiss.org. Alternatively, hard copies may be sent to *Survival*, IISS–US, 2121 K Street NW, Suite 801, Washington, DC 20037, USA.

The editorial review process can take up to three months. *Survival*'s acceptance rate for unsolicited manuscripts is less than 20%. *Survival* does not normally provide referees' comments in the event of rejection. Authors are permitted to submit simultaneously elsewhere so long as this is consistent with the policy of the other publication and the Editors of *Survival* are informed of the dual submission.

Readers are encouraged to comment on articles from the previous issue. Letters should be concise, no longer than 750 words and relate directly to the argument or points made in the original article.

ADVERTISING AND PERMISSIONS

For advertising rates and schedules

USA/Canada: The Advertising Manager, Taylor & Francis Inc., 530 Walnut Street, Suite 850, Philadelphia, PA 19106, USA Tel +1 (800) 354 1420 Fax +1 (215) 207 0050.

UK/Europe/Rest of World: The Advertising Manager, Routledge Journals, Taylor & Francis, 4 Park Square, Milton Park, Abingdon, Oxfordshire OX14 4RN, UK Tel +44 (0) 207 017 6000 Fax +44 (0) 207 017 6336.

SUBSCRIPTIONS

Survival is published bimonthly in February, April, June, August, October and December by Routledge Journals, an imprint of Taylor & Francis, an Informa Business.

Annual Subscription 2020

	UK, RoI	US, Canada Mexico	Europe	Rest of world
Individual	£162	$273	€ 220	$273
Institution (print and online)	£585	$1,023	€ 858	$1,076
Institution (online only)	£497	$869	€ 729	$915

Taylor & Francis has a flexible approach to subscriptions, enabling us to match individual libraries' requirements. This journal is available via a traditional institutional subscription (either print with online access, or online only at a discount) or as part of our libraries, subject collections or archives. For more information on our sales packages please visit http://www.tandfonline.com/page/librarians.

All current institutional subscriptions include online access for any number of concurrent users across a local area network to the currently available backfile and articles posted online ahead of publication.

Subscriptions purchased at the personal rate are strictly for personal, non-commercial use only. The reselling of personal subscriptions is prohibited. Personal subscriptions must be purchased with a personal cheque or credit card. Proof of personal status may be requested.

Dollar rates apply to all subscribers outside Europe. Euro rates apply to all subscribers in Europe, except the UK and the Republic of Ireland where the pound sterling rate applies. If you are unsure which rate applies to you please contact Customer Services in the UK. All subscriptions are payable in advance and all rates include postage. Journals are sent by air to the USA, Canada, Mexico, India, Japan and Australasia. Subscriptions are entered on an annual basis, i.e. January to December. Payment may be made by sterling cheque, dollar cheque, euro cheque, international money order, National Giro or credit cards (Amex, Visa and Mastercard).

Survival (USPS 013095) is published bimonthly (in Feb, Apr, Jun, Aug, Oct and Dec) by Routledge Journals, Taylor & Francis, 4 Park Square, Milton Park, Abingdon, OX14 4RN, United Kingdom.

The US annual subscription price is $1,023. Airfreight and mailing in the USA by agent named WN Shipping USA, 156-15, 146th Avenue, 2nd Floor, Jamaica, NY 11434, USA. Periodicals postage paid at Jamaica NY 11431.

US Postmaster: Send address changes to Survival, C/O Air Business Ltd / 156-15 146th Avenue, Jamaica, New York, NY11434.

Subscription records are maintained at Taylor & Francis Group, 4 Park Square, Milton Park, Abingdon, OX14 4RN, United Kingdom.

ORDERING INFORMATION

Please contact your local Customer Service Department to take out a subscription to the Journal: **USA, Canada:** Taylor & Francis, Inc., 530 Walnut Street, Suite 850, Philadelphia, PA 19106, USA. Tel: +1 800 354 1420; Fax: +1 215 207 0050. **UK/Europe/Rest of World:** T&F Customer Services, Informa UK Ltd, Sheepen Place, Colchester, Essex, CO3 3LP, United Kingdom. Tel: +44 (0) 20 7017 5544; Fax: +44 (0) 20 7017 5198; Email: subscriptions@tandf.co.uk.

Back issues: Taylor & Francis retains a two-year back issue stock of journals. Older volumes are held by our official stockists: Periodicals Service Company, 351 Fairview Ave., Suite 300, Hudson, New York 12534, USA to whom all orders and enquiries should be addressed. *Tel* +1 518 537 4700 *Fax* +1 518 537 5899 *e-mail* psc@periodicals.com *web* http://www.periodicals.com/tandf.html.

The issue date is August–September 2020.

The print edition of this journal is printed on ANSI-conforming acid-free paper.

Israel's Evolving Iran Policy

Dalia Dassa Kaye and Shira Efron

Concerns about Iran's nuclear ambitions have consumed Israeli decision-makers for decades. Another grave concern is what Israelis perceive as Iran's growing political and military influence in the region, particularly in Lebanon, Syria and Iraq. Capitalising on regional conflicts and political vacuums, Iran is building what Israel views as a 'land bridge' of friendly, largely Shia forces from Tehran to the Mediterranean. Never mind that Iran faces serious limitations to its regional power-projection capabilities and is domestically vulnerable after years of sanctions, repressive rule and poor governance.[1] Or that Israel remains the most powerful and well-equipped military force in the region, supported by its strategic ally, the United States. From the Israeli perspective, Iran's expanding missile capacity and network of non-state militia partners pose a grave threat. Iran's past support for terrorist attacks within Israel itself and against Israelis abroad, combined with inflammatory rhetoric expressing the intention to 'wipe Israel off the map', further elevates the Iranian menace in the Israeli psyche. In short, there is little debate in Israel about Iran's desire or ability to do it harm.

Until recently, however, views on how to deal with the Iranian nuclear challenge diverged. From fissures within the security establishment about the utility of military options and the wisdom of the Iranian nuclear agreement to concerns among political leaders about publicly opposing an American

Dalia Dassa Kaye is Director of the Center for Middle East Public Policy and Senior Political Scientist at the RAND Corporation. **Shira Efron** is a Policy Advisor at Israel Policy Forum.

Survival | vol. 62 no. 4 | August–September 2020 | pp. 7–30   DOI 10.1080/00396338.2020.1792095

president, Israel's positions on Iran policy were more divided over the past decade than is often understood.[2] While a consensus emerged about the need to counter Iran in Syria even before the 2015 Joint Comprehensive Plan of Action (JCPOA) – that is, the nuclear deal – Israeli views on Iran's nuclear programme remained contested.

The most significant divisions arose between Israel's political and security establishments, with the latter taking a less alarmist view of Iran and the nuclear agreement than Israel's political leaders, most notably Prime Minister Benjamin Netanyahu. As a former senior intelligence official noted, 'Israel's security establishment has seen Iran as a serious threat that needs to be managed. For Netanyahu, fearing Iran is like a religion.'[3] These cracks persisted into the first year of the Trump administration, when it was still unclear whether a US president openly hostile to the nuclear agreement would nonetheless remain in the deal. A number of prominent Israeli security officials and analysts, even those originally opposed to the JCPOA, were in favour of the US staying in the agreement and believed it was working to keep the Iranian nuclear challenge contained. Having delayed the nuclear threat, the JCPOA provided Israel with space to shift its attention to the more immediate and prevalent challenge the country faced from Iran, namely its growing influence in Syria.[4]

Once President Donald Trump decided to pull the US out of the JCPOA in 2018, though, domestic debates within Israel over Iran policies dissipated. A new consensus emerged in support of the Trump administration's 'maximum pressure' approach, which many Israelis hope may lead to the collapse of the Islamic Republic. The increased Israeli focus on Iranian entrenchment in Syria and the belief that the JCPOA had empowered Iran regionally brought the political and security communities into closer alignment and overshadowed previous differences over how to handle the nuclear threat and relations with Washington.

Notwithstanding a minority of Israeli analysts who question the effectiveness of the American maximum-pressure approach in achieving its stated goals, there is widespread optimism that the strategy is weakening Iran and its regional networks, particularly following the United States' killing of Iranian Islamic Revolutionary Guard Corps (IRGC) commander

Qasem Soleimani in early January. Even the analysts who question the merits of maximum pressure do not propose an alternative strategy.

The perception of Iranian vulnerability has only grown in the wake of the COVID-19 crisis, which has hit Iran particularly hard as its leaders blundered their response to the outbreak. Israelis are expressing confidence that the twin pressures of the pandemic and economic hardship are leading Iran to pull back its forces from Syria.[5] After an attempted Iranian cyber attack on Israeli water infrastructure in spring 2020, some Israeli analysts viewed Israel's successful retaliatory cyber attack, which shut down an Iranian port, as further evidence of Iranian vulnerability.[6] Such assessments reinforce Israeli support for continuing pressure on Iran despite calls for easing economic sanctions during the pandemic.[7]

It is also worth noting that during the years leading up to the JCPOA, the main opponents to a military strike on Iran were the heads of Israel's security services. This included former Israel Defense Forces (IDF) chiefs of staff Gadi

> *Israeli perceptions of Iranian vulnerability have grown*

Eisenkot, Gabi Ashkenazi and Benny Gantz, as well as Israeli intelligence leaders like ex-Mossad heads Meir Dagan (who died in 2016) and Tamir Pardo, and former Shin Bet chief Yuval Diskin. They mainly feared that a strike without American consent and coordination would not deliver the desired outcome. Today, like-minded individuals who fully back Netanyahu's views dominate the defence establishment. For instance, the Mossad director is Yossi Cohen, Netanyahu's confidant and former national security advisor. The current head of the National Security Council, Meir Ben-Shabbat, is also a close ally of the prime minister. Coming from the Shin Bet, he lacks relevant experience on Iran and in dealing with the international community.[8] But while many Israeli defence professionals still believe that reaching a new agreement with Iran would be the best course of action, they are discouraged from proposing alternative viewpoints by a leadership now tightly aligned with Netanyahu.[9] While newly appointed Defense Minister Gantz may change this discourse, no such change is now apparent.

The result is that Israel's Iran policies are now unusually cohesive, with hardly any divergence about the wisdom of Netanyahu's preferred policy.

With a US administration fully sympathetic with his strident hostility towards Iran and supportive of continued economic and military pressure on that country, Israel's political and security establishments have little to debate. Israelis largely agree that the best approach is for Israel to continue degrading Iran's capabilities in Syria while supporting the American maximum-pressure campaign against Iran through economic sanctions, military strikes in Iraq and Syria, and continued cyber warfare. Many in Israel believe Netanyahu's ultimate strategy is to encourage a US escalation with Iran that would prompt an American military strike against Iran's nuclear sites, which some Israelis believe would be far more effective than any strike the Israelis could carry out on their own.[10] The military option, off the table since 2013, is again a topic of national conversation.

Israel's Iran policies during the Obama administration

For decades, Israel has promoted efforts to expose and prevent an Iranian nuclear-weapons capability. Israeli leaders quickly condemned the final nuclear agreement between Iran and world powers in July 2015.[11] Netanyahu called it a 'stunning historic mistake' and noted that Israel was not bound by the agreement 'because Iran continues to seek our destruction'.[12] Avigdor Lieberman, then the Israeli foreign minister, compared the deal to the Munich agreement with Nazi Germany.[13] Moshe Ya'alon, the Israeli defense minister at the time, said the agreement was built on 'lies and deceit' and that it was a 'tragedy for all who aspire to regional stability and fear a nuclear Iran ... Instead of fighting terror with all its might, the free world has granted legitimacy to Iran's hateful, murderous ways.'[14] Former national security advisor and newly appointed Mossad head Yossi Cohen argued in January 2016 that Iran was an even more formidable threat following the nuclear agreement, saying that as it 'continues to call for Israel's destruction, it upgrades its military capabilities and deepens its grip in our area ... via its tentacles of terror'.[15]

However, such official reactions to the JCPOA masked important debates within Israel about its approach to the nuclear negotiations and the deal itself. Critiques of Netanyahu's opposition to the deal focused largely on how he managed his relationship with the United States during the nuclear negotiations and his public attempts to persuade Congress to derail the agreement. Analysts viewed Netanyahu's speech to both houses at the US Capitol in March 2015 as particularly damaging to Israel's relationship with Washington, jeopardising bipartisan support for Israel with his 'crude interference in American politics'.[16]

Even hardline Israeli leaders like Lieberman who were highly critical of the nuclear deal frowned on Netanyahu's public opposition to the US position that led Americans and others to 'simply laugh at us when we start to talk about Iran'.[17] Former national security advisor Giora Eiland viewed the JCPOA as a 'bad agreement', but argued that a confrontational approach with Washington should be abandoned in favour of a dialogue with the US whereby 'Israel can request returns in the defense world'.[18] Ephraim Sneh, a former minister in Labor governments and a long-time Iran hawk who adamantly opposed the JCPOA, was nonetheless critical of the rift Netanyahu created with the Obama administration by choosing 'to follow the interests of the Republican party rather than Israel's own security interests'.[19]

Disagreement also emerged within Israel about the merits of the deal itself, with Israel's security establishment maintaining a far less hostile view of the JCPOA than the political elite expressed. Some security analysts and officials even saw value in the agreement, and behind closed doors said that it represented the most viable means of ensuring Israel's security in the short to medium term.[20] In a speech to the Washington Institute for Near East Policy in September 2015 following the failure to thwart the deal in the US Congress, Gantz – currently defense minister, then IDF chief of staff – argued that while 'a better deal could have been reached ... I also see the half-full part of the glass here ... And I see the achievement of keeping away the Iranians for ten, fifteen years into the future – and postponing their capabilities of having a nuclear capability – and with the right price.'[21] Gantz went on to argue that it was a 'done deal' that in his assessment did not threaten Israel's security situation: 'We are the strongest country in the [Middle East]; we know how to take care of ourselves ... So I refuse to get hysterical on this.'[22] A former Israeli defence official similarly noted that the Iran issue had decreased in importance for members of the IDF general staff, some of whom believed that too much attention and resources had been invested on Iran.[23] Indeed, in a speech to the Institute for National Security Studies in Tel Aviv in January 2015, IDF Lieutenant-General Gadi Eisenkot, then chief of staff, referred to the nuclear agreement as a 'strategic turning point' that brought risks but also opportunities for Israel.[24]

Others in Israel's military and security community also viewed the JCPOA as successful in at least postponing the Iranian programme, and assessed it was a better outcome than the alternatives.[25] For example, while calling the nuclear agreement 'highly problematic', in part because it 'legitimizes Iran's status as a nuclear threshold state', former military-intelligence head Amos Yadlin saw gains at least in the short term.[26] Former Mossad head Efraim Halevy also argued that the agreement blocked the 'road to Iranian nuclear military capabilities for at least a decade'.[27] Israeli analyst and former general Shlomo Brom called the agreement an 'historic achievement' that shuts off 'Iran's pathway to a nuclear weapon for ten years or more' and that 'is good for Israel and its national security'.[28] Isaac Ben-Israel, chairman of the Israeli Space Agency, argued that 'the agreement is not bad at all, it's even good for Israel … The United States president said that the deal distances Iran from a nuclear bomb for a decade or two, and he is correct.'[29] Even the Israel Atomic Energy Commission, the important Israeli panel that advises the Israeli government on nuclear issues, reportedly endorsed the JCPOA, finding the agreement's inspection measures and constraints on Iranian plutonium and uranium enrichment sufficient to prevent Iran's ability to produce a nuclear bomb.[30]

Some Israeli analysts believe the reported fissures between the security and political establishment over the nuclear deal have been overblown. As one former Israeli security official put it, 'out of 600 ex-generals and officials, 500 were with Bibi [Netanyahu] on Iran, even if those same 500 would be against Bibi on Israeli–Palestinian issues'.[31] The fact remains that prominent voices in Israel's security establishment publicly countered Netanyahu's assessments of the agreement and the way he handled Israel's relationship with Washington.

Despite Israel's official opposition to the JCPOA, it is remarkable how, once the agreement became a reality, the nuclear issue quickly moved off the radar in Israel's political and public discourse. In October 2015, then-defense minister Ya'alon, who had forcefully argued against the agreement, acknowledged the new strategic context in a joint press conference with Ash Carter, the US secretary of defense: 'The Iran deal is a given. Our disputes are over. And now we have to look to the future.'[32] The Israeli intelligence community did not assess that Iran was cheating after the deal, and largely accepted it as a fait accompli.[33] The regional challenges from Iran became a much greater concern than the nuclear agreement, which many in Israel's security establishment had come to accept as largely functioning to contain Iran's nuclear programme.[34] Iran's expanding regional presence through Syria undoubtedly became Israel's greatest security concern.

Iran's regional presence became the greatest concern

When the Syrian civil war broke out in 2011, Israel refrained from intervening. Israeli analysts noted that the war at first actually served the country's interest by substantially weakening the Syrian army and bringing about the US-led effort to dismantle Syria's chemical-weapons arsenal in 2013. Like many other countries, Israel acknowledged the Syrian people's tragedy. It also offered humanitarian assistance to villages in the Syrian-administered portion of the Golan Heights in the hope that these areas would not be used as launch pads for attacks against Israel.[35] During the first years of the war, Israel kept its intervention to a minimum, enforcing two red lines by responding militarily to attacks on its territory and thwarting shipments of sophisticated arms from Iran and Syria to Hizbullah.

While the Israeli campaign in Syria to target Iranian intervention started well before the 2015 nuclear deal, it accelerated as the focus shifted from the nuclear negotiations and as Israel perceived a need to respond to Iran's growing regional posture and its increased ability to threaten Israel in conventional spheres. In 2015, under Eisenkot, the IDF published for the first time an unclassified version of its doctrine. The document introduced a military term now commonly used both in Israel and in the US: the 'campaign between the wars' or, in its Israeli acronymic form, *mabam*.[36] The *mabam*, conceptually an agile campaign, has evolved over time, but its underlying objective is to enable the IDF to enforce its red lines while avoiding escalation to full war. It was at this point that the Israeli concept of Iran building a land bridge to extend its influence from Tehran to Beirut through Iraq and Syria became a key talking point in Washington and within the US think-tank community.[37]

By 2016, Israel assessed that Iran sought to create a permanent presence in Syria, building camps, ports and civilian infrastructure to create a Syrian version of Hizbullah.[38] The *mabam* campaign started as a limited effort, but expanded rapidly in scale and depth. The campaign involved more than 1,000 targets throughout Syria, including Iranian weapons and rocket depots, Iran's command and control headquarters, intelligence and logistics sites, and key IRGC and Hizbullah personnel.[39] Israel had learned its lesson from Hizbullah in Lebanon and vowed not to let Iran establish another front in the Syrian Golan. The shifting balance in Syria led Israel to draw another red line at Iran's build-up of capabilities in Syria that could be used against Israel in a future war. In practice, enforcing Israeli red lines has meant numerous airstrikes in Syria, with no signature strikes in Lebanon but later an expansion to Iraq, as well as a diplomatic campaign to distance Iran, Shia militias and Hizbullah from Israel's border.[40]

Israel's actions in Syria have been constrained by Russia's presence in and air dominance over the country since its 2015 intervention. But Moscow's interests vis-à-vis Iran in Syria are also nuanced, and through an improvement of ties with Russian President Vladimir Putin, Netanyahu's government was able to deconflict its operations with Moscow and continue its campaign. Even an accidental downing of a Russian plane by Syrian air-defence systems following an Israeli strike in 2018 did not disrupt Israel's campaign beyond limiting its freedom of action for a brief period.[41]

In parallel with its military campaign, Israel has consistently appealed to the international community, and primarily to Russia, to keep the Iranians and Shia militias at least 40 miles (65 kilometres) from its Golan border. Despite international agreements, and notwithstanding reports that Russia agreed to heed Israel's requests,[42] these demands have not been met,[43] and Shia militias, including Hizbullah, continue to operate on the Syrian side of the Golan, deployed independently, or often embedded within the Syrian army.[44]

Israel's policy shift during the Trump administration

There is little doubt that Trump's hostile views of Iran and the nuclear deal were welcome news to Netanyahu. Based on discussions with Israeli officials and analysts, as well as reports from that period, it appears that while Netanyahu did actively lobby for the US withdrawal from the JCPOA, he was merely pushing on an open door. Netanyahu and Ron Dermer, Israel's ambassador to the United States, viewed Trump's election as an unexpected opportunity to derail the deal and adjust the United States' Iran policies. According to a former Israeli intelligence official, Trump's ascension to the White House precipitated a 'dramatic change', as Israel's political system, though not its professional echelon, began to actively work against the deal.[45]

They were preaching to the converted. As one former Israeli defence official put it, 'either Bibi conveyed to Trump that he's right or they were just thinking alike'.[46] Another former official observed that while Netanyahu was cautious, he saw Arab leaders in the Gulf pushing for a more aggressive stance against Iran when Trump took office. He no longer saw any reason to be constrained, finding Trump and his advisers to be in 'total sync' with his own views on Iran.[47] Other former intelligence officials similarly observed that while Netanyahu wanted Trump to get out of the deal, Trump himself vowed to withdraw from it during his election campaign and entered office with that intention. Thus, the two leaders were already 'on the same page'.[48]

Israel's exposure of a nuclear archive it captured from Iran, and Netanyahu's dramatic presentation of the material in spring 2018 just days ahead of Trump's decision to leave the deal, appeared to be coordinated with the US administration.[49] At that stage, the expectation in Israel was that the United States would withdraw from the agreement. Nevertheless, Israeli officials viewed the archive discovery and public presentation as important for shaping perceptions in Europe and globally. It failed to do so.[50] While the archive provided additional support for allegations that Iran had lied about its nuclear programme in the past, it did not provide new evidence that Iran was violating the JCPOA. The International Atomic Energy Agency also issued multiple reports confirming Iranian compliance even as the US threatened to withdraw from the agreement.

For this reason, and despite the anti-JCPOA positions of Netanyahu and his close advisers, some important voices in Israel were still arguing in favour of the United States staying in the deal and pushing back against Netanyahu's drive to scuttle the agreement. One former defence-intelligence official suggested that Israel's professional security experts saw the JCPOA as the best solution to a complex problem, particularly since a military attack on Iran was too risky.[51] Unlike Netanyahu, many in Israel's professional security establishment viewed Iran as a rational actor susceptible to containment, and saw the JCPOA as a useful mechanism for accomplishing that goal.[52] Even leaders such as former prime minister and IDF chief of staff Ehud Barak, who had once advocated military options, did not see the value of the US pulling back from the deal unilaterally. As he put it, 'even if America decides to pull out of it, no one will join – not the Chinese, not the Russians, not even the Europeans. It will serve the Iranians.'[53] In a similar vein, former Shin Bet director Carmi Gillon argued that 'doing away with the agreement is no real option. It simply removes from existence something that had been established, that presented certain assets and certain things that are tangible – and replacing that [with] nothing.'[54]

Once Trump formally withdrew the United States from the JCPOA in May 2018, however, debate within Israel ended. Even professional career officials who believed the JCPOA was better than the alternatives began reconsidering its problematic aspects. Those who still believe that reaching a new agreement is the best way forward are discouraged from voicing their opinions.[55]

Maximum pressure

Israel's ongoing concerns about Iran's regional provocations aligned well with the Trump administration's central complaint that the nuclear deal failed to address them. Secretary of State Mike Pompeo's 12-point list of grievances against Iran underscored that for the Trump administration, the nuclear and regional issues could no longer be uncoupled – a position long held by Netanyahu.[56] Connections between Israel's campaign between the wars in Syria and the Trump administration's maximum-pressure approach against Iran became more apparent in the two years following the US withdrawal from the JCPOA.[57]

Indeed, until mid-2018, Israel was not attacking Iranian targets directly in Syria, and instead had largely focused attacks against Iran's delivery of weapons to Hizbullah. But with what Israel saw as a shift in Iran's operational mode in Syria and under the cover of the US withdrawal from the nuclear deal and maximum pressure, Israel's campaign expanded to direct targeting of Iranian officials and assets in Syria. Israel's traditional stance of non-attribution for attacks in Syria also gave way to more open acknowledgement of military action directed against Iran there.[58] With unusual candour, Eisenkot told the *New York Times* that in 2018 alone, the IDF dropped 2,000 bombs in Syria.[59]

In 2018, Naftali Bennett, then the Israeli education minister, warned that such a shift was coming. He vowed that Israel would not let Syria turn into another front for Iran to launch proxy attacks on Israel and contended that Israel's approach of dealing solely with the proxies had proven insufficient. Referring to Iran as an octopus with tentacles, Bennett coined the term the 'octopus doctrine' and stated that from then on Israel should strike the beast's head in response to proxy attacks. He also linked the regional elements to the nuclear issue.[60]

By 2019, Israel had expanded its target list beyond Syria to Iranian targets in Iraq. Israel was worried about Iranian expansion in Iraq as Tehran faced greater constraints in the Syrian theatre due to Russian pressure, Israeli strikes, and Assad's and Hizbullah's desire to avoid escalation with Israel.[61] As Iran moved to Iraq, 'so did Israel'.[62] According to a former Israeli official, the US did not initially welcome the expansion of Israeli strikes to Iraq, but views changed in the White House as the Trump administration saw value in Israel working in parallel to confront Iran.[63] According to former senior US defence officials, while the Pentagon saw Israel's actions in Syria as shouldering the burden of rolling back Iran's influence, US Central Command initially opposed Israel's actions in Iraq, fearing that they would risk American lives.[64]

These policies blurred the distinctions between the nuclear agreement and the regional conflict, particularly as Iran itself began lashing out at regional targets in the Persian Gulf to raise the costs of the American pressure campaign and the reinstatement of sanctions. While it is not clear to what extent Israel and the United States are coordinating their respective attacks in Syria and Iraq against Iranian targets, there is certainly greater mutual awareness of the linkages between Israeli and American military actions against Iran. Though one of the stated American policy objectives of this pressure is a new agreement with Iran – a prospect that Netanyahu deeply opposes – many Israelis perceive the ultimate American goal as regime change in Tehran, on which they see close synergy among Trump's top advisers (particularly Pompeo) and Netanyahu's inner circle.[65] Former officials think Netanyahu too is hoping for regime change, and that every time there are protests on the streets he believes the regime will collapse, as do many in Washington.[66]

Despite confusion about policy aims and the rising costs of maximum pressure and US–Iran escalation, Israelis across the political spectrum support the Trump administration's approach to Iran. Many Israelis were surprised by the US decision to kill Soleimani, likening it to an unexpected gift.[67] In Israeli eyes, the strike offset grave Israeli disappointment when the US did not respond to the attacks on state-owned Saudi Aramco oil-processing facilities in September 2019 that were attributed to Iran. Israeli officials and analysts feared that American forbearance reflected an incli-nation to withdraw from the region, and regarded the Soleimani strike as restoring US deterrence. Despite some concern that his death may worsen the situation for pragmatists in Iran and increase pressure on Iraq to expel the United States, most Israeli analysts believe the killing – and the wider pressure campaign – is working, at least to the extent of degrading Iran's capabilities over the shorter term.

As one former Israeli defence official put it, Israel's post-Soleimani view of US Iran policy is 'so far so good' and 'what's not to like?'[68] In the Israeli calculus, Soleimani's death disrupted Iranian overconfidence and will force the Iranians to be more cautious, since they can no longer predict American responses.[69] The Israeli strategy is to 'ignite things' and force Iran to take steps, such as resuming its nuclear programme, that might lead to more robust American action against the country.[70] After fearing American pas-sivity, some Israelis even believe that the next logical US step would be a strike on Iran's nuclear facilities.[71]

The military option and current Israeli policy

Debates about an Israeli military option against Iran were prevalent through late 2012. According to a former Israeli national-security analyst, until then the Israeli military was ready to act, as Netanyahu and then-defense minister Ehud Barak supported a military attack against Iran even if the security establishment largely opposed it.[72] Whether or not the Israeli military was preparing military plans for actual use or merely for political influence, the military option faded when it became clear that the diplomatic track with Iran was serious.[73]

When the JCPOA was finalised in 2015, the prevailing view among Israeli analysts was that the military option was off the table as long as Iran was adhering to the deal. As one defence reporter put it, 'now, with the entire international community behind the agreement, it's unlikely that there is even one person in the top ranks of the defence establishment – including the chief of the Mossad, the director of the Shin Bet security service and the commander of the air force – who supports an attack on Iran'.[74]

With the Trump administration's withdrawal from the JCPOA, in the context of Israel's optimism about American pressure and its assessment that Iran's vulnerabilities are only increasing, military options to address Iran's nuclear programme have again become salient.[75] In summer 2019, former Israeli National Security Council head Yaakov Amidror stated at a public conference that Israel still needed to plan for a strike on Iran, and that Israel could not rely on or trust the international community to stop Iran from obtaining nuclear weapons.[76] In December 2019, Yisrael Katz, then the minister of foreign affairs, said that an Israeli strike on Iran was a possibility, contending that while US pressure was effective, the sophisticated attack on Saudi Aramco indicated that Iran remains strong and was deterrable only by military threats.[77] The same week, the IDF reported a test launch of a 'rocket engine propulsion system', which reportedly was part of a surface-to-surface *Jericho* ballistic missile, having a range of 4,000 km and capable of carrying nuclear warheads. The test occurred days after reports emerged that Iran had deployed missiles in Iraq and Yemen in violation of the Missile Technology Control Regime, and thus was interpreted as a direct warning to Tehran.[78]

The same month, IDF Chief of Staff Aviv Kochavi assessed that escalation between Israel and Iran was almost inevitable and could even result in war.[79] In early 2020, the IDF's Military Intelligence Directorate published an assessment recommending that, to capitalise on Soleimani's death, the IDF should increase strikes against Iranian forces in Syria to drive them out of the country. Some believe that Netanyahu's strategy supports escalation in order to trigger a US–Iran military confrontation, because he ultimately wants the United States to 'deal with Iran', including striking its nuclear targets.[80] Several Israeli analysts believe Israel could handle an escalation with Iran and would be willing to accept retaliation if the US decisively targeted Iran's nuclear sites.[81]

Reports of a replay of pitched debates between the political and defence establishments about the merits of military options against Iran's nuclear assets appear to be exaggerated.[82] There is far less defence and intelligence pushback than there was before 2012 on account of Washington's overall supportiveness of an aggressive Israeli policy, heightened concerns about Iran's regional activities and its resumption of the nuclear programme, and an Israeli security leadership more closely aligned with Netanyahu.

Public debates in Israel over its Iran policies have largely disappeared. Once the Trump administration decided to withdraw from the JCPOA and apply maximum pressure, Israelis across the political and security establishments embraced American policies. Israel's own military campaigns in Syria and beyond reinforce American pressure against Iran, and the views among the political leadership in both countries are more closely aligned than ever. While Israelis would not welcome a decision by Trump to negotiate a new deal with Iran, they do not believe such a scenario is likely, and many still view the ultimate outcome of maximum pressure as regime change in Tehran. But from Israel's perspective, the result of maximum pressure is less important than continuing the process of applying it.

Indeed, Israel's current Iran policy favours short-term gains and accords little attention to the long term. Many Israeli strategists see advantages in short-term planning, and the benefits of disruptive actions that alter the status quo. In addition, Netanyahu may want to capitalise on Trump's time in office to 'shake things up' in the hope that something better will emerge, because he is convinced that now is the time to deal with Iran and that it is his historic mission to do so.[83] At least officially, Israelis also appear confident that the current pressure is weakening Iran and curtailing its influence. The COVID-19 crisis is only increasing Israeli confidence that the Iranian leadership is vulnerable.[84]

The fact remains that undesirable Iranian actions have continued. Thus, Israeli confidence could be dangerous. Current official Israeli thinking, with no significant countervailing voices in Israel or the US to provide fallback options, may only encourage military escalation and support for more aggressive US military actions against Iran, with unknown or at least poorly thought-through results.

* * *

The wild card, of course, is the impending election in the United States. A transition in Washington from a Republican White House hawkish on Iran to a Democratic one led and substantially staffed by those who served in the administration that initiated and concluded the JCPOA would undoubtedly constrain Israel's options and affect its calculations. This is why the Netanyahu government is working so hard to lock in gains now, prior to the US elections, supporting policies against Iran that may make a return to the JCPOA and engagement with Iran more difficult, if not impossible, regardless of who is in the White House.

In spring 2020, Israel formed a unity government with Netanyahu as the prime minister for the first 18 months. Former IDF chiefs of staff Gantz and Ashkenazi became defense minister and foreign minister, respectively. Both have opposed Israeli military actions in Iran without coordination with Washington. Under Netanyahu, the tenor of Israel's Iran policy in the near to medium term will depend on his own legal situation, as he faces a trial for corruption charges, and on how the US election shapes up. Netanyahu could inflate the threat if his legal troubles appear grim and he perceives that the next US administration is not prioritising Iran.

If Joe Biden becomes president and attempts to bring the US back into the JCPOA and possibly even directly engages Iran, something close to déjà vu all over again may ensue. Netanyahu will reflexively resist such a change in Washington, just as he vehemently opposed Obama's Iran policies at first. Most likely Netanyahu would, as he did before, reach out directly to Jewish groups in the United States and friendly members of Congress to slow sanctions relief or any other measures he viewed as concessions to Tehran. Depending on political tensions, Gantz and Ashkenazi might choose not to push back against such steps, at least not publicly. At the same time, Israel would continue its military campaign against Iran in Syria, which is uncontested by Washington, although the IDF might need to scale back its kinetic strikes in Iraq. If these steps were unavailing, the Netanyahu government might try to provoke Iran.[85] The key would be to maintain a threat level and target list that would not directly place American personnel in harm's way, but that could nonetheless prompt a US response to Iranian escalation. This might involve covert Israeli action in Iran itself, including explosions at sensitive facilities, which would likely elicit an Iranian response but not necessarily pose a direct risk to US assets.[86]

Only a major shift in US policy, such as public rebukes to Israel for spoiling attempts to revive the nuclear agreement that portended long-term damage to the bilateral relationship, would be likely to rekindle debate in Israel about its approach to Iran. As matters stand now, a policy of escalation seems to be the favoured tactic on all sides, imposing few costs on Israel and preserving the legacy of the longest-serving prime minister in Israel's history. If Israel does conclude that the United States is determined to reach an agreement with Iran, it will likely shift its focus from attempting to derail such an agreement to trying to shape it. Israel might then work with Arab Gulf countries to pressure Washington into linking agreement on sanctions relief and nuclear issues to Iranian concessions on ballistic missiles and regional activities. Given the post-JCPOA evolution of US and Israeli policies on Iran, Biden might be more likely than Obama was to consider such a linkage, particularly if it attracted European support. By the same token, Iran's leadership might be less likely to consider it.

Notes

1   See Michael Wahid Hanna and Dalia Dassa Kaye, 'The Limits of Iranian Power', *Survival*, vol. 57, no. 5, October–November 2015, pp. 173–98; and Steven Simon and Jonathan Stevenson, 'Iran: The Case Against War', *New York Review of Books*, vol. 66, no. 13, 15 August 2019.

2   See Dalia Dassa Kaye, *Israel's Iran Policies After the Nuclear Deal* (Santa Monica, CA: RAND Corporation, 2016), https://www.rand.org/pubs/perspectives/PE207.html.

3   Author phone interview with a former senior Israeli intelligence official, 10 April 2019.

4   Amir Rapaport, 'A Year After the Implementation of the Nuclear Agreement with Iran', *Israel Defense*, 5 January 2017, translated by the authors from the original Hebrew, https://www.israeldefense.co.il/he/node/28148; and author interview with former senior Israeli defence official, Tel Aviv, 29 January 2020.

5   See Ben Caspit, 'Iran Seems to Reconsider Military Entrenchment in Syria', *Al-Monitor*, 5 May 2020, https://www.al-monitor.com/pulse/originals/2020/05/israel-syria-iran-russia-us-donald-trump-bashar-al-assad.html.

6   Judah Ari Gross, 'Cyberattack on Port Suggests Israeli Tit-for-tat Strategy, Shows Iran Vulnerable', *Times of Israel*, 19 May 2020, https://www.timesofisrael.com/cyberattack-on-port-suggests-israeli-tit-for-tat-strategy-shows-iran-vulnerable/.

7   See Amos Yadlin and Ari Heistein, 'Calls to Reduce Pressure on Iran's Regime Are Reckless and Misguided', *Times of Israel*, 7 April 2020, https://www.timesofisrael.com/calls-to-reduce-pressure-on-irans-regime-are-reckless-and-misguided/.

8   Amir Rapaport, 'The Former Reporter from Dimona Who Will Soon Become Head of the NSC', *Israel Defense*, 18 August 2017, translated by the authors from the original Hebrew, https://www.israeldefense.co.il/he/node/30767.

9   Author interview with former senior national-security official, Tel Aviv, 29 January 2020; and author phone interview with senior defence official, 20 April 2020.

10 Author interview with multiple former senior Israeli defence officials, Tel Aviv, 28–29 January 2020.

11 For official statements and the full text of the agreement, see 'Joint Comprehensive Plan of Action', US Department of State, https://2009-2017.state.gov/documents/organization/245317.pdf. See also Dassa Kaye, *Israel's Iran Policies After the Nuclear Deal*.

12 Barak Ravid, 'Netanyahu: Iran Nuclear Deal Makes World Much More Dangerous, Israel Not Bound By It', *Haaretz*, 14 July 2015, http://www.haaretz.com/israel-news/1.665821.

13 Moran Azulay, 'Negotiators Reach Historic Nuclear Agreement with Iran', Ynet News, 14 July 2015, http://www.ynetnews.com/articles/0,7340,L-4679591,00.html.

14 'Israeli Leaders, Some Jewish Groups Condemn Final Iran Nuclear Deal', Jewish Telegraphic Agency, 14 July

2015, http://www.jta.org/2015/07/14/
news-opinion/united-states/
israeli-leaders-jewish-groups-
condemn-final-iran-nuclear-deal-2.

15 Ben Caspit, 'New Mossad Chief
Brings Touch of Bond, Lots of
Reality to the Job', *Al-Monitor*, 11
January 2016, http://www.al-monitor.
com/pulse/originals/2016/01/
israel-mossad-yossi-cohen-new-chief-
mideast-chaos-challenge.html.

16 Akiva Eldar, 'Why Bibi Is
Personally Responsible for Iran
Policy Failure', *Al-Monitor*, 14
July 2015, http://www.al-monitor.
com/pulse/originals/2015/07/
iran-agreement-powers-netanyahu-
bush-clinton-obama-israel.html#.

17 Marissa Newman, 'Liberman:
Netanyahu Incapable of Stopping
the Iran Deal', *Times of Israel*, 24 July
2015, http://www.timesofisrael.com/
liberman-netanyahu-incapable-of-
stopping-the-iran-deal/.

18 Yaakov Lappin, 'Eiland Calls for
Discreet Talks with DC to Ensure
Long-term Obligations', *Jerusalem Post*,
15 July 2015, http://www.jpost.com/
Israel-News/Politics-And-Diplomacy/
Eiland-calls-for-discreet-talks-
with-DC-to-ensure-long-term-
obligations-409006.

19 Mazal Mualem, 'Former
Israeli Minister Calls Removal
of Iran Sanctions a "Black
Day"', *Al-Monitor*, 18 January
2016, http://www.al-monitor.
com/pulse/originals/2016/01/
ephraim-sneh-deputy-defense-
minister-iran-nuclear-agreement.html.

20 Author phone interview with senior
defence official, 20 April 2020.

21 Rebecca Shimoni Stoil, 'Former

IDF Chief Says "Hysteria" Over
Iran Deal Is Unwarranted', *Times
of Israel*, 25 September 2015,
https://www.timesofisrael.com/
former-idf-chief-says-hysteria-over-
iran-deal-is-unwarranted/.

22 Benny Gantz, 'Israeli National
Security in a Changing Regional
Environment', 8th Annual Zeev Schiff
Memorial Lecture on Israeli National
Security, Washington Institute for
Near East Policy, 25 September 2015,
http://www.washingtoninstitute.
org/policy-analysis/view/
israeli-national-security-in-a-
changing-regional-environment.

23 Author interview with former
Israeli defence official, Tel Aviv, 17
January 2016.

24 For analysis of Eisenkot's speech, see
J.J. Goldberg, 'Israel's Top General
Praises Iran Deal as "Strategic
Turning Point" in Slap at Bibi',
Forward, 26 January 2016, http://
forward.com/opinion/331714/
israels-top-general-praises-iran-deal-
as-strategic-turning-point-in-slap-at/.

25 One former defence official argued
that there was no better alternative to
postponing an Iranian bomb for five
to ten years, and said he did not think
there was a better deal than what was
agreed to in the JCPOA. Interview
with former defence official, Tel Aviv,
17 January 2016.

26 Amos Yadlin, 'Following the
Problematic Nuclear Agreement:
Scenarios and Recommendations',
INSS Insight No. 722, Institute
for National Security Studies, 20
July 2015, http://www.inss.org.
il/?id=4538&articleid=10100.

27 Interview with Efraim Halevy, *PBS*

NewsHour, PBS, 21 August 2015, http://www.pbs.org/newshour/bb/expecting-iran-try-cheat-need-deal-says-former-mossad-chief/.

28 Hardin Lang and Shlomo Brom, '6 Biggest Myths about the Iran Nuclear Deal', *National Interest*, 29 July 2015, http://nationalinterest.org/feature/6-biggest-myths-about-the-iran-nuclear-deal-13443.

29 Quoted in Mazal Mualem, 'Israeli Media Drowns Out Pro-Iran-deal Voices', *Al-Monitor*, 21 July 2015, http://www.al-monitor.com/pulse/originals/2015/07/netanyahu-herzog-lapid-iran-nuclear-deal-ben-israel-expert.html.

30 Chaim Levinson, 'Israel's Nuclear Advisory Panel Endorses Iran Deal', *Haaretz*, 22 October 2015, http://www.haaretz.com/israel-news/.premium-1.681918.

31 Author interview with former senior Israeli military official, Tel Aviv, 13 January 2016.

32 Barbara Opall-Rome, 'Israeli DM: Iran Deal Is Done, Time to Look Ahead', *Defense News*, 28 October 2015, http://www.defensenews.com/story/defense/policy-budget/leaders/2015/10/28/israeli-dm-iran-deal-done-time-look-ahead/74754218/.

33 Author interview with former intelligence official, Tel Aviv, 28 January 2020.

34 A former Israeli defence official suggested that the predominant IDF and Mossad assessment (and that of most security professionals in Israel) was that the JCPOA has pushed the nuclear issue off the table for at least ten years. Author interview with former Israeli defence official, Tel Aviv, 17 January 2016. Despite the consensus that the JCPOA effectively put the Iran nuclear issue on the backburner for up to a decade, some Israeli arms-control experts continued to argue against the agreement. See, for example, Yaakov Lapin, 'A Deal with Gaping Failures', *Jerusalem Post*, 18 July 2015, http://www.jpost.com/Middle-East/A-deal-with-gaping-failures-409287. While noting some positive nuclear rollbacks in the agreement, Ariel E. Levite (a former deputy general at the Israeli Atomic Energy Commission) similarly expressed concern over several elements of the agreement, including its acceptance of continued research and development on advanced centrifuges, and its mechanisms for verifying Iranian compliance and for reimposing sanctions should Iran violate the agreement. See Ariel E. Levite, 'The Good, the Bad and the Ugly Nuclear Agreement', *Haaretz*, 17 July 2015, http://carnegieendowment.org/2015/07/17/good-bad-and-ugly-nuclear-agreement/idjg.

35 Amos Harel, 'Israel Is Changing Its Approach to Syria War amid Assad's Battleground Advances', *Haaretz*, 21 February 2016, https://www.haaretz.com/israel-news/.premium-israel-is-changing-its-approach-to-syria-war-1.5407077.

36 Lt-Gen. Gadi Eisenkot, 'IDF Strategy', August 2015, available in Hebrew at https://www.amutatmabal.org.il/?CategoryID=180&ArticleID=367.

37 See Jackson Diehl, 'Why Iran Won't Give Up Syria', *Washington Post*, 2 August 2015, https://www.washingtonpost.com/opinions/why-iran-wont-give-up-syria/2015/08/02/

b9269fa2-360c-11e5-9d0f-7865a67390ee_story.html; and Franc Milburn, 'Iran's Land Bridge to the Mediterranean: Possible Routes and Ensuing Challenges', *Strategic Assessment*, vol. 20, no. 3, October 2017, https://www.inss.org.il/publication/irans-land-bridge-mediterranean-possible-routes-ensuing-challenges/.

38 Several former defence and intelligence officials we spoke with articulated this view of Iranian intentions in Syria, which they claim is held at the highest levels of Israel's military and security leadership.

39 See Ilan Goldenberg et al., 'Countering Iran in the Gray Zone', Center for New American Security, 14 April 2020, https://www.cnas.org/publications/reports/countering-iran-gray-zone; and Michael Herzog, 'Iran Across the Border: Israel's Pushback in Syria', Washington Institute for Near East Policy, Policy Notes No. 66, July 2019, https://www.washingtoninstitute.org/uploads/Documents/pubs/PolicyNote66-Herzog-WEB-4.pdf.

40 Herzog, 'Iran Across the Border: Israel's Pushback in Syria'.

41 Daniel Byman, 'Israel's Four Fronts', *Survival*, vol. 61, no. 2, April–May 2019, pp. 167–88.

42 See Alexander Fulbright, 'Israel, Russia Said to Reach Secret Deal on Pushing Iran Away from Syria Border', *Times of Israel*, 28 May 2018, https://www.timesofisrael.com/us-russia-reach-syria-agreement-to-distance-iran-from-golan-heights-reports/; and David M. Halbfinger and Ben Hubbard, 'Netanyahu Says Putin Agreed to Restrain Iran in Syria', *New York Times*, 12 July 2018, https://www.nytimes.com/2018/07/12/world/middleeast/syria-israel-putinnetanyahu.html.

43 Amos Yadlin and Zvi Magen, 'The Netanyahu–Putin Meeting: What Was Agreed, and What Are Russia's Intentions?', Institute for National Security Studies, INSS Insight No. 1,149, 18 March 2019, https://www.inss.org.il/publication/netanyahu-putin-meeting-agreed-russias-intentions/.

44 See Avi Issacharof, 'Iranian Camouflage: At the Golan Heights, Hizbullah Gives Orders to the Syrian Army', Walla! News, 23 June 2019, translated by the authors from the original Hebrew, https://news.walla.co.il/item/3243028; and Tal Lev Ram, 'IDF: A Commander in the Syrian Army Is Helping Hizbullah Deploy on the Golan', *Maariv*, 10 April 2020, translated by the authors from the original Hebrew, https://www.maariv.co.il/news/military/Article-759291.

45 Author interview with former intelligence official, Tel Aviv, 28 January 2020. According to this former official, Dermer made daily visits to the White House to convince the administration to withdraw from the JCPOA. It was clear to the intelligence community this was a Netanyahu–Dermer effort, as neither had confidence in the professional system. Dermer told this official directly that he was confident Trump would leave the deal.

46 Author interview with former defence official, Tel Aviv, 27 January 2020.

47 Author interview with former National Security Council official, Tel Aviv, 27 January 2020.

48 Author interview with former intelli-

gence official, Tel Aviv, 27 January 2020.

49 Author interview with former intelligence official, Tel Aviv, 27 January 2020. See also David M. Halbfinger, David E. Sanger and Ronen Bergman, 'Israel Says Secret Files Detail Iran's Nuclear Subterfuge', *New York Times*, 30 April 2018, https://www.nytimes. com/2018/04/30/world/middleeast/ israel-iran-nuclear-netanyahu.html.

50 While Israel's removal of the 'atomic archives' from Iran was a daring intelligence mission and brought to light more details on Iran's past nuclear behaviour, most international arms-control analysts did not see the material as contradicting intelligence assessments that Iran had given up its efforts to develop a nuclear-weapons programme. See, for example, Oren Liebermann, 'What Did Netanyahu Reveal About Iran's Nuclear Program? Nothing New, Experts Say', CNN, 3 May 2018, https://www.cnn. com/2018/05/01/middleeast/israel- iran-nuclear-evidence-analysis/index. html. Former Israeli intelligence officials we spoke with also did not view the archive material as contradicting these international assessments.

51 Author interview with former defence official, Tel Aviv, 27 January 2020.

52 Author interview with former defence official, Tel Aviv, 27 January 2020.

53 Mark Landler, 'Ehud Barak, Israeli Hawk and No Friend of Iran, Urges Trump to Keep Nuclear Deal', *New York Times*, 11 October 2017, https:// www.nytimes.com/2017/10/11/us/ politics/trump-ehud-barak-iran- nuclear-deal.html.

54 Quoted in George J. Mitchell, 'Israeli Experts Defend the Iran Nuclear Deal', *Boston Globe*, 13 October 2017.

55 Author phone interview with former senior intelligence official, 20 April 2020.

56 See 'After the Deal: A New Iran Strategy', Speech by Secretary of State Michael R. Pompeo at the Heritage Foundation, 21 May 2018, https://www.state.gov/ after-the-deal-a-new-iran-strategy/.

57 See Amos Yadlin and Assaf Orion, 'The Campaign Between Wars: Faster, Higher, Fiercer?', Institute for National Security Studies, INSS Insight No. 1,209, 30 August 2019, https://www.inss.org.il/publication/ the-campaign-between-wars-faster- higher-fiercer/.

58 Tal Snyder, 'Election Panic or End of the Ambiguity Era: Israel Reveals Its Strikes Outside of Its Borders', *Globes*, 25 August 2019, translated by the authors from the original Hebrew, https://www.globes.co.il/news/article. aspx?did=1001298349.

59 Bret Stephens, 'The Man Who Humbled Qassim Suleimani', *New York Times*, 11 January 2019, https://www. nytimes.com/2019/01/11/opinion/gadi- eisenkot-israel-iran-syria.html.

60 Naftali Bennett, address, Institute for National Security Studies, 12th Annual Conference, 30 January 2018, translated by the author from the original Hebrew, https://www.inss.org.il/ person/bennettnaftali/.

61 Author interview with former intelligence official, Tel Aviv, 28 January 2020.

62 Author interview with former defence official, Tel Aviv, 28 January 2019.

63 Dalia Dassa Kaye, 'Trump Must Not Give Israel a Blank Check in the Middle East', *National Interest*, 15 September 2019; and author interview

with former intelligence official, Tel Aviv, 28 January 2020. After meeting with US Secretary of Defense Mark Esper, Israel's then-defense minister Naftali Bennett stated publicly that Israel was working in tandem with Washington to confront Iran in Iraq and Syria. See Nati Yefet and Judah Ari Gross, 'Bennett: US Agreed to Counter Iran in Iraq While Israel Fights It in Syria', *Times of Israel*, 10 February 2020, https://www.timesofisrael.com/us-agreed-to-fight-iran-in-iraq-israel-to-counter-tehran-in-syria-bennett-says/.

64 Author interview with retired senior US defence official, Tel Aviv, 29 January 2020.

65 Author interview with former National Security Council official, Tel Aviv, 27 January 2020.

66 Author interview with former intelligence official, Tel Aviv, 27 January 2020.

67 Author interview with former National Security Council official, Tel Aviv, 27 January 2020.

68 Author interview with former defence official, Tel Aviv, 28 January 2019.

69 Author interview with former defence official, Tel Aviv, 28 January 2019.

70 Author interview with former intelligence official, Tel Aviv, 28 January 2020.

71 Author interview with former senior Israeli defence official, Tel Aviv, 28 January 2020.

72 Author interview with former National Security Council official, Tel Aviv, 27 January 2020.

73 Author interview with former Israeli defence official, Tel Aviv, 17 January 2016. This former official said that after April 2013, when US negotiations with Iranians in Oman were serious, the Americans told Israeli leaders that they should start preparing for an agreement.

74 Amos Harel, 'Why Netanyahu Deserves Credit for Iran Nuclear Deal', *Haaretz*, 18 July 2015, http://www.haaretz.com/israel-news/.premium-1.666413.

75 For an overview of previous debates about military options against Iran, see Ronen Bergman and Mark Mazzetti, 'The Secret History of the Push to Strike Iran', *New York Times*, 4 September 2019, https://www.nytimes.com/2019/09/04/magazine/iran-strike-israel-america.html.

76 'Panel Discussion: Iran – Putting the Genie Back in the Bottle', Herzliya Conference, 1 July 2019, https://www.idc.ac.il/he/research/ips/pages/2019/hc2019-live.aspx.

77 David Goldberg, 'Foreign Minister Yisrael Katz: "Israeli Strike in Iran Is an Option; We Will Work with Saudi Arabia"', JDN, 8 December 2018, translated by the authors from the original Hebrew, https://www.jdn.co.il/news/1239536/.

78 Yossi Melman, 'Why Would Israel Reportedly Have Missiles That Reach Beyond Iran', *Haaretz*, 11 December 2019, https://www.haaretz.com/middle-east-news/.premium-israel-jericho-missile-test-iran-pakistan-india-yossi-melman-1.8251584.

79 Amos Harel, 'Analysis: Israel–Iran Collision Almost Inevitable, IDF Chief Makes Clear', *Haaretz*, 28 December 2019, https://www.haaretz.com/israel-news/.premium-israel-iran-collision-inevitable-idf-lebanon-syria-iraq-gaza-1.8318914.

80 Author interview with former intelli-

gence official, Tel Aviv, 27 January 2020.

81 Several former officials and analysts we spoke with made this point, and they appeared confident in the ability of Israel to withstand the aftermath of a US military attack on Iran.

82 We did not find strong support in our own interviews for a report that suggested a replay of previous debates. See Yonah Jeremy Bob, 'The Coming Giant Internal Israeli War Over a Nuclear Iran, a 2010 Rematch', *Jerusalem Post*, 12 April 2020, https://www.jpost.com/Israel-News/The-coming-giant-internal-Israeli-war-over-a-nuclear-Iran-A-2010-rematch-624452.

83 Author interview with former intelligence official, Tel Aviv, 29 January 2019.

84 It is important to note that despite the economic implications of the COVID-19 crisis, some leading Israeli analysts do not believe that it has weakened the Iranian regime. Rather, they see the refusal of Washington to approve a loan to Tehran as empowering the hardliners and increasing the anti-American stance in Iran. See 'Live Discussion: Iran in the Days of Coronavirus – Implications for Israel's National Security', Institute for National Security Studies, 20 April 2020, discussion conducted in Hebrew, https://www.inss.org.il/he/event/iran-coronavirus/.

85 Author phone interview with former senior Israeli intelligence official, 20 April 2020.

86 Author phone interview with a former senior Israeli intelligence official, 20 April 2020.

The Military and the Constitution Under Trump

Kori Schake

In the midst of the largest public protests in 50 years, widespread concern about the polarisation of politics, police brutality and racism, and fear about the usurpation of democratic institutions in the United States, the country last month experienced an extraordinary affirmation of military faithfulness to the Constitution. When forced to choose between a president improperly if not illegally pushing it into a repressive and politicised domestic role, and the founding document's protection of liberty and equality, the American military chose the latter course and preserved its relationship with civil society.

Remember Lafayette Square

President Donald Trump considered invoking federal authority to enforce the law and putting the military on the streets to restore order. While that decision was under consideration, riot police forcibly cleared protesters and the president paraded through Lafayette Square, near the White House, with the leaders of the agencies representing coercive force: the attorney general, the secretary of defense, and the chairman of the Joint Chiefs of Staff, who was wearing combat fatigues.

Both the policy and the performance occasioned an outcry. Five former secretaries of defense (including one of Trump's own), three former chair-

Kori Schake leads the foreign- and defence-policy team at the American Enterprise Institute and was deputy director of the IISS. She edited, with Jim Mattis, *Warriors and Citizens: American Views of Our Military* (Hoover Institution Press, 2016).

Survival | vol. 62 no. 4 | August–September 2020 | pp. 31–38   DOI 10.1080/00396338.2020.1792096

men of the Joint Chiefs of Staff and an avalanche of civil-society voices objected. Within two days, Secretary of Defense Mark Esper belayed his call to 'dominate the battlespace' and made public his opposition to invoking the Insurrection Act of 1807.[1] General Mark Milley, chairman of the Joint Chiefs of Staff, issued a directive affirming the military's fidelity to the Constitution and released a video apologising for his failure to uphold the apolitical character of the US military. While reportedly fuming in private, even the president was compelled to conform with this dispensation, giving an anodyne graduation speech at the US Military Academy at West Point and saying he was fine with General Milley's expression of regret.[2]

It was a striking assertion of constitutional propriety on the military's part, and arguably the most important episode in American civil–military relations since Harry Truman fired General Douglas MacArthur for insubordination in 1951. A commander-in-chief attempting to exercise his statutory authority and cynically manoeuvre the military into endorsing his policy choices was instead deserted by civilian and military leaders who committed themselves to the higher authority of the Constitution and repudiated the president's policies. Civic pressure pushed the president himself to validate their opposition.

Trump would not have been the first president to invoke the Insurrection Act, which allows the federal government to supersede the authority of state governors and deploy US armed forces in the United States in limited circumstances. Dwight D. Eisenhower did so to desegregate schools in 1957, and George H.W. Bush to quell the Los Angeles riots in 1992 (although in that case, California's governor and the Los Angeles mayor requested the federal troops). And Trump certainly would not have been the first president to use the military for political purposes. Every president does that in one way or another, because the American military is comfortably the most popular American institution. Presidents crave pictures of themselves with troops, routinely pander to military audiences, amass endorsements from veterans and their service groups, and enlist officers in uniforms rather than civilians in suits to justify their decisions on wars.

What made Trump's actions different was the attempt to use the military domestically to suppress political protest protected by the First

Amendment to the Constitution. For the military, it conjured nightmares of public rejection after the fatal Kent State shootings by National Guardsmen in 1970, activating institutional protectiveness of their symbiosis with the public.

Civil–military relations, American style

In every free society, the military must be conscious that it is sustained by public affirmation. While American military leaders sometimes complain that the military is used as a laboratory for 'politically correct' policies that may impede its combat effectiveness or affront its martial culture, they resolutely did not want to be thrust into the middle of a roiling domestic dispute about police brutality and systemic racism. As of 2015, those from racial- and ethnic-minority groups made up 40% of the active-duty American military.[3] The US military has worked hard to prevent racism in its ranks. The only other instance in which the military has publicly dissociated itself from the White House during Trump's presidency arose when he mused about 'good people on both sides' after a violent white-supremacist rally in Charlottesville, Virginia, in 2017.[4]

Military officers generally don't get to choose whether to support legal orders from the commander-in-chief. They can either obey orders or resign their commissions. Nor should the military sit in judgement of the policy choices or comportment of elected civilian leaders. In this case, however, two extraordinary circumstances prompted the rejection of Trump's policy. Firstly, the president and his senior military adviser, General Milley, violated the norm that the American military does not participate in partisan politics. Secondly, Trump, Esper and Milley militarised the US government's response to a domestic protest. These two factors were crystallised in the president's photo-op in Lafayette Square.

Civil–military relations in the United States are different than they are in most other countries. The military has a degree of structural and cultural influence in American policymaking that is rare in free societies. Militaries in other democracies tend to be more domesticated, less salient in policymaking and less popular. About 82% of Americans trust the military, a proportion several times the levels for any other organisations in political or civic life.[5] Thanking people in uniform for their service is a secular sacrament in American civic life, expected of every politician and practised by much of the population.

There are two main drivers of popular support for the US military. Firstly, the military is accurately considered to be a reliable conveyor belt into the middle class. This has been true since the end of the Second World War, when the GI Bill began subsidising education and home mortgages for veterans; it has been emphatically true in the last three decades as other means of advancement have stalled. While wages have stagnated in most occupations, Congress has raised them for the military every year since at least 2007, and required increases exceeding the US Department of Labor's index of pay in private industry.[6] A whopping 48% of Americans think military pay should be raised further, and only 4% consider it too high.[7] As a result, 84% of military enlistees are paid more than civilians at similar skill levels.[8] Veterans also receive preferential hiring for government jobs, and comprise 31% of all federal employees.[9]

> The public blames political leaders for wars

This does not mean Americans actually know much about their military. Most Americans are off by a factor of six in estimating its size, for example.[10] Most have no direct experience of the military: 45 years into an all-volunteer force, the armed forces constitute less than half of one per cent of the population. The Posse Comitatus Act of 1878 (which generally precludes the domestic use of the military), the availability of the National Guard to state governors and the physical consolidation of troops onto a few large stateside bases have ensured that the only actual exposure most Americans have to the military arises when it supports civilian authorities during natural disasters.

Actually winning wars has less to do with public support than one might imagine. Public backing for the military as an institution endured through the Korean, Vietnam, Iraq and Afghanistan wars. It has even marginally increased for troops fighting so-called endless wars because the public – usually correctly – blames political leaders for the choice of going to war and for errant strategy.

The second driver of public support is that the active-duty military has largely remained aloof from domestic US politics. Being apolitical is a norm that the military cherishes, understanding that it is crucial for maintaining professionalism and objectivity across politically divergent administrations. Yet the American public's commitment to an apolitical military is waning. The public increasingly favours political endorsements and activism by veterans, as displayed by retired generals Michael Flynn and John Allen when they spoke at political conventions in 2016. Reflecting the polarisation of American politics, the public has begun to judge the military as it does the Supreme Court: appropriately apolitical when it supports its policy preferences, but unduly biased and politicised when it opposes them. This is a particularly acute problem for the military because of the low level of public knowledge about the profession and its practices. The political biases that the public seems to want the military to adopt would in fact destroy precisely what the public has traditionally valued in the military.

As the work of Peter Feaver and Jim Golby has demonstrated, when the military is perceived as associating itself with particular policies, this damages public support for the military as an institution.[11] Surveys conducted during the current protests reinforce Feaver and Golby's findings. According to the advocacy group More in Common, 77% of Americans agreed with the statement that 'if America uses its military to act like law enforcement, we risk drawing the military into politics'.[12]

That is precisely what Trump attempted to do. In what may be a 'back from the brink' moment for civil–military relations, the American public saw the military at the centre of a domestic political debate, and recoiled. The More in Common survey indicated that 86% of Americans subsequently supported Esper's statement opposing Trump's stance. General Milley's apology, not his walk with Trump to Lafayette Square, will surely be his legacy. Anecdotally, the president's position may have ended up reducing voter support for him from within the military.[13]

Perhaps even more telling, all of the military service chiefs condemned the police killings, supported protesters and affirmed their commitment to the Constitution in advance of General Milley, who was effectively correcting his behaviour to align with theirs. Even with General Milley's remarkable apology, there have been mutterings of resentment among senior officers and veterans that he put himself in such a compromising position. Anticipating ambushes is, after all, something soldiers are trained for. General Milley fell far short of the example his Australian counterpart, Lieutenant-General Angus Campbell, set in asking permission for military officers to leave a press conference that turned political last year.[14] Also significant was the restrained and platitudinous West Point graduation speech that Trump delivered as the crisis was winding down. He said: 'As long as you remain loyal, faithful and true, then our enemies don't even stand a chance. Our rights will never be stolen. Our freedoms will never be trampled.'[15] However formulaic and patronising the rhetoric, civil–military experts were greatly relieved to see this president, who revels in corroding the norms and institutions of democracy in America, conform to the traditional constraints of his office.

Trump did find other outlets for utilising the military for partisan purposes, opposing the renaming of army bases in the southern United States that currently memorialise secessionist generals. But support for renaming is strong and bipartisan in Congress: both the House of Representatives and the Senate Armed Services committees included the provision in defence legislation.[16] To prevent it, Trump would have to veto the annual defence-spending bill, which would be politically unpopular, especially since support for the military is a central plank in his re-election bid.

Joe Biden, the presumptive Democratic presidential nominee, has also been reckless about the military's role in society, angling to associate himself with the virtue of the military's professionalism while politicising the institution. Expressing his fears that Trump will try to steal the 2020 presidential election, Biden said, 'I promise you, I'm absolutely convinced, [US troops] will escort him from the White House.'[17]

*   *   *

The fact remains that, with numerous mistakes along the way, American leaders of the military ultimately reinforced the best traditions of US civil–military relations. They stayed out of partisan politics, protected their profession from encroachment and appealed to the people for affirmation. The American public is left with the view of its military as disciplined professionals conscientiously cognisant of constitutional constraints even as politicians try to exploit them. Their political self-discipline has bolstered what the public most respects about the military, even if it isn't always what it wants from the military in the moment. As General Milley said in his apology: 'We must hold dear the principle of an apolitical military that is so deeply rooted in the very essence of our republic. And this is not easy. It takes time and work and effort, but it may be the most important thing each and every one of us does every single day. And my second piece of advice is very simple. Embrace the Constitution, keep it close to your heart. It is our North Star. It's our map to a better future.'[18]

Notes

1   Esper is quoted in, for example, Thomas Gibbons-Neff et al., 'Former Commanders Fault Trump's Use of Troops Against Protesters', *New York Times*, 2 June 2020, https://www.nytimes.com/2020/06/02/us/politics/military-national-guard-trump-protests.html.

2   Quoted in Brooke Singman, 'Trump Responds to Milley Apology for Lafayette Square Photo Op', 12 June 2020, https://www.foxnews.com/politics/trump-responds-to-milley-apology-for-lafayette-square-photo-op.

3   Kim Parker, Anthony Cilluffo and Renee Stepler, '6 Facts About the U.S. Military and Its Changing Demographics', Pew Research Center, 13 April 2017, https://www.pewresearch.org/fact-tank/2017/04/13/6-facts-about-the-u-s-military-and-its-changing-demographics/.

4   Alex Ward, 'US Military Chiefs: No Room for Racists and Bigots in the Services', Vox, 16 August 2017, https://www.vox.com/2017/8/16/16158880/military-tweets-charlottesville-navy-army-marine-corps-air-force-national-guard.

5   More in Common, 'Hidden Tribes Live: U.S. Military and Domestic Activities', 11 June 2020.

6   US Department of Defense, 'Military Compensation', https://militarypay.defense.gov/Pay/Basic-Pay/AnnualPayRaise/.

7   Hoover Institution, 'Warriors and Citizens Crosstabs 2', pp. 11, 27, https://www.hoover.org/sites/default/files/pages/docs/civ-mil_1_tabs.pdf.

8   James Hosek et al., *Military and Civilian Pay Levels, Trends, and Recruit Quality* (Santa Monica, CA: RAND Corporation, 2018), p. xiv, https://www.rand.org/content/dam/rand/pubs/research_reports/RR2300/

RR2396/RAND_RR2396.pdf.

9 Office of Personnel Management, 'OPM Releases Veteran Employment Data', News Release, 12 September 2017, https://www. opm.gov/news/releases/2017/09/ opm-releases-veteran-employment-data/#:~:text=Veterans%20now%20 represent%20approximately%20 one,initiative%20was%20 implemented%20in%202009.

10 Hoover Institution, 'Warriors and Citizens Crosstabs 2', pp. 66–7.

11 Jim Golby and Peter Feaver, 'Military Prestige During a Political Crisis: Use It and You'll Lose It', *War on the Rocks*, 5 June 2020, https:// warontherocks.com/2020/06/ military-prestige-during-a-political-crisis-use-it-and-youll-lose-it/.

12 More in Common, 'Hidden Tribes Live: U.S. Military and Domestic Activities'.

13 See Jennifer Steinhauer, 'Trump's Actions Rattle the Military World: "I Can't Support the Man"', *New York Times*, 12 June 2020, https://www. nytimes.com/2020/06/12/us/politics/ trump-polls-military-approval.html.

14 See, for instance, Tom Bowman, 'When Political Partisanship and the Military Collide', NPR, 17 June 2020, https://www. npr.org/2020/06/17/878587105/ when-political-partisanship-and-the-military-collide.

15 'Donald Trump West Point Commencement Speech Transcript', Rev Transcripts, 13 June 2020, https:// www.rev.com/blog/transcripts/ donald-trump-west-point-commencement-speech-transcript.

16 Connor O'Brien, 'Scrubbing Confederate Names from Army Bases Gains Steam in Congress, but Fight with Trump Looms', *Politico*, 11 June 2020, https://www.politico.com/ news/2020/06/11/pentagon-rename-military-confederate-bases-313383.

17 Sarah Mucha and Eric Bradner, 'Biden "Absolutely Convinced" Military Would Escort Trump from White House If He Loses and Refuses to Leave', CNN, 11 June 2020, https:// www.cnn.com/2020/06/11/politics/ joe-biden-donald-trump-military-white-house/index.html.

18 'General Mark Milley Keynote Speech Transcript: Apologizes for Photo Op With Trump', Rev Transcripts, 11 June 2020, https://www.rev.com/ blog/transcripts/general-mark-milley-keynote-speech-transcript-apologizes-for-photo-op-with-trump.

Iran and Mr Bolton

Mark Fitzpatrick

John Bolton's preoccupation with Iran is well known. For years, he has publicly advocated airstrikes and regime change as the only solutions to Iran's nuclear threat.[1] Serving as national security advisor to President Donald Trump from April 2018 to September 2019, Bolton continued to push singularly aggressive policies, as recounted in *The Room Where It Happened: A White House Memoir*, his insider exposé of those tempestuous 17 months.[2]

An obsession

No topic takes up more space in Bolton's book than Iran, which he mentions 755 times.[3] Iran has more entries in the index than any other proper noun except 'Pompeo, Mike'. Bolton considers Iran to be a top-tier threat, together with China, Russia and North Korea. Chiding former US secretary of defense James Mattis for inferring that this rank order in the National Security Strategy meant Iran was a 'fourth tier' threat, Bolton said it came after the other three only 'because we did not yet believe it had nuclear weapons'.[4]

Bolton recounts how, in the first hours of his first day on the job on 8 April 2018, he raised the issue of Iran with his British counterpart, Mark Sedwill, in the middle of a telephone consultation about dealing with Syria's use of chemical weapons. He told Sedwill that the United States would be

Mark Fitzpatrick is an IISS associate fellow, was executive director of IISS–Americas from 2015 through 2018, and headed the IISS Non-Proliferation and Nuclear Policy Programme for 13 years. He had a 26-year career in the US Department of State, including as deputy assistant secretary of state for non-proliferation, working under John Bolton. This article is adapted from the author's 1 July 2020 post on Politics and Strategy: The *Survival* Editors' Blog.

Survival | vol. 62 no. 4 | August–September 2020 | pp. 39–46   DOI 10.1080/00396338.2020.1792098

pulling out of the 2015 Iran nuclear deal, whose formal name – the Joint Comprehensive Plan of Action (JCPOA) – Bolton allows to appear only once in his book.[5] On that first afternoon, Bolton told National Security Council staff, who 'had been working feverishly to save the deal', to prepare to exit it within a month. In his words, 'there was no way ongoing negotiations with the UK, France and Germany would "fix" the deal'.[6] Good-faith US diplomacy with allies be damned.

Bolton was even more firmly fixated on stopping any diplomacy with Iran. He twice prepared to resign if Trump followed through on his impulse to meet with Iranian Foreign Minister Javad Zarif.[7] Whether or not regime change was the United States' declared goal, 'there would be no "new" Iran deal and no "deterrence" established as long as Iran's current regime remained'.[8]

A 'turning point' that hastened what Bolton insists was his resignation – Trump says he fired the man – was Trump's last-minute decision to refrain from bombing Iranian targets in response to the 20 June 2019 downing of an uninhabited US reconnaissance drone, on the grounds that it might result in 150 Iranian casualties. This act of forbearance, says Bolton, was 'the most irrational thing I ever witnessed any President do'.[9] Bolton has been in public life for half a century, working for four Republican administrations, including the one that in 2003 invaded Iraq on a false pretext at the cost of 4,400 American and perhaps half a million Iraqi dead. Yet to him, nothing was more ludicrous than declining to spark another Middle East conflict because Iran had shot down an uninhabited vehicle that it contended violated its airspace.

Bolton sees an Iranian bogeyman almost anywhere he looks. In the first chapter of the book, we learn that the efforts of several of Trump's national-security principals to preserve the Iran nuclear deal, despite Trump's campaign promise to withdraw from it, was the 'most palpable manifestation' of the administration's policy incoherence and why he, Bolton, was needed in the White House.[10] In the chapter on China, he writes that he 'was consumed with Iran's growing threat'.[11] In the one on Syria, Bolton insists that Iran was a more serious threat than the Islamic State.[12] In contrast to what he saw as Mattis's mistake in focusing on jihadist terrorism, Bolton boasts that 'Iran was my main concern'.[13]

Regarding Afghanistan, Bolton acknowledges that preventing the resurgence of the Islamic State and al-Qaeda was a top priority, but no more important than 'remaining vigilant against the nuclear-weapons programs in Iran and Pakistan'. It appears unclear why these objectives should be co-equal or what preventing nuclear weapons in Iran has to do with Afghanistan, but then he talks about the need to preserve US military bases in Afghanistan.[14] Although he does not explicitly say so, the implication is that the US would need the bases to mount attacks against Iran. Bolton rails against the State Department for negotiating objectives that 'were completely detached from what I considered to be our real objectives'.[15] But if preparing for military action against Iran was an objective, launching strikes from Afghanistan would be both logistically fraught and totally contrary to the bilateral security agreement with that country.

Unsupportable conclusions

Many of Bolton's references to Iran are false or unsupportable accusations. In June 2018, Bolton told Russian President Vladimir Putin that Iran was in violation of the 2015 nuclear deal.[16] In fact, not until summer 2019 did Iran exceed the deal's uranium-enrichment limits in response to the US breaking its own commitments to the accord. Bolton does not say why he believed otherwise a year earlier, notwithstanding repeated findings to the contrary by the International Atomic Energy Agency.[17] Bolton is also flatly wrong in concluding that Iran's retaliatory walk back from the nuclear deal was 'proving' that its key objective was nuclear weapons.[18] What it proved, rather, was Iran's intention to maintain a nuclear hedging strategy and its determination not to be played for a sucker in unilaterally honouring the agreement.

Bolton's claim that Iran is engaged in chemical- and biological-weapons work stretches the data to a near breaking point.[19] The State Department's most recent arms-control compliance report speaks of 'concerns' in this regard raised by Iran's activities, but draws none of the unqualified conclusions that Bolton asserts.[20] His claim, which he has been making for a decade, that Iran financed North Korea's construction of the Syrian plutonium-production reactor that Israel destroyed in 2007, rests on an unsupported article by a former German official known for his alarmist assertions.[21] Bolton's claim, with 'near certainty', that Iran financed North Korea's sale of chemical-weapons equipment and precursor chemicals to Syria rests on even flimsier evidence.[22]

Iran and North Korea have certainly cooperated closely on missile development dating back 25 years. Claims that their cooperation extended to the nuclear realm are far weaker.[23] Bolton assumes that Iran obtained nuclear-weapons designs from Pakistani proliferator A.Q. Khan (because Khan sold one to Libya).[24] But where is the evidence? One might give Bolton the benefit of the doubt here, given that he had access to the most secret US intelligence. Bolton, however, was insisting on the same Iranian misdeeds when he was a private citizen without such intelligence access.[25]

Some of Bolton's claims may be true. The North Korean, Syrian and Iranian regimes are bad actors in terms of non-proliferation, human rights and other international norms. Shackled by US sanctions, they may naturally find it useful to turn to one another for weapons help that they cannot get elsewhere. But acting on unsupported assumptions can lead to perdition. The 2003 invasion of Iraq on the tendentious and slipshod assessment that Saddam Hussein was still developing weapons of mass destruction should have taught policymakers a lesson about leaping to conclusions. Bolton, though, has never acknowledged that the Iraq intervention was a disastrous unforced error or expressed contrition for his role in it. The last time Bolton was in government before his recent stint, in the George W. Bush administration, he came under fire for cherry-picking intelligence, claiming, in the best-known case, that Cuba had a biological-weapons programme.[26] Especially post-Iraq, US intelligence agencies have been careful about interpreting data, issuing caveats about what is known, surmised and remains under study. Not Mr Bolton.

It is particularly ironic that while Bolton rightly criticises Trump's inattention to intelligence briefings, he himself misuses intelligence assessments to leap to unsupportable conclusions. No, the Islamic Republic of Iran is not a top-tier threat. It is a problematic middle power whose reach is limited to the Middle East. It does not pose a threat to the US homeland. Its threat can be contained through diplomacy and deterrence. Salutary though it is that Bolton contributed to exposing Trump's impeachable misconduct in dealing with Ukraine and other matters, the United States is almost certainly safer now that Bolton is a private citizen.

*   *   *

Bolton has still left a menacing strategic imprint on the Trump White House. Secretary of State Pompeo, his ideological soulmate, and Bolton acolytes on the National Security Council staff continue to push for harsher sanctions against Iran to try to goad it into ending the JCPOA. The thinly veiled endgame remains regime collapse.[27] A recent step in this strategy was seeking an extension of the ban on arms to and from Iran that is set to expire in October. This effort is likely to fail.[28] The administration will then probably seek to trigger the sanctions snap-back provision of UN Security Council Resolution 2231, which was adopted in July 2015 in conjunction with the JCPOA. Few if any other Security Council members believe that the US, having left the accord, has standing to invoke snap-back sanctions. Even if the US were to succeed, few countries would implement sanctions they consider illegitimate.[29]

The Trump administration's strategy could yield the termination of the JCPOA once and for all, as intended, given that Iran has vowed to pull out of the deal if UN sanctions are restored. Tehran has also threatened to withdraw from the Nuclear Non-Proliferation Treaty for good measure. For Bolton and his like-minded colleagues, that would be even better: it could be cast, however speciously, as proof of Iran's intent to possess nuclear weapons. And that, of course, would at last provide the *casus belli* that Bolton seems to want. Avoiding war may then depend on an 'irrational' decision on the part of the president.

Notes

1   See, for example, John R. Bolton, 'To Stop Iran's Bomb, Bomb Iran', *New York Times*, 26 March 2015, https://www.nytimes.com/2015/03/26/ opinion/to-stop-irans-bomb-bomb-iran.html; and 'John Bolton on Iran', *The Iran Primer*, US Institute of Peace, updated 10 September 2019, https://

iranprimer.usip.org/blog/2018/mar/22/ john-bolton-iran.

2   John R. Bolton, *The Room Where It Happened: A White House Memoir* (New York: Simon & Schuster, 2020).

3   See Rachel Marsden, 'Good Thing John Bolton's Influence Culminates Only in a Book', *Minneapolis StarTribune*, 24 June 2020, https://www.startribune.com/ good-thing-john-bolton-s-influence-culminates-only-in-a-book/571465722/.

4   Bolton, *The Room Where It Happened*, p. 373.

5   *Ibid.*, pp. 20, 47.

6   *Ibid.*, p. 49.

7   *Ibid.*, pp. 420–2.

8   *Ibid.*, p. 391.

9   *Ibid.*, p. 403.

10 *Ibid.*, pp. 19–20.

11 *Ibid.*, p. 300.

12 *Ibid.*, p. 192.

13 *Ibid.*, p. 196.

14 *Ibid.*, pp. 428–9.

15 *Ibid.*, p. 428.

16 *Ibid.*, p. 132.

17 See, for example, Kelsey Davenport, 'IAEA Says Iran Abiding by Nuclear Deal', *Arms Control Today*, April 2019, https://www. armscontrol.org/act/2019-04/news/ iaea-says-iran-abiding-nuclear-deal.

18 Bolton, *The Room Where It Happened*, p. 395.

19 *Ibid.*, p. 66.

20 US Department of State, 'Adherence to and Compliance with Arms Control, Nonproliferation and Disarmament Agreements and Commitments', August 2019, https://www.state. gov/wp-content/uploads/2019/08/ Compliance-Report-2019-August-19-Unclassified-Final.pdf.

21 See Bolton, *The Room Where It Happened*, p. 28. On the article in question, see 'Report: Iran Financed Syrian Nuke Plans', Associated Press, 19 March 2009, http://www. nbcnews.com/id/29777355/ns/ world_news-mideast_n_africa/t/ report-iran-financed-syrian-nuke-plans/#.XvyhmyhKhPY.

22 Bolton, *The Room Where It Happened*, p. 30.

23 *Ibid.*, p. 27. The most serious claim, reported by the *Süddeutsche Zeitung* in August 2011, is that North Korea transferred to Iran a specialised computer program that simulates whether a nuclear bomb would explode, and which may have been part of a larger $100 million deal for nuclear training and information and missile technology. See 'Two Recent Media Reports to Note on Iran's Nuclear Program', Institute for Science and International Security, 29 August 2011, https:// isis-online.org/isis-reports/detail/ two-recent-media-reports-to-note-on-irans-nuclear-program/.

24 Bolton, *The Room Where It Happened*, p. 28.

25 See, for instance, John Hayward, 'John Bolton: If North Korea Gets Nuclear Missiles, "Iran Could Have that Capability the Next Day by Writing a Check"', Breitbart, 28 April 2017, https://www.breitbart.com/ radio/2017/04/28/john-bolton-if-north-korea-gets-nuclear-missiles-iran-could-have-that-capability-the-next-day-by-writing-a-check/.

26 See Sebastian Rotella, 'John Bolton Skewed Intelligence, Say People Who Worked with Him', ProPublica, 30 March 2018, https://www.propublica.

org/article/john-bolton-national-
security-adviser-intelligence.

27 See Mark Dubowitz, 'Build an Iranian
Sanctions Wall', *Wall Street Journal*,
2 April 2019, https://www.wsj.com/
articles/build-an-iranian-sanctions-
wall-11554246565.

28 See Carol Morello, 'U.S. Finds Little
Support for Extending Arms Embargo
Against Iran', *Washington Post*, 30 June
2020, https://www.washingtonpost.
com/national-security/us-finds-little-
support-for-extending-arms-embargo-
against-iran/2020/06/30/073e3666-
bb08-11ea-86d5-3b9b3863273b_story.
html.

29 See Mark Fitzpatrick, 'Why Is US
Pushing Unworkable Plan to Renew
Iran Arms Ban?', *Al-Monitor*, 14
May 2020, https://www.al-monitor.
com/pulse/originals/2020/05/
trump-push-plan-renew-iran-
arms-ban-nuclear-deal-jcpoa.
html#ixzz6MSHrvcZR.

Don't Fear China's Belt and Road Initiative

Christopher Mott

China's Belt and Road Initiative (BRI) is an ambitious state effort to link Asia and Europe economically through massive investments in infrastructure, primarily in developing nations that often struggle to secure such funds in capital markets. The United States has viewed the project warily for fear that it could increase Chinese influence. However, BRI loans might not pay off for China, and, where they do, the US might benefit from increased trade. The BRI could also counter extremism and facilitate state-building in several unstable regions. Additionally, the BRI does not significantly narrow Washington's diplomatic options or bind countries like Russia permanently to Chinese interests. Overt opposition from the United States, however, might cause countries involved in the project to align more closely with Beijing.

Perceptions of the BRI

With the BRI, China has undertaken a massive infrastructure project to facilitate international trade and expand its links with partner nations. The BRI offers a large-scale construction programme aimed at updating old infrastructure and building entirely new facilities to reinvigorate inland Eurasian trade. For countries that are often on the periphery of world trade networks, it is an opportunity to increase their commerce substantially.

Christopher Mott is a fellow at Defense Priorities and author of *The Formless Empire: A Short History of Diplomacy and Warfare in Central Asia* (Westholme Publishing, 2015).

Survival | vol. 62 no. 4 | August–September 2020 | pp. 47–55   DOI 10.1080/00396338.2020.1792097

The BRI's investment and development plan aims to expand trade and logistical capacity in up to 138 nations, at least in theory. It specifically targets an inland-Eurasia-focused grouping of 'one belt economies': Mongolia, Russia, the former Soviet Republics in Central Asia, the Caucasus, Turkey and a variety of Central, Eastern and Southern European states. In addition, the BRI seeks to net in 'one road economies', tracking the historical Maritime Silk Road, by way of projects focused on Southeast Asia, the Indian Ocean and East and West Africa. Railroads and highways are the initial focus of the first group, and ports the second.[1] The goals are cast as policy-coordination efforts among participant governments, communication facilitation on macro-issues related to commerce between the signatories, facilities' connectivity via standardised infrastructure, integration of finance mechanisms among nations and a general reduction of trade barriers across the board.[2]

The total cost of this undertaking to China is estimated to reach between $4 and $8 trillion dollars by the projected completion of the project in 2049, with $900 billion in annual investment required to meet targets. These numbers would stress the Chinese economy, and so far the project has struggled to reach proposed funding levels.[3] By 2017, China had invested $340bn. If that rate continued, the target goal of $1trn by 2025 could be realised. If increased, state spending on the project could reach $2trn by 2030.[4]

US commentators warn that the project will cost the United States influence across the world, believing that as China gains control over smaller nations, it will establish itself as the world's pre-eminent international deal-broker.[5] Multiple think tanks and commentators have raised concerns about how the Chinese might assert economic control over much of the planet and exclude the US from entire regions.[6]

These fears are misplaced. The BRI poses no real threat to the US position on the world stage. In fact, certain facets of the BRI may indirectly enhance US diplomatic options by reducing instability and nurturing development in parts of the world where US influence is limited. Furthermore, the arrival of the BRI has already prompted some countries to increase their own alternative investments in regional infrastructure to compete with Beijing.[7]

Potential benefits for Eurasia

The BRI may well reduce trade costs by streamlining infrastructure standards and customs practices among its partner countries while reducing trade barriers. Given that the Chinese made massive economic gains under US-backed trade policies in the past, the BRI could allow the US to do the same by piggybacking on Beijing's programmes. Rendering pre-existing trends more efficient at generating commerce could open opportunities for all actors doing business in the region.

Development can also help make states more governable and responsible to their citizens. The absence of economic opportunity enhances the appeal of extremist groups.[8] Expanding infrastructure in regions where extremist non-state actors operate is no panacea, but it can limit their appeal. Kazakhstan's post-Soviet development has enhanced its internal stability, while its neighbour Uzbekistan – which has struggled to develop – hosts Central Asia's largest jihadist recruitment drive.[9]

Afghanistan will not be able to rely on American largesse indefinitely. But powerful neighbouring countries have an interest in preventing state failure conducive to transnational insecurity and disorder. China and Pakistan already have close ties and considerable interests in Afghanistan. Beijing is in a better position than Washington to assist Afghanistan.[10] A hypothetical Chinese-led and Pakistani-assisted project operating in conjunction with the Afghan government could secure long-term benefits for that historically unstable region.

The BRI could also solidify the economic sovereignty of beneficiary states, as foreign development assistance helped countries such as Egypt, Yugoslavia and some non-aligned countries bolster their independence during the Cold War. Increased levels of development fuelled through infrastructure and trade can enable smaller countries to attract investment from multiple competing powers, in turn increasing their ability to shop around for better deals and shrink their dependence on a single source. Already Japan has begun to compete with China on projects in countries signed up to the BRI programme by offering alternative and competitive investments in infrastructure.

Countries recovering from conflict, such as Pakistan and Tajikistan, tend to be dependent on larger patrons. Pakistan's internal fragility, for instance, causes it to lean heavily on Chinese support, especially for defence. But should it become a more important conduit of international trade from Central Asia through its newly upgraded and integrated ports on the Indian Ocean, it would be better able to diversify its sources of foreign assistance. Tajikistan is the least developed nation in Central Asia, and since the Tajik civil war Russia has maintained a large and influential military presence in the country. Tajikistan is also incredibly rich in hydropower, of which it is a net exporter. The BRI-driven expansion in pan-regional infrastructure could increase Tajikistan's trading options and decrease its dependence on Moscow.

Other countries with significant interests in the Indian Ocean could also benefit. As part of the BRI, China has taken out a 99-year lease on a new port in Hambantota, Sri Lanka, and undertaken its development. At first blush, this venture seems illustrative of Chinese economic predation, whereby Sri Lanka becomes more dependent on Chinese investment and subservient to its interests. In fact, however, the deal has alerted Japan and India to the need to invest in Sri Lanka to prevent China from gaining too much strategic traction there.[11]

In any case, evidence that the BRI is winning China massive goodwill in beneficiary countries is inconclusive. China often stipulates that its own companies and labourers must get many of the jobs created by BRI-related projects, which generates some resentment. So far, the BRI's largest effect in Central Asia seems to be to encourage public discussion on how much Chinese influence is desirable. China can help build infrastructure and promote prosperity, but it is not necessarily buying long-term leverage that would exclude other powers from competing with Beijing to wield their own diplomatic weight.

Potential American opportunities

The landlocked nations that comprise much of the BRI's present coverage have little direct connection to US security or prosperity. Accordingly, it seems unlikely the United States could offer them realistic alternatives for development. The risks would outweigh the rewards for non-local actors, and even local actors are not guaranteed profitability from more speculative investments.

While the potential benefits to Beijing are real, the BRI carries enormous financial risk in the form of publicly guaranteed debt. This will be the major source of funding for many countries on the BRI priority list. According to the World Bank, almost two-thirds of the countries affected by the BRI have elevated debt vulnerabilities, and over one-third are in danger of or actually in debt distress. Many projects will not work out and pay off for China, likely undermining smaller nations' relationships with Beijing. The likelihood of such uneven results suggests that China will struggle to transform BRI investments into hegemonic reach.[12]

The BRI may also lead to private investment in places previously regarded as economic backwaters. The massive expansion of infrastructure during the Cold War in places like Singapore, Malaysia and the Gulf states greatly increased the international prominence of those countries. Owing money to China also gives smaller powers some situational leverage with Beijing as they enter a newly competitive investment market. At the same time, China's political compulsion to keep a project profitable significantly limits its financial options, as does its incentive to buoy the ability of the host country to raise investment elsewhere to ease its financial burden.[13]

While no reprise of the Sino-Soviet split of the 1960s is likely now, the BRI could ultimately increase rather than decrease Sino-Russian rivalry.[14] Russia has strong defence ties with India, which is sceptical about the BRI but a potential beneficiary of its trade promotion. Dating back to Indian independence, the Soviet Union and now Russia has been a reliable arms supplier to the Indian state. Since the 1962 border conflict through today's Himalayan border disputes, Beijing and New Delhi have had an uneasy relationship. Customary cooperation between Pakistan and China is a constant concern for India. For geopolitical reasons, Russia remains compelled to balance between India and China, and the expansion of the BRI will not change this dynamic.[15] In this light, it seems premature at best to anticipate that the BRI will lock in a permanent and robust Sino-Russian alliance.[16]

Policies that push Beijing and Moscow together are more likely to create a long-term anti-American front than BRI projects in Eurasia. A US effort to malign and undermine the BRI would be perceived as hostile, and might alienate smaller nations and drive them closer to China. Increased Chinese influence in a region of limited importance to US security is a far safer – and potentially even profitable – outcome. As an oceanic trading power, the United States benefits by maximising the prosperity of other nations, be they allied or not. In particular, US policies should not discourage American firms from pursuing attractive investment opportunities in BRI countries. Because of the private nature of such transactions and the greater distance of the United States from BRI nations compared to China, small nations would likely see US investments as less predatory than Chinese ones.

*　　*　　*

The BRI is an example of a larger phenomenon: as states get richer, they tend to invest more heavily abroad in ways that advance their interests. But as the junior partners in such arrangements receive more funds, they are better able to act autonomously when it comes to competitive diplomacy. This means that policymakers in Washington would be wise to expand trade relationships and be more sparing in deploying sanctions that could drive potential partners away. Nations, especially secure superpowers, should not enter bidding wars for influence in regions with little strategic pay-off.

The BRI could bring a variety of outcomes to the smaller Eurasian states, none of which substantially endangers US security. Greater levels of development may increase trade to the region and reduce violent extremism. They probably will not seriously compromise the sovereignty of the smaller participant states, and may help some strengthen their regional negotiating positions by playing China off against other potential patrons.

The general principle stands that China's development of international trade links and relationships is not an automatic zero-sum loss for the United States. Chinese investment does not preclude investment by private US companies, and the more patrons a smaller country has, the less likely it is to be 'bought out' by a single foreign nation.

The United States' geographical distance from Eurasian states means that they are likely to view it as a less threatening partner than China. Washington policymakers should not squander this advantage by taking a confrontational or obstructionist approach to the international infrastructure projects of other powers. An overwrought American reaction to the BRI would only transform it from an opportunity for the United States into an unnecessary threat.

Notes

1 See World Bank Group, *Belt and Road Economics: Opportunities and Risks of Transport Corridors* (Washington, DC: International Bank for Reconstruction and Development/ The World Bank, 2019).

2 See Organization for Economic Cooperation and Development, 'China's Belt and Road Initiative in the Global Trade, Investment and Finance Landscape', OECD Business and Finance Outlook 2018, https://www. oecd.org/finance/Chinas-Belt-and-Road-Initiative-in-the-global-trade-investment-and-finance-landscape.pdf.

3 Atif Ansar and Bent Flyvbjerg, 'Too Much of a Good Thing: China's Infrastructure Boon Threatens Its Economic Prosperity', Reconnecting Asia, 7 December 2016, https:// reconasia.csis.org/analysis/entries/ too-much-good-thing/.

4 Jonathan E. Hillman, 'How Big Is China's Belt and Road?', CSIS, April 2018, https://www.csis.org/analysis/ how-big-chinas-belt-and-road.

5 See Alek Chance, 'American Perspectives on the Belt and Road Initiative', Institute for China–America Studies, November 2016, https://chinaus-icas.org/ wp-content/uploads/2017/02/ American-Perspectives-on-the-Belt-and-Road-Initiative.pdf; Dane Chomorro, 'Belt and Road: China's Strategy to Capture Supply Chains

from Guangzhou to Greece', *Forbes*, 12 December 2017, https://www. forbes.com/sites/riskmap/2017/12/21/ belt-and-road-chinas-strategy-to-capture-supply-chains-from-guang-zhou-to-greece/#4935555e6237; and Frederick Kempe, 'China Is Making a Global Power Play and the US Response Is Coming Up Short', CNBC, 26 April 2019, https://www. cnbc.com/2019/04/26/china-is-making-a-global-power-play-and-the-us-response-is-coming-up-short.html.

6 See Daniel Kliman, 'China's Power Play: The Role of Congress in Addressing the Belt and Road', Center for a New American Security, 12 June 2019, https://www.cnas.org/ publications/congressional-testimony/ chinas-power-play-the-role-of-congress-in-addressing-the-belt-and-road; and Jeff M. Smith, 'China's Belt and Road Initiative: Strategic Implications and International Opposition', Heritage Foundation, *Backgrounder* no. 3,331, 9 August 2018, https://www.heritage.org/sites/ default/files/2018-08/BG3331_2.pdf.

7 See Parag Khanna, 'Washington Is Dismissing China's Belt and Road. That's a Huge Strategic Mistake', *Politico*, 30 April 2019, https:// www.politico.com/magazine/ story/2019/04/30/washington-is-dismissing-chinas-belt-and-road-thats-a-huge-strategic-mistake-226759.

8   Iffat Idris, 'Youth Vulnerability to Violent Extremist Group in the Indo-Pacific', GSDRC Helpdesk Research Report, September 2018, https://gsdrc.org/wp-content/uploads/2018/10/1438-Youth-Vulnerability-to-Violent-Extremist-Groups-in-the-Indo-Pacific.pdf.

9   Edward Lemon, Vira Miranova and William Tobey, 'Jihadists from Ex-Soviet Central Asia: Where Are They? Why Did They Radicalize? What Next?', *Russia Matters*, 7 December 2018, https://www.russiamatters.org/analysis/jihadists-ex-soviet-central-asia-where-are-they-why-did-they-radicalize-what-next.

10   Ben Blanchard, 'China, Pakistan to Look at Including Afghanistan in $57 Billion Economic Corridor', Reuters, 26 December 2017, https://www.reuters.com/article/us-china-pakistan-afghanistan/china-pakistan-to-look-at-including-afghanistan-in-57-billion-economic-corridor-idUSKBN1EK0ES.

11   John Herskovitz and Iain Marlow, 'China Faces New Competition as Japan, India Eye Sri Lanka Port', Bloomberg, 21 May 2019, https://www.bloomberg.com/news/articles/2019-05-21/japan-india-in-deal-at-belt-and-road-colombo-port-nikkei.

12   See Ileana Cristina Constantinescu and Michele Ruta, 'How Old Is the Belt and Road Initiative? Long Term Patterns of Export to BRI Economies', World Bank Group, *MTI Practice Notes*, no. 6, December 2019, http://documents.worldbank.org/curated/en/984921545241288569/pdf/How-Old-is-the-Belt-and-Road-Initiative-Long-Term-Patterns-of-Chinese-Exports-to-BRI-Economies.pdf; and Francois De Soyres et al., 'How Much Will the Belt and Road Reduce Trade Costs?', World Bank Group, *Policy Research Working Paper*, no. 8,614, October 2018, http://documents.worldbank.org/curated/en/592771539630482582/How-Much-Will-the-Belt-and-Road-Initiative-Reduce-Trade-Costs.

13   Tobias Harris, '"Quality Infrastructure": Japan's Robust Challenge to China's Belt and Road', *War on the Rocks*, 9 April 2019, https://warontherocks.com/2019/04/quality-infrastructure-japans-robust-challenge-to-chinas-belt-and-road/.

14   Merlin Linehan, 'Mutual Suspicion Stalls China and Russia Cooperation', Frontera, 28 June 2016, https://frontera.net/news/asia/whats-future-sino-russian-relations/.

15   Stephen Kotkin, 'The Unbalanced Triangle: What Chinese–Russian Relations Mean for the United States', *Foreign Affairs*, vol. 88, no. 5, September/October 2009, pp. 130–8.

16   Melinda Lui, 'Xi Jinping Has Embraced Vladimir Putin – For Now', *Foreign Policy*, 3 October 2019, https://foreignpolicy.com/2019/10/03/xi-jinping-has-embraced-vladimir-putin-for-now/.

Noteworthy

Pandemic

'The greatest asset we have in this crisis is the trust and adherence of the public. You want trust? You need to be open with people. This isn't open. It is reminiscent of Stalinist Russia. Not a good look.'

> Stephen Reicher, a member of the UK government's Scientific Advisory Group for Emergencies (SAGE), responds to the redaction of a report that contained criticisms of potential government policies with respect to the COVID-19 pandemic.[1]

'It's clear this virus cannot be eradicated in Germany. There's consensus on that – at least until there's a vaccine or a treatment. We will have to try to build this virus into our everyday lives, changing our behaviour to reduce its transmission. We find ourselves in a new normality.'

> Lars Schaade, the vice-president of the Robert Koch Institute, a public-health institution in Germany, comments on the country's experience with COVID-19.[2]

'In China, after making painstaking efforts and enormous sacrifice, we have turned the tide on the virus and protected the life and health of our people. All along, we have acted with openness, transparency and responsibility ... We have released the genome sequence at the earliest possible time. We have shared control and treatment experience with the world without reservation. We have done everything in our power to support and assist countries in need.'

> Chinese President Xi Jinping announces a $2 billion donation toward fighting the pandemic in a statement during the virtual opening of the 73rd World Health Assembly on 18 May 2020.[3]

'[China's] commitment of $2 billion is a token to distract from calls from a growing number of nations demanding accountability for the Chinese government's failure to meet its obligations under international health regulations to tell the truth and warn the world of what was coming.'

> John Ullyot, spokesman for the US National Security Council.[4]

'We will be today terminating our relationship with the World Health Organization and redirecting those funds to other worldwide and deserving urgent global public health needs.'

> US President Donald Trump announces the withdrawal of US support for the World Health Organization (WHO), ten days after delivering a letter to WHO Director-General Tedros Adhanom Ghebreyesus warning that the US would cut its funding of the organisation if reforms were not made within 30 days.[5]

'It was never about reforming the WHO. That was all lies. It was always about distraction and scapegoating. Leaving castrates our ability to stop future pandemics and elevates China as the world's go-to power on global health. What a nightmare.'

> US Senator Chris Murphy.[6]

'From tomorrow, we will be able to turn the page on the crisis that we have lived through. This does not mean that the virus has completely disappeared or that we can lower our guard ... but like you I am happy about this victory over the virus.'

> French President Emmanuel Macron announces the end of COVID-19 restrictions in France beginning on 15 June 2020.[7]

Survival | vol. 62 no. 4 | August–September 2020 | pp. 56–58   DOI 10.1080/00396338.2020.1792099

Law and order?

'I can't breathe.'

George Floyd, an African American, pleads for assistance during his arrest in Minneapolis, Minnesota, shortly before his death in police custody on 25 May 2020.[8]

'I couldn't believe that they committed a modern-day lynching in broad daylight.'

Philonise Floyd, brother of George Floyd.[9]

'I am your president of law and order and an ally of all peaceful protesters.

[…]

I am mobilizing all available federal resources – civilian and military – to stop the rioting and looting, to end the destruction and arson and to protect the rights of law-abiding Americans, including your Second Amendment rights.

[…]

If a city or state refuses to take the actions necessary to defend the life and property of their residents, then I will deploy the United States military and quickly solve the problem for them.'

US President Donald Trump issues a statement from the Rose Garden of the White House on 1 June after the US Park Police and the National Guard confronted protesters outside the building.[10]

'I have watched this week's unfolding events, angry and appalled. The words "Equal Justice Under Law" are carved in the pediment of the United States Supreme Court. This is precisely what protesters are rightly demanding. It is a wholesome and unifying demand – one that all of us should be able to get behind. We must not be distracted by a small number of lawbreakers. The protests are defined by tens of thousands of people of conscience who are insisting that we live up to our values – our values as people and our values as a nation.

[…]

We must reject any thinking of our cities as a "battlespace" that our uniformed military is called upon to "dominate." At home, we should use our military only when requested to do so, on very rare occasions, by state governors. Militarizing our response, as we witnessed in Washington, D.C., sets up a conflict – a false conflict – between the military and civilian society. It erodes the moral ground that ensures a trusted bond between men and women in uniform and the society they are sworn to protect, and of which they themselves are a part. Keeping public order rests with civilian state and local leaders who best understand their communities and are answerable to them.

[…]

Donald Trump is the first president in my lifetime who does not try to unite the American people – does not even pretend to try. Instead he tries to divide us. We are witnessing the consequences of three years of this deliberate effort. We are witnessing the consequences of three years without mature leadership. We can unite without him, drawing on the strengths inherent in our civil society. This will not be easy, as the past few days have shown, but we owe it to our fellow citizens; to past generations that bled to defend our promise; and to our children.'

Former US defense secretary James Mattis criticises the White House's response to the protests in a statement released on 3 June 2020.[11]

Sources

1 Stephen Reicher (@ReicherStephen), tweet, 8 May 2020, https://twitter.com/ReicherStephen/status/1258727943062372358.

2 Kate Connolly, 'Coronavirus Part of New Normality, Says Germany Agency as Briefings Cease', *Guardian*, 7 May 2020, https://www.theguardian.com/world/2020/may/07/coronavirus-part-of-new-normality-says-german-agency-as-briefings-cease.

3 'Full Text: Speech by President Xi Jinping at Opening of 73rd World Health Assembly', Xinhua, 18 May 2020, http://www.xinhuanet.com/english/2020-05/18/c_139067018.htm.

4 Andrew Jacobs, Michael D. Shear and Edward Wong, 'U.S.–China Feud over Coronavirus Erupts at World Health Assembly', *New York Times*, 18 May 2020, https://www.nytimes.com/2020/05/18/health/coronavirus-who-china-trump.html?action=click&module=Spotlight&pgtype=Homepage.

5 White House, 'Remarks by President Trump on Actions Against China', 29 May 2020, https://www.whitehouse.gov/briefings-statements/remarks-president-trump-actions-china/.

6 Chris Murphy (@ChrisMurphyCT), tweet, 29 May 2020, https://twitter.com/ChrisMurphyCT/status/1266455066657148929.

7 Victor Mallet, 'Emmanuel Macron Lifts Most Coronavirus Restrictions', *Financial Times*, 14 June 2020, https://www.ft.com/content/cba9ddeb-72eb-4b6d-b23f-4284bc0383ca?emailId=5ee6e74ac1ccff0004dc1091&segmentId=22011ee7-896a-8c4c-22a0-7603348b7f22.

8 Christine Hauser, Derrick Bryson Taylor and Neil Vigdor, '"I Can't Breathe": 4 Minneapolis Officers Fired After Black Man Dies in Custody', *New York Times*, 26 May 2020, https://www.nytimes.com/2020/05/26/us/minneapolis-police-man-died.html.

9 Martin Pengelly, 'George Floyd's Brother Says Trump "Kept Pushing Me Off" During Phone Call', *Guardian*, 31 May 2020, https://www.theguardian.com/us-news/2020/may/31/george-floyd-brother-philonise-floyd-trump-phone-call#maincontent.

10 White House, 'Statement by the President', 1 June 2020, https://www.whitehouse.gov/briefings-statements/statement-by-the-president-39/.

11 Jeffrey Goldberg, 'James Mattis Denounces President Trump, Describes Him as a Threat to the Constitution', *Atlantic*, 3 June 2020, https://www.theatlantic.com/politics/archive/2020/06/james-mattis-denounces-trump-protests-militarization/612640/.

Port Investments in the Belt and Road Initiative: Is Beijing Grabbing Strategic Assets?

Jordan Calinoff and David Gordon

In 2013, as President Xi Jinping rose to the leadership of the world's second-largest economy, he signalled a bold shift in China's global strategy. In Xi's new vision, China was ready to rejoin the ranks of the world's leading powers, touching every corner of the globe with its economic might. At the centre of Xi's campaign has been the Belt and Road Initiative (BRI), a massive economic-development programme covering scores of countries in regions ranging from Southeast Asia through South and Central Asia into Europe, the Middle East and Africa. China has described the BRI, sometimes known as 'One Belt, One Road', as a purely economic endeavour to expand mutually beneficial infrastructural linkages – through the belt, an overland series of projects recreating the ancient Silk Road; and the road, an ambitious chain of expanding and upgrading ports and infrastructure to facilitate access to global sea lanes.

While Beijing has vigorously denied that there is any strategic geopolitical motivation behind the BRI, most analysts view the effort as having parallels with the United States' Marshall Plan for the reconstruction of Europe following the Second World War. In this view, the BRI seeks to fuse China's own strategic ambitions as a global power with expanding opportunities for

Jordan Calinoff is a political-risk and macroeconomic analyst who has worked for a variety of hedge funds and asset managers. He started his career as an investigative journalist based in Shanghai, China. **David Gordon** is Senior Adviser for Geo-economics and Strategy at the IISS, and a former director of policy planning at the US State Department.

Survival | vol. 62 no. 4 | August–September 2020 | pp. 59–80   DOI 10.1080/00396338.2020.1792134

a wide range of global partners. A much sharper critique of the BRI posits that the effort is broadly neocolonial, bullying recipient countries for China's own gain and, in particular, seeking to wrest control from recipient governments of strategic ports around the world through 'debt-trap diplomacy'.

In this article, we compare the dynamics of debt-trap transactions in real estate – so-called 'lend-to-own' deals – to the evolution of several major Chinese efforts at port development under the BRI, including the case of Hambantota Port in Sri Lanka, which is the most commonly cited example of Beijing's purported pattern of seizing strategic assets. We find that these cases do not support the debt-trap-diplomacy hypothesis. Nor do they support Beijing's claims that the BRI lacks strategic intent. Rather, they highlight the importance to Beijing of minimising its vulnerability to US dominance of the sea lanes linking China to the oil-exporting countries of the Middle East, a vulnerability Beijing is seeking to overcome not by seizing assets, but by becoming a durable and reliable ally to a set of countries that share two attributes: they are located next to global sea lanes, and they can be assisted by China in increasing their leverage against more powerful external actors.

The BRI and rising Chinese nationalism

In the BRI's early days, President Xi and other Chinese leaders cast it in multilateralist language as a programme that would enhance globalisation by bridging the infrastructural gaps limiting ties between Asia, the Middle East and Europe, to the benefit of all. But as Xi's overall approach took on a more nationalist tone, so did the BRI. While many expected that China would use as a financing mechanism the new Asian Infrastructure Investment Bank (AIIB) – initiated by Beijing at roughly the same time as the BRI and which includes dozens of partner countries – Beijing decided to pursue the BRI solely through bilateral mechanisms. It placed Chinese companies in charge, including a high proportion of state-owned enterprises.

In contrast to the Marshall Plan, which was funded by US grants to recipient governments, the BRI has been primarily funded through long-term loans, the terms of which generally have not been disclosed. The propaganda department of the Chinese Communist Party was given responsibility for promoting the BRI, and has insisted that the programme, unlike the 'imperialistic' Marshall Plan, is devoid of any strategic intent beyond promoting expanded 'win–win' economic ties between China and recipient countries.[1] Not surprisingly, the combination of non-transparent terms, overwhelming reliance on Chinese contractors and the vociferous denial of any strategic interest (even if perfectly legitimate) on the part of China has served to increase the level of concern and scepticism directed at the BRI.

While the BRI was cast in triumphalist terms in Chinese domestic media and by many recipient governments, a counter-narrative was developed by critics of China, both in the West and in Asia. In their view, the BRI is a manifestation of Beijing's ever-expanding global ambitions under Xi: an economic scheme that will ultimately enable China to gain strategic assets. Serving as the linchpin for such criticisms is the notion of debt-trap diplomacy, a phrase coined by Indian scholar Brahma Chellaney.[2] He writes:

> Through its $1 trillion 'one belt, one road' initiative, China is supporting infrastructure projects in strategically located developing countries, often by extending huge loans to their governments. As a result, countries are becoming ensnared in a debt trap that leaves them vulnerable to China's influence.[3]

By this logic, Beijing, through purposefully extending loans to debt-ridden island states in the Indian Ocean and beyond, would convert economic and financial dominance into political leverage, forcing vulnerable partners to hand over strategically valuable concessions such as land, ports and natural resources.

Are BRI ports a debt trap?

So which is it? Is the BRI China's win–win attempt to create a more interconnected, highly developed world? Or is it a cynical attempt to enable China to gain control over key elements of the global commercial infrastructure?

The latter view seems to have taken particularly strong hold with respect to the BRI's maritime-infrastructure projects. In February 2019, General Joseph Votel, then-commander of US Central Command, said in remarks to the US Senate that 'if left unchecked, the expanding global reach of China's economic and military initiatives … will pose a significant challenge to U.S. prosperity, security, and regional stability'.[4] He urged the US government 'to be watchful of [China's] developing relationships with other partners across the region, particularly in the maritime environment'.[5]

A wide swath of academic analysis now suggests, à la Chellaney, that the BRI's maritime strategy is using economic objectives to simultaneously achieve geopolitical objectives. A recent report for the Kiel Institute for the World Economy by Sebastian Horn, Carmen Reinhart and Christoph Trebesch quantifies the financing China is offering developing countries, revealing that the scope of BRI lending is far greater than has been reported. The authors claim that China's overseas lending has soared from $500 billion in the early 2000s to more than $5 trillion today – an amount that exceeds the total combined lending of the IMF and the World Bank. The authors also claim that perhaps up to half of that debt has not been publicly disclosed.[6] While the authors posit that the scale of China's exposure to BRI debtors – they estimate that China now holds 40% of the public debt of the world's poorest countries[7] – creates something of a debt trap for Beijing as well as its partners, it could also provide the basis for China to engage in 'debt-for-equity' swaps and for the emergence of a new form of colonialism with 'Chinese characteristics'.

Indeed, the most aggressive of China's critics claim that, beyond seeking to achieve economic goals or even to influence other countries' policies through the leverage gained from a high debt burden, Beijing is using the BRI to seize *strategic* foreign assets, specifically ports. Malaysia's former prime minister Mahathir Mohamad initially emerged as one of the strongest proponents of this theory. In April 2018, Mahathir stated: 'Lots of people don't like Chinese investments. We are for Malaysians. We want to defend the rights of Malaysians. We don't want to sell chunks of this country to foreign companies who will develop whole towns.'[8] A few months later, he excoriated the BRI while standing next to China's Premier Li Keqiang, saying: 'You don't want a situation where there's a new version of colonialism happening because poor countries are unable to compete with rich countries in terms of just open, free trade.'[9]

Although Mahathir tempered his criticism as Beijing accommodated his demand to renegotiate the terms of projects signed before he regained office in May 2018, those senior US officials most critical of China have taken up the asset-seizure theory with gusto. Peter Navarro, director of the White House National Trade Council, elaborated on this in a speech at the Hudson Institute in July 2018, saying:

> There's debt-trap financing to developing countries. This speaks to the way that China is, in many cases, able to gain control, not just of the resources of a country, like copper or cobalt, but also of infrastructure. China will lend a bunch of money to these countries that they really can't afford to borrow and then foreclose on that loan.

He continued by citing a common example, asking: 'Anybody know the Hambantota issue, the Sri Lanka issue? I believe that's the one where the Chinese basically gained ownership of that port.'[10]

Hambantota: lend-to-own in geopolitical context

Navarro's comments draw parallels between China's behaviour towards its BRI partners and a tactic that is well known in real-estate investing: the lend-to-own strategy. In the real-estate version, hard-money lenders – wealthy individuals, family offices or specialised funds – offer borrowers high-interest loans with the expectation that the borrower will likely default, allowing the lender to foreclose on a valuable piece of property. While perfectly legal, the strategy is viewed as ethically dubious, even in the ultra-capitalistic world of real-estate investing. The question is whether the case of Sri Lanka's Hambantota Port and other BRI port projects actually fit the lend-to-own model, as Navarro and other critics contend.

There are three key elements of the lend-to-own investment strategy: a desperate or corrupt borrower; an above-market, high-interest loan agreement; and a profitable or strategically important property offered as collateral. The suggestion concerning China's BRI maritime strategy is that Beijing is using lend-to-own to acquire strategically important ports around the globe, and especially in Asia. The transactions around Sri Lanka's Hambantota Port are often cited as a case in point.

Hambantota is located on the southern tip of Sri Lanka, a key sea lane for trade between India and China through which 70,000 to 80,000 ships pass every year.[11] While a port had long been discussed for this underdeveloped area, it had also been viewed as economically unfeasible, especially after the area was decimated in the 2004 Indian Ocean tsunami. That changed in 2005 when Sri Lanka elected Mahinda Rajapaksa as president, who began searching for financing to develop Hambantota, his home region, into the second-largest urban centre in the country. Rajapaksa first reached out to India, Sri Lanka's closest ally, but was rebuffed. He then approached the United States, the World Bank and other potential investors, none of which expressed much enthusiasm. Eventually, China's Export–Import (Exim) Bank agreed to step into the breach.

China was an attractive lender to Rajapaksa for reasons beyond its willingness to finance the project. Firstly, China did not impose conditions for reform, transparency or other governance-related issues – a boon for a new president looking to reward allies. Secondly, China offered a comparatively good rate. Moreover, as Jerry Lou, Morgan Stanley's China strategist, said to the *New York Times* in 2010, Chinese 'companies are … competitive because they have acquired a lot of expertise in building large infrastructure projects in China … Chinese companies have become the biggest suppliers to ports of cranes used to move shipping containers, displacing South Korean and Japanese companies.' He described China as a 'game-changer' for the world's construction industry.[12]

Over the next several years, Hambantota, which became part of the BRI programme after it was launched by Xi, was built up and opened for business. Use of the port's facilities was initially poor, seeming to confirm sceptics' fears about its commercial viability. As late as 2018, the project appeared to be a white elephant, and few expected China, through its state-owned China Merchants Group, to make the needed investments to attract profitability. A Bloomberg News report observed that

> the port has a long way to go before it worries competitors in Singapore, Malaysia and the Middle East. Even with more traffic, Hambantota is only handling about one ship a day – not enough to even register on China

Merchants' own data showing cargo handling volumes for February. It didn't make a United Nations' list of the world's top 40 container terminals.[13]

The construction of Hambantota coincided with a massive international debt binge by Sri Lanka. By 2017, the interest payments from Sri Lanka's debts – along with the resource drain from an unprofitable port – had created an unsustainable financial burden for the country. Colombo sought a major restructuring of Hambantota's debt with China. In exchange for writing off the debt, Sri Lanka transferred 80% control of the port in a 99-year lease to China Merchants Port Holdings Company along with 1,235 acres (500 hectares) of land.[14]

From a cursory examination of this transaction, China's 'seizure' of the port appears to fit most, if not all, of the criteria of a lend-to-own strategy. Firstly, the Hambantota project began with a borrower that could be described as both desperate and corrupt. Not only had Sri Lanka been unable to find any reasonable lenders other than China's Exim Bank for the port's construction, but then-president Rajapaksa was born and raised in the Hambantota region, giving him a strong political motivation to support a project that could create 50,000 well-paying jobs and untold numbers of sweetheart deals within his hometown constituency. The Rajapaksa family has been accused and investigated for corruption, including for allegedly taking money from the China Harbour Engineering Company (CHEC) for Rajapaksa's re-election campaign.[15] Secondly, about one-third of the total loan was thought to be above market for similar developing-country infrastructure projects at the time. China's Exim Bank offered a $307 million loan for the first phase of construction at a rate of 6.3%.[16] Finally, the location of Hambantota, on a key sea lane for China's trade with India and a deep-water outpost within the Indian Ocean, makes the port a potentially strategically significant asset for China.

Critics of the project highlighted these points to suggest that not only was there more than a whiff of corruption around Hambantota, but that China's broader BRI ports strategy was a cynical attempt to seize strategic assets at the expense of the governments and citizens of host countries. However, a closer examination of Hambantota reveals a much more complicated picture.

Broadening the lens on Hambantota

While Sri Lanka did match the profile of a desperate, corrupt borrower to some extent, China's loans accounted for only a small proportion of a much wider debt binge. Driven by low interest rates as international investors searched for yields in a post-quantitative-easing world, Sri Lanka took on a massive amount of debt, which by 2018 totalled $66bn.[17] The Hambantota project amounted to only $1.1bn of that debt. While China is Sri Lanka's largest bilateral creditor, it only accounts for an estimated 9–15% of the country's outstanding debt. For context, Japan accounts for approximately 10% and international sovereign bonds for around half of the country's debt, with Americans holding two-thirds of the bonds' value and Asians only 8%.[18]

The Hambantota Port saga needs to be examined from a subregional geopolitical perspective. Sri Lanka appears to have turned to China at least partially because Colombo perceived it was becoming overly dependent on India, another regional power that appeared poised to deepen Sri Lanka's dependence. Sri Lanka has long had complicated relations with India, and it approached China to balance against its northern neighbour's dominance of maritime trade and the prospect of that dominance substantially increasing.

In 2017, 42% of Sri Lanka's container throughput was from India's trans-shipment trade.[19] Furthermore, Sri Lanka was worried that India's massive $50–125bn Sagar Mala port- and logistics-development programme would leave Sri Lankan ports less competitive in the region and further deepen the country's dependence on India.[20] A report from Sri Lanka's Lakshman Kadirgamar Institute of International Relations and Strategic Studies expressed the urgency of a Sri Lankan upgrade to its port infrastructure and competitiveness under the threat of Sagar Mala:

> As foreign flagged vessels will now be allowed to transport goods from one Indian port to another, Sri Lanka's ports might no longer play a major role in transshipping these goods. This could be a major blow as the Sri Lankan shipping industry relies heavily on its transshipment role. As such, both port expansions under Sagar Mala as well as the liberalisation of Indian shipping regulations could deteriorate the feeder

network that Sri Lanka has been able to maintain, thereby undermining its competitiveness as a hub.[21]

The fear of deepening Indian dominance also led Sri Lanka to reject India's attempt to buy the airport near Hambantota Port, which would have limited the attractiveness of Hambantota as a port of call for Chinese naval vessels. All of this coincided with the refusal of India to increase its military cooperation with Rajapaksa's planned offensive against the rebel Tamil Tigers, while China was more than willing to sell Sri Lanka new weapons.[22] These considerations reinforce the view that Sri Lanka wanted to use China to balance against – and increase its leverage with – India.

While the terms of the debt structure and interest rates around Hambantota are not entirely in the public domain, an examination of the available data suggests that China's loans to Sri Lanka are far from egregious. According to a report by Hong Kong-based academics Barry Sautman and Yan Hairong:

> Sri Lanka must pay interest averaging 6.3 per cent on international sovereign bonds and the principal must be fully repaid, on average, within seven years. In contrast, more than two-thirds of the value of Chinese state funds lent to Sri Lanka from 2001–2017 (including two-thirds of the Hambantota port loans) were at 2 per cent interest, and mostly repayable over 20 years.[23]

The small relative proportion of Chinese loans in Sri Lanka's overall debt profile, in combination with the relatively benign terms of those loans, is not consistent with a lend-to-own pattern.

Lend-to-own arrangements usually feature an impending debt-service default and a resulting ownership transfer, but Sri Lanka was not facing a debt-servicing default on Hambantota Port, and China did not execute a foreclosure or even a debt-for-equity swap. Instead, the port's debt, along with additional funds, were swapped into a 99-year lease. The deal was driven by Sri Lanka's overall national debt burden, and the arrangement with China meant that Sri Lanka was better able to service loans with far higher interest rates, mostly to Western firms and international bond holders.

Thus, although Hambantota is often cited by critics of China's BRI port strategy, it fails to support either the narrow lend-to-own parallel or the broader debt-trap hypothesis. Indeed, it can legitimately be argued that, despite the criticism it has drawn, Hambantota has led to a win–win situation for China and Sri Lanka. China has gained long-term operational control over the port, while Sri Lanka retains ownership and full sovereignty over the port zone.

The long-term lease was probably important in giving the port's Chinese operator, China Merchants, greater confidence in further investment, which, as mentioned, was crucial for improving the port's commercial outlook. For Sri Lanka, in addition to the balance-of-payments boost provided by the deal, the Hambantota project is leading to knowledge transfer, a narrowing of the maritime-infrastructure gap with India and a real, if limited, improvement of the country's long-term economic potential. According to Pabasara Kannangara of the Lakshman Kadirgamar Institute:

> By March 2019 the port had already reached 20 per cent of its total RORO [roll-on/roll-off] throughput for 2018, signalling a strong positive outlook. CM Ports has made efforts to improve efficiency by implementing best practices and processes. As a result, Hambantota Port was able to sign two Terminal Service Agreements early in 2019 with major shipping lines Hyundai Glovis and Hoegh Autoliner, both expected to bring in big volumes from the European and Indian markets.[24]

The geopolitics of Hambantota are subtle, and suggest that Beijing is playing a different, longer game than the debt-trap scheme cited by its critics. China has gained another friend in South Asia, but has not aggressively pushed to dominate Sri Lanka's external relations. Indeed, one of Sri Lanka's benefits from the deal is that India has responded by paying more attention to its southern neighbour, which was a goal of Sri Lanka's all along. For its part, there is little evidence that Beijing is undertaking an aggressive effort to shift Colombo's focus on balancing China and India. Shantanu Roy-Chaudhury has noted that

Colombo needs to tread carefully on how it manages its defense relations. Growing too close to China could create problems with India while leaning too much in favor of India could affect Chinese military sales to the country and other aspects of their bilateral relationship. For Colombo, it is therefore imperative to try and maximize its own gains while not antagonizing either of the large powers.[25]

Both India and China have accommodated themselves to this approach.

Beijing's port diplomacy as a 'win–win'

The Hambantota case is not an exception. China's international port investments elsewhere reinforce the conclusion that Beijing is not aggressively seeking ownership or control of the facilities that form part of the BRI. A comprehensive survey of BRI projects by the Rhodium Group shows that Hambantota is the only BRI project that could even partially be considered an asset seizure.[26] This is not to suggest that geopolitical considerations are not major drivers of Beijing's approach to port development. They clearly are, but in a much different way than the debt-trap/lend-to-own hypothesis suggests.

In many cases, countries on the receiving end of China's port investments have lobbied for these projects as a way to balance against larger regional or global powers, much as Sri Lanka sought support from Beijing to enhance its leverage vis-à-vis India. Djibouti chose to balance its dependence on the United States by allowing China to build the Doraleh Port. Gwadar Port in Pakistan was partially driven by Islamabad's desire to give the appearance of a naval alliance with China to balance against India's bilateral naval dominance. China's upgrading of Greece's Piraeus Port can be seen as assisting Athens to balance the European Union's dominance over Greece's economy and politics.

Most recently, Beijing's renewal of its commitment to a major BRI programme in Myanmar – including the building of a deep-sea port at Kyaukpyu – was signed during a two-day trip to Myanmar by President Xi in January. The agreement came at a time of intense criticism of Myanmar by Western countries and a concomitant drop in financial commitments. In 2013, the EU had removed sanctions against Myanmar after Aung San Suu Kyi's election to Myanmar's parliament, which led to a massive uptick in employment in the vitally important garment industry. By late 2018, however, the EU was threatening to reimpose sanctions because of state violence against the country's minority Rohingya population.[27] Similarly, the US in mid-2018 imposed extensive sanctions on Myanmar's military leaders and cooled ties that had been warming during the previous five years.[28] Myanmar's leaders clearly believed that improving ties with China could serve as an insurance plan against the possible re-isolation of the country.

In each of these cases, China provided recipient government partners not just opportunities for economic development (and the attendant corruption), but also geopolitical benefits in the form of increased leverage over, or decreased vulnerability to, more powerful external actors. This suggests that China is using its port-development projects not for short-term gain through asset-seizing, but for building longer-term partnerships underpinned by overlapping or complementary geopolitical agendas. It is too early to assess whether these port investments will be win–win in economic terms, but they are already providing desirable geopolitical outcomes both for China and for the recipient countries.

The micro-financial data around specific port projects reinforces this view. The Rhodium Group survey shows that for most of the projects that have become unprofitable or never reached profitability, China has either completely written off the debt, or refinanced or deferred it at preferential rates – hardly the actions of a country set on colonial-style asset seizures.[29] Thus, a common feature of China's BRI port projects is an effort to enhance partnerships with countries for whom Chinese investments can provide a significant boost to their own geopolitical status.

BRI ports and Beijing's energy insecurity

A second feature of many BRI port projects is that they will mitigate what China's leaders have long viewed as one of their country's greatest weaknesses: energy insecurity. China is the world's leading importer of crude oil, and foreign sources provided more than 70% of China's crude-oil consumption in 2018. What is particularly concerning for Beijing is that the vast bulk of China's energy imports pass through the extremely narrow Malacca Strait, where the US Navy has the ability to interdict passage and thereby threaten one of Beijing's most vital lifelines. This vulnerability was famously summarised as China's 'Malacca Dilemma' by then-president Hu Jintao in 2003.[30]

For Hu, the dilemma for Beijing was that it lacked both an alternative to its dependence on the strait and the capacity to counter the US military advantage in the region. China is using the BRI to try to ease this dual vulnerability, both directly and indirectly. The most direct elements of its strategy are the port projects in Gwadar and Kyaukpyu. At each of these ports, the medium-term plan is to develop oil and natural-gas pipelines to transport large volumes overland to China. For Kyaukpyu, the planned pipeline capacity is 400,000 barrels per day, or about 4–5% of China's total crude-oil imports.[31] For Gwadar, the initial capacity will be 1m bpd, with the option to increase this further.[32] Together, these projects could redirect nearly 20% of China's oil imports away from the Malacca Strait.

Although the BRI allows China to finally address its energy-security interests under a broader and less threatening 'developmental' banner, China's interest in both Gwadar and Kyaukpyu pre-dated the BRI. In fact, China's efforts to address its energy vulnerabilities in the maritime space began under Hu. As early as 2004, the US Pentagon began using the phrase 'string of pearls' to describe Chinese efforts to build strategic relationships along the sea lanes from the Middle East to the South China Sea. Even then, port development was a theme of Beijing's approach. By the middle of the last decade, China had focused its efforts on creating four major port projects, creating or enhancing facilities at Hambantota, Gwadar, Kyaukpyu and Chittagong in Bangladesh. From an energy-security perspective, Gwadar and Kyaukpyu were the most important because of the linkages to existing or proposed large pipeline projects.

Kyaukpyu

China has been working on developing a large deep-water port at Kyaukpyu, on the western coast of Myanmar, for nearly a decade. While the port is touted as a key initiative of the BRI, China has long pushed for a facility in the area as a way to improve its energy security. There are already operational oil and gas pipelines from western Myanmar to China's southern Yunnan province. With the addition of the port, larger shipments of energy products from the Middle East can be transported directly to China while bypassing the Malacca Strait.[33] The initial plan for Kyaukpyu was to build a massive $7bn special economic zone, including an industrial park, as well as the deep-water port. After pushback from the Myanmar government over the high price tag and the resulting debt overhang, China scaled back the project to $1.3bn for the first phase, with Chinese state-owned firms contributing 70% and Myanmar's government investing the remaining 30%.[34]

Progress on Kyaukpyu has been stop-and-go, however, reflecting the shifting relationships between Myanmar and China on the one hand, and Myanmar and Western powers on the other, in the aftermath of the transition away from military dictatorship. Myanmar's leader, Aung San Suu Kyi, had been cautious about Kyaukpyu, worried that she might lose her ability to balance between China and the West. It is only in recent months, after Myanmar's estrangement from the West over its persecution of the Rohingya, that a new set of agreements around the development of Kyaukpyu has been reached with China.

Gwadar

Gwadar Port is the 'crown jewel' in the China–Pakistan Economic Corridor (CPEC), the maritime entrepôt for the rail and road linkages between the Indian Ocean and the underdeveloped regions of western China and Central Asia, reducing the costs of linking up these regions with global sea lanes by shortening the transportation distances by thousands of kilometres. Port development at Gwadar will address two major Chinese security interests by securing alternative pathways to the Malacca Strait for oil to reach China, and by promoting growth and stability in western China and along China's vast western border region.

The China–Pakistan relationship has dramatically deepened in the past decade, especially as relations between Washington and Islamabad have soured and the former has moved to expand and deepen its ties with India.

As Pakistan and China have become closer, and in response to Pakistan's deepening economic and financial challenges, Beijing has moved to ease the terms of Pakistan's BRI projects, especially those attached to Gwadar. China has converted several infrastructure loans into interest-free grants and cut rates on other loans to far below market rates. Specifically, China slashed the interest rate from 3% to 1.6% on $3.8bn of infrastructure loans related to various Gwadar projects. In addition, China has recast its $140m loan for the construction of the highway to the Gwadar Port and the $230m loan for the construction of the Gwadar International Airport as interest-free grants.[35] This behaviour is the opposite of what would be expected under the lend-to-own hypothesis, which holds that creditors use debtors' financial distress to gain control of the assets in question.

Chittagong

China's intended port project at Chittagong, Bangladesh, has not yet been built. In contrast with relatively unstable and challenging regional geopolitical circumstances in Myanmar, Pakistan and Sri Lanka, Bangladesh has long-standing and cordial political and security relations with its closest regional partner, India. This has been particularly true during the 11 years that Sheikh Hasina has been Bangladesh's prime minister. Hasina's rule has also been marked by strong economic growth of 6% per year for the decade. During this time, Bangladesh's economic ties with China have dramatically deepened, and bilateral relations have been smooth.

Still, Bangladesh has rebuffed repeated offers by China for a port project at Chittagong, even as Beijing has facilitated some $10bn in BRI projects elsewhere in the country, including the first bridge across the Padma River that will connect Bangladesh's western and eastern coastal zones. Hasina declined China's offers to build Chittagong Port for two reasons, both intimately connected with regional geopolitics. Firstly, India made clear that it did not want the project to go forward; and secondly, Bangladesh did not want to deepen strategic relations with the principal patron of its own regional rival, Pakistan. Instead, Bangladesh has signed an agreement with Japan's foreign-aid agency to construct modest additional port facilities at Matabari, near Chittagong.[36]

Piraeus

China's port-building activities under the BRI have not been confined to geographic settings where energy security is directly at stake. In Europe, China has pursued equity ownership in the Port of Piraeus in Greece. Beijing probably views Piraeus as a key way of expanding the BRI initiative to Europe. With additional overland projects, Piraeus can become the BRI's gateway to the economies of Eastern and Southern Europe. China began its involvement in 2009, winning a 35-year concession to upgrade and run the port through the country's largest shipping firm, the China Ocean Shipping Company (COSCO). In 2016, COSCO went further, purchasing 51% of the port. COSCO also agreed to spend €600m on further development, obtaining partial financing from the European Investment Bank.[37]

The Piraeus case shows that if China was truly driven to own BRI-developed ports, it could use a far more direct strategy than lend-to-own or debt-trap diplomacy – it could simply purchase the equity of these projects through its multinational companies, just as the US, Japan and European nations often do. While there was some local pushback in Greece to China's involvement, Piraeus's successful economic outcomes quickly dispelled any criticism:

> Before COSCO took over, the port's container handling record was at 1.5 million TEUs [twenty-foot equivalent units]. These figures rose to 3.692 million containers in 2017. As a result, revenue and profits soared. In 2017, the Athens stock exchange listed company (OLP) almost doubled its pre-tax profits from 11 to 21.2 million euros.[38]

While Greece might not technically qualify as a developing country like the others profiled here, Greece's eagerness to join China's BRI fits the pattern of nations using Chinese largesse to balance against other large powers – in this case the EU. Greece has the highest unemployment rate in Europe, and is constantly in what Athens sees as a humiliating tug of war with Northern European countries for fiscal assistance. Piraeus's upgrade alone will create an estimated 10–13,000 jobs, and the follow-on, China-backed $9.5bn Hellenikon Airport resort project, could create an additional 75,000 jobs once operational.[39]

In exchange for Chinese investment, Greece joined the '17+1 Cooperation' group linking China and Central and Eastern European countries; and Athens has defended Beijing's human-rights record against EU censure.[40] Greece has long been something of an ideological maverick in Europe, so it should not be surprising that it has offered China some broader political support in exchange for its economic assistance. Greece will be one of several countries standing in the way of Germany's hopes to forge a stronger and tougher European consensus on China during the second half of 2020 when it holds the EU presidency.

* * *

The extent, scale and perseverance of Beijing's port-development activities are one of the strongest indicators that the BRI, in contrast to Beijing's claims, has powerful geopolitical drivers, goals and attributes. Among these are the aims of mitigating China's vulnerability to the Malacca dilemma; expanding economic and military ties as a mechanism to begin to erode the long-standing US maritime dominance in the region; and making friends and influencing people more broadly, to paraphrase Dale Carnegie.

A key element of BRI port projects that has made them attractive to recipient governments is that they provide geopolitical as well as economic benefits. China has been extremely effective in using port investments to enhance the geopolitical standing of host governments vis-à-vis stronger regional states. Any adoption by China of aggressive and hostile investor strategies such as lend-to-own would only be counterproductive. Moreover, while BRI projects are mostly funded through loans that are less concessional than those offered by multilateral development banks, China has shown flexibility on financing and restructuring, especially in circumstances (as in Gwadar) where the projects directly promote Beijing's own key goals. The fact that the largest multilateral development banks and most major non-Chinese donors (Japan being a partial exception) have eschewed large-scale port-development projects has given Beijing leverage as the 'only game in town' for such investments. In a recent interview, Aboubaker Omar Hadi, the head of Djibouti's port authority, explained that his country had accepted Chinese investment because

> We [had] no choice. Did the rest of the world give us a chance or choice? If Japan offers us the same, if Europe or the U.S. offers us the same, [there would be] no issue. We are pro-our country, pro-our continent. We are not pro-other foreign country.[41]

The financial scale and uniqueness of the BRI has allowed China to establish 'privileged creditor' status, much to the chagrin of other official and commercial creditors.

China's actual BRI port strategy is much more challenging for the United States and Beijing's other Western rivals than the imagined strategy of debt-trap diplomacy and asset-grabbing through lend-to-own. There is no doubt that BRI loans have contributed, sometimes heavily, to the debt challenges facing a growing number of recipient countries, especially in the context of the coronavirus-induced global economic crisis. But that does not justify the assertion that creating debt difficulties was central to Beijing's aims in creating the BRI. If the evidence supported the debt-trap hypothesis, the US and others would have a strong prima facie case for discouraging countries considering BRI projects involving potentially strategic assets such as ports. But lacking supporting evidence, the accusation of debt-trap diplomacy becomes little more than an ideological stick, which may be of some use to opponents of incumbent governments in BRI recipient countries, but with little value beyond that. The accusation in itself is an affront to those countries that are cooperating with China on various projects, more likely reinforcing Beijing's influence than challenging it. Much more effective are critiques that focus on Beijing's lack of transparency, accountability and sustainability in BRI projects generally, as well as efforts to enhance, and bring to scale, non-Chinese-dominated financing alternatives to address the large-scale infrastructure needs of the developing world.

Notes

[1] This article does a good job detailing the extensive measures the Chinese Communist Party has taken to control the narrative around the BRI: Nadège Rolland, 'Mapping the Footprint of Belt and Road Influence Operations', Sinopsis, 8 December 2019, https://sinopsis.cz/en/

rolland-bri-influence-operations/.

2   See Brahma Chellaney, 'China's Debt
     Trap Diplomacy', Project Syndicate,
     23 January 2017, https://www.
     project-syndicate.org/commentary/
     china-one-belt-one-road-loans-
     debt-by-brahma-chellaney-2017-01;
     and Brahma Chellaney, 'China
     Ensnares Vulnerable States in a
     Debt Trap', Nikkei Asian Review,
     20 February 2018, https://asia.nikkei.
     com/Politics/International-relations/
     China-ensnares-vulnerable-states-in-a-
     debt-trap.

3   Chellaney, 'China's Debt Trap
     Diplomacy'.

4   'Statement of General Joseph L.
     Votel, Commander, U.S. Central
     Command, Before the Senate
     Armed Services Committee', 5
     February 2019, p. 12, https://www.
     centcom.mil/Portals/6/Documents/
     Transcripts/Votel020519.pdf.

5   US Central Command, 'Senate Armed
     Services Committee Hearing on U.S.
     Central Command', 11 February
     2019, https://www.centcom.mil/
     MEDIA/Transcripts/Article/1754626/
     general-joseph-votel-senate-armed-
     services-committee-hearing-on-us-
     central-comm/.

6   Sebastian Horn, Carmen Reinhart
     and Christoph Trebesch, 'China's
     Overseas Lending', Kiel Working
     Paper no. 2,132, June 2019, pp. 2, 8–9,
     https://www.ifw-kiel.de/fileadmin/
     Dateiverwaltung/IfW-Publications/
     Christoph_Trebesch/KWP_2132.pdf.

7   Ibid., p. 5.

8   Anisah Shukry and Yudith Ho,
     'Malaysia's Mahathir Pledges
     to Review China Investment if
     Re-elected', Bloomberg News, 8

April 2018, https://www.bloomberg.
com/news/articles/2018-04-08/
mahathir-pledges-to-review-china-
investment-after-malaysia-vote.

9   'Mahathir Warns Against New
     "Colonialism" During Visit to
     China', Bloomberg News, 20 August
     2018, https://www.bloomberg.
     com/news/articles/2018-08-20/
     mahathir-warns-against-new-
     colonialism-during-visit-to-china.

10   'White House National Trade Council
     Director Peter Navarro on Chinese
     Economic Aggression', Hudson
     Institute, 9 July 2018, https://www.
     hudson.org/research/14437-full-
     transcript-white-house-national-trade-
     council-director-peter-navarro-on-
     chinese-economic-aggression.

11   See 'Hambantota Port Complex: Will
     Sri Lanka Realize the Dream?', 9
     February 2010, released by WikiLeaks
     as Cable 10COLOMBO103_a,
     https://wikileaks.org/plusd/
     cables/10COLOMBO103_a.html.

12   Vikas Bajaj, 'India Worries as China
     Builds Ports in South Asia', New York
     Times, 15 February 2010, https://www.
     nytimes.com/2010/02/16/business/
     global/16port.html.

13   Iain Marlow, 'China's $1 Billion
     White Elephant', Bloomberg News, 17
     April 2018, https://www.bloomberg.
     com/news/articles/2018-04-17/
     china-s-1-billion-white-elephant-the-
     port-ships-don-t-use.

14   See Eric Bellman, 'Sri Lanka, Deep
     in Debt, Turns Increasingly to China
     for Loans', Wall Street Journal, 29
     January 2019, https://www.wsj.
     com/articles/sri-lanka-deep-in-debt-
     turns-increasingly-to-china-for-
     loans-11548774001.

15 See Ranga Sirilal and Shihar Aneez, 'Rajapaksa Comeback Bid Checked by Sri Lanka Bribery Probe', Reuters, 24 July 2015, https://www.reuters.com/article/us-sri-lanka-rajapaksa/rajapaksa-comeback-bid-checked-by-sri-lanka-bribery-probe-idUSKCNoPY1PK20150724.

16 'China's Debt Trap? The True Story of Hambantota Port', Hellenic Shipping News, 21 May 2019, https://www.hellenicshippingnews.com/chinas-debt-trap-the-true-story-of-hambantota-port/.

17 Ministry of Finance, Sri Lanka, 'Annual Report 2018', p. 6, http://treasury.gov.lk/documents/10181/12870/Finance+Ministry+Annual+Report+2018+English+updated.pdf/. Total government debt in 2018 was about 12trn Sri Lankan rupees or around $66bn.

18 Barry Sautman and Yan Hairong, 'The Truth About Sri Lanka's Hambantota Port', South China Morning Post, 6 May 2019, https://www.scmp.com/comment/insight-opinion/article/3008799/truth-about-sri-lankas-hambantota-port-chinese-debt-traps.

19 Pabasara Kannangara, 'Sri Lanka's Port Development and the Role of BRI', Asia Dialogue, 24 May 2019, https://theasiadialogue.com/2019/05/24/sri-lankas-port-development-and-the-role-of-the-bri/.

20 See Ministry of Shipping, Government of India, 'Sagar Mala Concepts and Objectives', http://sagarmala.gov.in/about-sagarmala/vision-objectives.

21 Pabasara Kannangara, 'Sagarmala: India's New Port Development Strategy and Its Implications for Sri Lanka', Lakshman Kadirgamar Institute of International Relations and Strategic Studies, 13 February 2019, https://www.lki.lk/publication/sagarmala-indias-new-port-development-strategy-and-its-implications-for-sri-lanka/.

22 See 'China and Sri Lanka: Between a Dream and a Nightmare', Diplomat, 18 November 2016, https://thediplomat.com/2016/11/china-and-sri-lanka-between-a-dream-and-a-nightmare/.

23 Sautman and Hairong, 'The Truth About Sri Lanka's Hambantota Port'.

24 Kannangara, 'Sri Lanka's Port Development and the Role of BRI'.

25 Shantanu Roy-Chaudhury, 'India–China–Sri Lanka Triangle: The Defense Dimension', Diplomat, 12 July 2019, https://thediplomat.com/2019/07/india-china-sri-lanka-triangle-the-defense-dimension/.

26 Agatha Kratz, Allen Feng and Logan Wright, 'New Data on the "Debt Trap" Question', Rhodium Group, 29 April 2019, https://rhg.com/research/new-data-on-the-debt-trap-question/.

27 See Laurence Norman, 'Myanmar's Economy in Peril as EU Weighs Trade Punishment over Rohingya', Wall Street Journal, 5 October 2018, https://www.wsj.com/articles/myanmars-economy-in-peril-as-eu-weighs-trade-punishment-over-rohingya-1538750348.

28 See Edward Wong, 'US Imposes Sanctions on Myanmar Military over Rohingya Atrocities', New York Times, 17 August 2018, https://www.nytimes.com/2018/08/17/us/politics/myanmar-sanctions-rohingya.html.

29 Kratz, Feng and Wright, 'New Data on the "Debt Trap" Question'.

30 See Wen Han, 'Hu Jintao Urges

Breakthrough in Malacca Dilemma', *Wen Wei Po*, 14 January 2004.

31 Lee Yimou, 'Beset by Delays, Myanmar–China Oil Pipeline Nears Start Up', Reuters, 21 March 2017, https://www.reuters.com/article/us-myanmar-china-oil/beset-by-delays-myanmar-china-oil-pipeline-nears-start-up-idUSKBN16S0XF.

32 Gwadar Central, 'Crude Oil Pipeline Requires 10 Billion Dollars Investment', 10 September 2018, https://gwadarcentral.com/crude-oil-pipeline-requires-10-billion-dollars-investment/.

33 See Myo Aung Myanmar, 'The Good, the Bad and the Ugly: Kyaukpyu Port Project Myanmar with China', November 2018, https://www.researchgate.net/publication/328902204_THE_GOOD_THE_BAD_AND_THE_UGLY_KYAUKPHYU_PORT_PROJECT_MYANMAR_WITH_CHINA.

34 Laura Zhou, 'China Sees Myanmar as Stepping Stone to Indian Ocean, Energy Security', *South China Morning Post*, 15 January 2020, https://www.scmp.com/news/china/diplomacy/article/3046218/china-sees-myanmar-stepping-stone-indian-ocean-energy-security.

35 'China Converts $230 Million Loan for Gwadar Airport into Grant', GEO Pakistan News, 23 September 2015, https://www.geo.tv/latest/6270-china-converts-230m-loan-for-gwadar-airport-into-grant.

36 See David Brewster, 'Bangladesh's Road to the BRI', Lowy Institute, 30 May 2019, https://www.lowyinstitute.org/the-interpreter/bangladesh-road-bri.

37 George Georgiopoulos, Angeliki Koutantou and Renee Maltezou, 'China, Greece Agree to Push Ahead with COSCO's Piraeus Port Investment', Reuters, 11 November 2019, https://www.reuters.com/article/us-greece-china/china-greece-agree-to-push-ahead-with-coscos-piraeus-port-investment-idUSKBN1XL1KC.

38 Zhang Zhen Kai, *China's 'Belt and Road' Initiative and Its Spatial Impacts in Europe*, Master's thesis, Politecnico de Milano, 2019, p. 43, http://docplayer.net/185950435-Politecnico-di-milano.html.

39 See Catherine Wong, 'Why Greece Is Banking on China's Modern-day Silk Road to Help Its Economic Recovery', *South China Morning Post*, 26 December 2017, https://www.scmp.com/news/china/diplomacy-defence/article/2125506/why-greece-banking-chinas-modern-day-silk-road-help-its.

40 See Shi Zhiqin, 'Xi's Visit Can Propel Greece's Role in BRI', *Global Times*, 11 November 2019, https://www.globaltimes.cn/content/1169675.shtml.

41 Akane Okutsu, 'Djibouti Has "No Choice" but China for Infrastructure Development', Dehai News, 1 September 2019, http://www.dehai.org/dehai/dehai-news/334831.

COVID-19 and the EU Economy: Try Again, Fail Better

Erik Jones

The last financial crisis was traumatic for the European Union. The response was slow, the damage was deep and the new arrangements made to prevent the next crisis from occurring remain incomplete.[1] Now, all too quickly, the wolf is at the door again. This time it came in the form of the novel coronavirus. The global pandemic struck a European economy that still has not fully recovered from the divisions that emerged between North and South, or the general weakness of its own macroeconomic performance. Worse, new political rifts have emerged between voters and politicians, West and East, Europe and America.[2] The challenge Europe faces may be existential. As François Heisbourg recently noted: 'To a significant degree, the EU's future is riding on its ability to handle the COVID-19 crisis.'[3]

Heisbourg also pointed out that 'the EU has proven to have strong survival instincts' and suggested that 'the EU could be one of the bigger geopolitical surprises of the crisis'.[4] Europe is adaptive, not static. European leaders have made mistakes, they have failed, progress has faltered, and yet the project as a whole has remained viable. This resilience is due partly to political determination and partly to a lack of alternatives. A world without the EU would be a much poorer, more conflictive and less innovative place. Moreover, the EU is a self-correcting and problem-solving organisation, even if the results may not always look like outright success.

Erik Jones is Professor of European Studies at the Paul H. Nitze School of Advanced International Studies (SAIS), Johns Hopkins University; Senior Research Associate at the Istituto per gli Studi di Politica Internazionale in Milan; and a contributing editor to *Survival*.

Survival | vol. 62 no. 4 | August–September 2020 | pp. 81–100   DOI 10.1080/00396338.2020.1792124

The two most important revelations of the last European crisis were the vulnerability of European financial markets to disintegration, and the link that vulnerability forges between the European Central Bank (ECB) and European sovereign-debt markets.[5] Both lessons are on full display in the current crisis, and they inform the actions of the ECB and the complex negotiations on European fiscal efforts. But it is unclear whether greater awareness of these realities will produce an effective policy response.

A crisis of confidence

The last financial crisis showed that European financial markets are difficult to hold together and relatively easy to pull apart.[6] Although lack of competitiveness, weak public finances and excessive borrowing in the private sector impaired European economies and could stand improving, financial-market disintegration was the main driver of the crisis.[7] The problem in Europe is not country-specific, but rather structural.[8] Disintegration occurs as investors react to uncertainty by trying to move their investments from assets that are harder to sell or higher in risk to assets that are more liquid and less risky. This is the so-called 'flight to quality' or 'flight to liquidity'.[9]

Europe, unlike other parts of the world, has one large regional economy composed of smaller national economies. As European financial markets integrated to form it, investors in countries with more savings moved some of that money into countries with greater opportunities for investment. Thus, Belgian, Dutch, French and German banks invested in countries such as Greece, Ireland, Italy, Portugal and Spain. Those same northern European banks also invested heavily in the United States and elsewhere, often in complex financial instruments and sometimes in instruments underpinned by subprime mortgages. When those northern European banks began to lose money on their US investments – and investments in other countries such as the United Kingdom – in 2007 and 2008, they began to worry about their exposure in countries such as Greece, Ireland, Italy, Portugal and Spain.[10]

For the northern European banks, reducing that exposure threatened to collapse asset prices and increase losses. Initially, therefore, it made sense to wait and see how bad and widespread the downturn would be. As the crisis moved across the Atlantic in late 2008, however, waiting no longer seemed like a viable option, so many of the northern European banks moved more quickly. Many collapsed, and some needed state assistance. The economies of Ireland and Greece suffered significant damage. Eventually, Spain and Italy also took major hits as northern European investors liquidated their holdings. During summer 2011, for example, foreign investors sold significant amounts of Italian sovereign debt and pulled almost €200 billion out of Italy.[11]

This 'sudden stop' dynamic precipitated the disintegration of European financial markets, as savers and investors that had worked across national boundaries no longer remained in sync.[12] Some countries lost huge volumes of capital. Beyond that, local firms could no longer borrow at the same price as those in other countries. Different national rates of interest prevailed – high in the countries that investors fled, low in the countries to which they flocked. This effect was especially pronounced in the yields on sovereign-debt instruments – typically regarded as the safest form of investment – which rose in countries that investors bolted from and fell in countries where they landed.

The ECB cannot influence macroeconomic activity in those parts of Europe that experience a sudden stop. The reason is simple. The ECB's standard instrument for influencing macroeconomic activity is interest rates, which the bank lowers to stimulate economic activity and raises to slow it down. When European financial markets disintegrate, however, the impact of a rate cut is heavily skewed towards safe-haven countries, where interest rates are already falling due to the influx of capital. Central-bank policy cannot effectively lower interest rates in the countries that have experienced a sudden stop because the ECB first needs to convince international investors to stop liquidating their positions and taking money out of those countries.

During the worst phase of the last crisis, in 2012, the monetary-transmission mechanism was broken. That is, the ECB's changing interest rates in Germany had no impact in Italy or Spain. Accordingly, the ECB has since focused on strengthening the link between interest rates set in Germany and those in other parts of the euro area.[13] To do so, the task was to restore investor confidence in the safest assets in Italy and Spain, which had experienced large-scale capital flight.[14] Mario Draghi, then the ECB president, promised to buy 'unlimited' amounts of distressed-country sovereign debt in order to preserve the functioning of the monetary-transmission mechanism. By implication, he reassured international investors that there was a floor below which the value of their sovereign-debt holdings would not fall. This convinced investors to buy Italian and Spanish sovereign debt rather than to sell it. The spread between Italian and Spanish sovereign debt, on the one hand, and German sovereign debt, on the other hand, narrowed, and the most acute phase of the European crisis came to an end.

The facility created by the ECB to safeguard the monetary-transmission mechanism was never used. Renewed market confidence was enough to reverse the flight to quality from Italy and Spain to Germany (and elsewhere). Unfortunately, that success was only partial in terms of restoring European financial-market integration and the monetary-transmission mechanism. As a result, the ECB has struggled to meet its policy targets. Furthermore, the impact of the last crisis on the financial institutions of those countries that were most affected – Cyprus, Greece, Ireland, Italy, Portugal and Spain – was dramatic, and their recovery uneven. Among remedial policies, the most important has been to encourage investors to take on risk. To do this, the ECB began to purchase low-risk assets – in particular, sovereign debt – in large volumes, driving up the price of these assets and driving down their yield. Here the goal is to get investors to move their money into riskier assets and to restore market confidence in distressed-country sovereign debt.

During the present pandemic, worries about the danger of sudden stops and the importance of preserving the monetary-transmission mechanism were initially overshadowed by concerns about the scale of the ECB's public-sector purchase programme and its implications for fiscal policy in different European countries. The two biggest policy shocks to hit the European economy during the first weeks of the pandemic came from a fundamental misunderstanding of the relationship between European monetary and fiscal policy.

The first shock came on 12 March, when Christine Lagarde, Draghi's successor, stated that the ECB was not responsible for closing the spread between the sovereign-debt instruments issued by different national governments.[15] The second arose in early May, when Germany's Federal Constitutional Court declared that the ECB had failed to consider the economic and fiscal implications of its monetary-policy decisions to ensure that they were 'proportionate'.[16] Market participants reacted to both developments by, among other things, selling Italian sovereign debt and buying German sovereign debt. Once again, it looked as though European financial markets might disintegrate in ways that would be very damaging to economic performance in the countries, like Italy, that investors fled. If left unchecked, this dynamic could repeat the damage of the last crisis in a way that could break the euro as a common currency.

The pandemic

The rapid spread of the novel coronavirus in northern Italy in late February and early March 2020 caught the ECB in a period of self-reflection. Draghi, the outgoing ECB president, pushed through an expansive package of monetary-policy measures in September 2019. As a result, Lagarde, Draghi's successor, planned to use her first months in office to undertake a comprehensive policy review. The onset of the pandemic forced her to jump into action. Before the 12 March monetary-policy meeting, Lagarde and her team recognised the importance of a powerful response. The question was how to sustain European economic performance during the shock that would occur when national governments locked down their populations to halt the spread of the virus. No precedent was available for guidance. They did recognise that while the threat of the virus was universal, the shock would be felt more strongly in some countries than others.

ECB economists designed their policy response to be as flexible as possible. They expanded the size of the asset-purchase programme by €120bn without spreading that money out into monthly purchases, allowing the ECB to spend as much money as necessary on short notice. The ECB also insisted that it would purchase as much as required across national jurisdictions. Finally, Lagarde made it clear that the emphasis on flexibility would last for as long as the crisis demanded.[17]

The trouble came when a journalist asked for the reason behind the flexibility, and whether in particular the ECB would help close the spread between Italian and German sovereign debt. Lagarde fell back on the idea that there is a clear distinction between monetary policy and fiscal policy, and that closing the spreads was the responsibility of other institutions. She also distinguished her position from Draghi's 'whatever it takes' stance, stating that she did not feel obliged to do anything unusual or dramatic in response to the pandemic.[18] Draghi, however, had made his extraordinary commitment precisely because of the widening of the spread between German and Italian (and Spanish) sovereign debt. Moreover, he did so not because he was trying on principle to intervene in fiscal policy but because the divergence threatened to break the interbank lending mechanisms that made it possible for the ECB to transmit its monetary policy across the euro-area economy.

Lagarde quickly corrected her misstatement.[19] Nevertheless, the pressure in the markets continued to increase until 18 March, when the ECB announced the creation of a new pandemic emergency-purchase programme.[20] That new programme would make €750bn available to purchase assets on a flexible basis to restore order to European sovereign-debt markets and ensure the smooth functioning of the monetary-transmission mechanism. It was only a partial success. Speculative pressure against Italian sovereign debt ebbed and flowed in subsequent weeks, mainly because Italy lacked sufficient fiscal space to mount an effective economic response to the pandemic. As a result, the Italian government lobbied extensively for support from the rest of Europe.

The institution most readily available to support Italy is the European Stability Mechanism (ESM), an intergovernmental organisation established by most (but not all) EU member states in 2012 to bail out national governments that needed fiscal resources. But the ESM cannot lend money unconditionally. The Italian government would have to qualify to borrow by showing longer-term debt sustainability and access to financial markets, and by accepting lending conditions. From Italy's perspective, borrowing from the ESM would mean sacrificing national sovereignty and accepting the kind of humiliation that successive Greek governments experienced during the last crisis.[21] The current government might choose that route, but it would be unlikely to last long if it did. A government formed by the opposition parties on the Italian right would almost surely trigger a confrontation with the rest of Europe and turmoil in the bond markets, similar to that which began to surface when the main right-wing Italian political party was in the coalition government from June 2018 to August 2019.[22]

Italian public finances are now under considerably more stress as a result of the pandemic than they were during the last government. European policymakers may find themselves between a rock and a hard place, their only choice being to either force the Italian government to accept support that could bring down the governing coalition, or leave it to its own resources with similar effect. Given that European leaders knew about the fragility of European financial markets from the last crisis, why didn't the EU already have an institutional solution in place?

The EU's lack of cohesion

The EU's failure to build the institutions necessary to avoid the financial-market disintegration that Europeans experienced between 2009 and 2012 was the result of profound disagreements among European governments. During the last crisis, national leaders recognised the need for financial stability. They created a new array of institutions to provide general oversight for European banks, insurance companies and financial markets. Then they gave the ECB specific responsibility for supervising European financial institutions. They wrote a common rule book on responsible bank conduct, and established a framework for deciding when and how misbehaving banks should be disciplined. And they built the ESM as a permanent mechanism to underwrite national public finances when the costs of responding to a crisis became too great for any national government to manage alone.[23]

But there was also substantial disagreement among European capitals. They differed over the need to issue common public-debt instruments or create a shared 'risk-free' asset. They bickered about the conditions under which national governments could discipline or bail out their own banks, how much of their own government's sovereign debt banks could hold, who would pay the costs of winding up failing banks and how best to insure the deposits in those institutions. Finally, they disagreed on what national governments should have to do whenever their own finances got into trouble and how quickly or automatically they might receive financial support from the ESM or the ECB.[24]

The upshot was that investors saw the risks associated with one country, like Germany, very differently from the risks associated with another, like Italy. Investors who discern national differences, of course, may be an important source of market discipline.[25] In response to a common shock like the coronavirus, however, the overriding need is for the EU to hang together. During the last crisis, in creating the space for European policymakers to complete institutional reforms so that the next crisis could be avoided, the ECB also afforded European policymakers the latitude to agree to disagree, and in some cases to withdraw support for key arrangements, such as the direct recapitalisation of stricken banks.[26]

The question remains whether the ECB's actions by themselves can restore market confidence this time around. The answer lies partly in the recognition that the Italian government is not strong enough to accept the kind and degree of oversight necessary to qualify for ECB assistance. The programme Draghi created to do 'whatever it takes' is only available to governments that agree to accept the conditions for ESM support. No Italian politician wants to face the voters after having ceded control over domestic policymaking to European institutions or to other governments, particularly Germany.[27]

The alternative would be for EU member states to accept responsibility for one another's debt or for debt that they would incur in common. This 'mutualisation' of sovereign debt is controversial but not entirely implausible.[28] The first step would be to identify or create an institution that is able to borrow money on the markets. The European Investment Bank, the ESM and the European Commission all have that ability. Every participating government would need to contribute some capital (or guarantee access to some flow of income) to that institution. In addition, every government would have to agree to make sure that the debt were repaid, even if that meant covering any losses by dipping into the capital and topping it up as necessary.

Other aspects of the proposition are more problematic. Politicians disagree about whether the government that spends the money should also be the government that repays the money. When the Irish government borrowed money to bail out its banks in 2008 and 2009, for example, not all the banks it saved were Irish. Dublin was also rescuing investors from other countries. The ECB prevented the Irish government from forcing those investors to share in the costs of saving the banks.[29] That raised legitimate questions about why the Irish government should be responsible for all the money that it borrowed. The debate about conditionality is also ongoing. Heavy restrictions make intuitive sense when it could be argued that the national government is responsible for its financial trouble, as was the case with Greece in the last crisis, but not so much when the national government obviously finds itself caught up in forces that are beyond its control, as Ireland did.[30]

Monetary versus fiscal policy

Relying on the ECB is the politically expedient way to avoid such conflicts. Nevertheless, counting on the ECB to share risks across countries comes at a cost. The ECB faces market-pricing risk that a special-purpose debt agency like the ESM does not. Once the ESM sells its own bonds, the purchasers bear any risk from price fluctuations. When the ECB purchases sovereign debt, its position resembles that of a private investor.[31] It is true that the representatives of the national central banks agreed that they would be responsible for purchasing their own government's sovereign debt, and that they would hold any risks associated with those purchases on their own balance sheets rather than sharing them across the euro system. This arrangement seems sensible, but it could go horribly wrong if one or more governments loses access to financial markets and no longer qualifies for ECB purchases.[32]

Relying on the ECB to stabilise European financial markets involves not only higher routine risks associated with the purchase or holding of debt instruments, but also higher catastrophic risks associated with the possibility that one or more of the debtors to which it is exposed will default. Nevertheless, the governments of the euro area would rather accept a higher mutualised risk in the ECB than they would face if they agreed to mutualise risks through an institution specifically designed to raise credit. That trade-off makes sense only because the ECB's balance sheet is large enough that it can prevent individual governments from getting into so much trouble in financial markets that they have no choice but to default. This is certainly the expectation, at least as long as Europe remains in this crisis.

How the ECB will manage its balance sheet after the crisis has passed remains to be seen. Now that the bank has taken on the task of mutualising risk across the euro area, its balance-sheet decisions will directly affect not only financial-market stability and price inflation but also government finances, which the ECB was not designed to influence. In particular, the bank has to decide in what proportions it should purchase across jurisdictions and categories, how much it can purchase of any issue or from any issuer, when it can relax restrictions it sets on its own policies and when it is safe to reimpose those restrictions. The trade-offs it faces are politically sensitive, and create winners and losers across the single currency. The ECB's decision to prevent the Bank of Cyprus from extending emergency liquidity assistance to the country's two largest banks in March 2013 is one illustration; the bank's decision to pull its waiver on the credit-rating requirements for the use of Greek sovereign debt as collateral in February 2015 is another. The ECB is ill-equipped to navigate such acutely political territory.[33]

The EU's calculus began to shift when the European Council met on 23 April to address the pandemic. At that meeting, members confirmed a European Commission initiative to support national unemployment-insurance programmes, whereby the commission would borrow money in the markets and then lend it to governments in need. They also approved a European Investment Bank programme to support lending to small and medium-sized enterprises, and an ESM plan to make loans available to national governments to pay for healthcare expenses related to the pandemic. Finally, the council asked the commission to set out a road map for the creation of a 'recovery fund' on an urgent basis.[34] Each of these short-term policy actions involved some form of mutualisation. The call for a new recovery fund suggested that even more risk-sharing might follow. Whether this would be enough to address the crisis adequately and take pressure off the ECB was uncertain.

Consider the role of the ESM. It was created to bail out insolvent governments, not to help finance a government facing a pandemic. That is why the requirement for conditions on lending is written into the institution's founding documents. It is also why the Italian government is so reluctant to rely on the ESM for credit. The European Council tried to get around this dilemma in its 23 April decision by imposing the lightest possible form of conditionality. The ESM also declared all governments in the euro area qualified to borrow, and the European Commission promised that the oversight on any lending would be minimal. Nevertheless, many Italians were still wary of the ESM.[35] Furthermore, market participants could not see how the Italian government could respond effectively to the macroeconomic downturn without accessing ESM financing, and continued to put pressure on Italian bonds, which the ECB had to ease by buying them.[36]

By late April, Italian ten-year government bonds yielded approximately 230 basis points (or 2.3%) more than German ten-year bonds.[37] The Italian bonds have a lower Standard & Poor's credit rating (BBB) than their German counterparts (AAA). A loan-based stabilisation programme, such as the one provided by the European Commission to backstop national unemployment systems or European Investment Bank support for small and medium-sized enterprises, could alleviate some of the pressure in the very short term, but it could not reshape the financial context. Neither could an emergency ESM loan to national governments to fund healthcare, even though such a loan would cost the Italian government less than borrowing from the markets.

It will still be harder for Italian firms to survive the pandemic than it will be for German firms. Economic conditions across the two countries will diverge, and the two economies will not work together as closely as they did. Efforts to make Italian government finances look more like German ones would only exacerbate the divergence. Arguing that Italians should pull themselves up by their own bootstraps does not change the fact the results look more like disintegration than integration, particularly from an Italian perspective.

Law and economics

The gap between Italy and Germany can be bridged only through direct transfers or more indirect support from the ECB. Transfers are politically controversial. The ECB is more politically expedient – or at least it was until Germany's Federal Constitutional Court raised fundamental questions about the legality of such actions. The timing of the German court's decision that the ECB had overreached had little or nothing to do with the rapid spread of the novel coronavirus or the introduction of the ECB's new pandemic emergency-purchase programme. The German court was responding to a complaint filed in 2015 after the start of the large-scale asset-purchase programme. During its deliberations, the court sought guidance from the Court of Justice of the European Union as to whether the ECB exceeded its mandate by purchasing large amounts of sovereign debt. Specifically, the German court expressed concern that having a central bank purchase sovereign debt might constitute monetary financing, which would go against specific EU treaty provisions. The European court responded in December 2018 that the ECB was acting within its mandate.

The German court held that the European court's ruling was 'incomprehensible' and could not be applied in German law. The court went on to argue that the ECB's actions may cross the boundary between monetary policy and fiscal policy. According to the court, if a central bank purchases large amounts of sovereign debt, promises to hold that debt to maturity and commits to reinvest the principal of maturing assets in purchasing still more debt, that is tantamount to monetary financing that helps governments pay their obligations. Such a policy, said the court, might benefit some governments more than others. Furthermore, if the goal of the purchases is to reduce the yields on a particular country's sovereign debt, they risk blunting market incentives that encourage governments to get their fiscal accounts in order.

The Federal Constitutional Court has no real leverage over the ECB. But it does enjoy considerable sway over Germany's federal government and the Bundestag, which have some leverage over the German central bank (or Bundesbank). The German court has demanded that the German federal government request that the ECB issue by early August a new decision on the public-sector purchase programme, taking into account the fiscal and other economic implications of its monetary actions. Otherwise, the German court opined, the German government should instruct the Bundesbank to withdraw from the programme and to sell off its sovereign debt, which would violate its European treaty commitments. The federal government and the German parliament could ignore the ruling of the court, but that would create a dangerous German constitutional precedent.

In this difficult context, French President Emmanuel Macron and German Chancellor Angela Merkel came together on a proposal for a European Recovery Fund. On 18 May, the French and German governments published a joint proposal to allow the European Commission to borrow money against an expanded European budget to direct expenditure of €500bn over the three years starting in January 2021.[38] The expenditure would help defray the costs of the crisis in some of the countries that were hardest hit as well as investing in new infrastructure, industrial support and strategic initiatives related to the introduction of digitalisation and green technology. If the budget were agreed before the end of this calendar year, the spending could be frontloaded to occur even sooner. Markets reacted favourably, as the spread between Italian and German long-term sovereign-debt instruments fell sharply. The governments of some of the smaller northern European states were less enthusiastic.[39] They worried that an expanded budget would create transfers across countries, and reduce incentives for the governments of Italy and Spain to undertake necessary reforms. In these concerns, the old debates about risk mutualisation continued to resonate. But the fact that Germany agreed with France on the need for greater common borrowing suggested that the balance was shifting towards more decisive action.

Markets reacted favourably to the French–German proposal

The European Commission announced its proposal – called 'Next Generation EU' – on 27 May.[40] That proposal goes beyond the French and German one by adding €250bn in loans on top of the €500bn in new spending. Importantly, the commission proposed financing this package by issuing debt that it would repay only gradually, largely out of its own resources. That would mark a significant increase in the commission's fiscal capacity. It would also rely on the commission's gaining the power to raise additional revenues through taxation. This would be a significant departure from past commission practice in terms of both borrowing and revenue. The European Council agreed to negotiate this proposal alongside its talks about the seven-year budget to start on 1 January 2021.

Guarded optimism

As of summer 2020, there appeared to be a realistic chance that the ambitions set out by the European Commission would crystallise into firm commitments. In early June, the German coalition government agreed to add €130bn to its national fiscal response to the pandemic.[41] At roughly the same time, the ECB decided to add €600bn to its pandemic emergency-purchase programme, to extend that programme to June 2021 and to maintain or roll over any holding in the programme through 2022.[42] Both actions underscored European determination.

The German stimulus package reflects the kind of leadership that was missing in early European responses to the last crisis. The German economy is Europe's largest, and it is an open economy that determines the fortunes of the region to an extraordinary degree. Economic confidence in Germany will spread. But it will take time for fiscal stimulus there to have a significant impact on other countries, in which new spending is considerably lower as a percentage of national income.

Fiscal efforts can blunt the terrible impact of the crisis, but they remain primarily stopgap measures. The bulk of the policy response still falls to the ECB as it tries to ensure that firms across the euro area have enough access to credit to survive. Despite its initial hesitations in early March, the ECB has internalised that lesson. As a result, it does 'whatever it takes' more quickly and decisively. Lagarde stated at the start of her 4 June press conference:

> the Governing Council remains fully committed to doing everything necessary within its mandate to support all citizens of the euro area through this extremely challenging time. This applies first and foremost to our role in ensuring that our monetary policy is transmitted to all parts of the economy and to all jurisdictions in the pursuit of our price stability mandate.[43]

The monetary effort, immense though it is, cannot by itself solve the economic problems of the euro area. Also required is a common European fiscal response to complement national and ECB measures. The European Commission's proposal is key. Only three months into the pandemic, the proposal offers a comprehensive package. This is a significant improvement over Europe's response to the last crisis.[44] But the commission will be able to forge an agreement only if Europe's leaders can resolve or set aside the controversies that prevented them from fully implementing the institutional response they had agreed to during the last crisis.

Not Hamilton but Madison

The European Commission's proposal attracted widespread attention both as a response to the pandemic and for what it might imply for the future of the EU. Many commentators questioned whether the proposal might signal a major leap forward in the integration process. They frequently drew parallels to the move by Alexander Hamilton to absorb the obligations of the original American states into the federal government. They wondered whether we might finally be seeing the emergence of a federal Europe with fiscal powers similar to those found in the United States.

This progressive interpretation of the commission's proposal overstates the parallels. European integration is not a matter of either yes or no, forward or backward, progress or regress. Integration and disintegration take place at the same time. This tension does not invalidate the European project, any more than the costs of free trade negate its overall desirability. Europeans can take inspiration from James Madison, particularly his 'Federalist Paper No. 10'. Madison begins the essay arguing: 'Among the numerous advantages promised by a well-constructed Union, none deserves to be more accurately developed than its tendency to break and control the violence of faction.'[45] He is extolling the virtues of political pluralism as opposed to the vices associated with fixed political interests and coalitions. He also points to a constitutional arrangement that balances the distinctiveness of individual states with the need for harmony across the union.

European monetary integration has always had to strike a balance between diversity and union. Early sceptics focused narrowly on the theoretical principles underpinning an optimum currency area, concluding that Europe could not fulfil them and that the euro would never work economically.[46] Europe's leaders built the single currency anyway, and the question became whether it would be stable. On this score, diversity turned out to have its advantages. Every national government sees something distinctive in the euro, and each has had to make different and painful adjustments to join it. Leaving it would be at least as difficult. There is every reason to believe that the single currency will hold together.[47]

The last crisis seemed to validate this point. No matter what kind of pressure came to bear on countries like Cyprus or Greece, their governments preferred to stay in the euro. There was, however, an important caveat: 'the greatest threat' to Europe's economic and monetary union was not that one country might drop out, but rather that the economic and monetary union would become a battleground for opposing political coalitions and thereby risk the collapse of the EU itself. Certainly that was the concern that Martin Feldstein raised in 1997. He noted that 'economic disagreements could contribute to a more general distrust among the European nations. As the political union developed, new conflicts would reflect incompatible expectations about the sharing of power and substantive disagreements over domestic and international policies.'[48]

In the 1990s, Feldstein's arguments came across as sensationalist naysaying. Now they are harder to dismiss. The tense relationship that has emerged between the Dutch and Italian governments is one illustration; the tentative consolidation of northern and southern European countries into rival blocs is another; and the decision of Germany's Federal Constitutional Court to scrutinise the ECB's monetary policy is a third. The bleeding of conflict over macroeconomic policy into 'more general distrust among the European nations' has undoubtedly become a salient aspect of European politics.

Nevertheless, there is still a strong political argument that, per Madison, diversity makes for a better union. Cleavages are an inevitable part of politics, particularly with respect to the distribution of wealth, income or property. Rich and poor, debtor and creditor, are inescapable divisions. It is 'the principal task of modern legislation' to find some way to balance these competing interests.[49] The rub is that democracy ensures that these divisions find direct expression in the legislative process: the interested parties are both making the decisions and reaping their benefits, or suffering their costs. Such a system is inherently prone to abuse given that individuals are consistently tempted to regard personal interest as more important than the general interest. The cure of non-democratic government, of course, is worse than the disease.

The trick is to find some way to temper the natural inclinations of the most powerful actors to impose their will on the rest. The theoretical solution is a republican form of government in which interests are balanced locally so that decisions made at the centre can focus more clearly on the good of the whole. It is all the more viable when the interests channelled through any given representative are many, and when the union as a whole is large. Both conditions exist in Europe. The member states' governments represent a wide variety of interests domestically, and the EU comprises a broad range of member states. The challenge for Europeans is to make use of these natural advantages.

*   *   *

The burgeoning bankruptcy and unemployment precipitated by the global pandemic will not resolve themselves automatically through the smooth functioning of the market. The problem of macroeconomic adjustment requires a political solution agreed at the European level and then sold back to national electorates. That is the lesson of the current crisis, and the EU appears to have learned it. Now Europe's leaders need to make it clear to their many constituencies that they can ensure both diversity and solidarity only by resisting factional politics at the European level while strengthening discretionary authority for macroeconomic governance. History suggests that this is eminently feasible. Europe's political survival has derived from the willingness of its people to learn collectively from their mistakes.[50] As Samuel Beckett knew, failure usually isn't fatal. Indeed, failing better is a form of progress that Europeans – and the EU – can live with.

Notes

[1] This essay draws on Erik Jones, R. Daniel Kelemen and Sophie Meunier, 'Failing Forward? The Euro Crisis and the Incomplete Nature of European Integration', *Comparative Political Studies*, vol. 48, no. 7, December 2015, pp. 1,010–34.

[2] See, for example, Veronica Anghel,

'Together or Apart? The European Union's East–West Divide', *Survival*, vol. 62, no. 3, June–July 2020, pp. 179–202.

[3] François Heisbourg, 'From Wuhan to the World: How the Pandemic Will Reshape Geopolitics', *Survival*, vol. 62, no. 3, June–July 2020, p. 18.

[4] *Ibid.*, p. 20.

5   See, for example, Maurice Obstfeld, *Finance at Centre Stage: Some Lessons of the Euro Crisis* (Brussels: European Commission, 2013).

6   Erik Jones, 'Forgotten Financial Union: How You Can Have a Euro Crisis Without a Euro', in Matthias Matthijs and Mark Blyth (eds), *The Future of the Euro* (Oxford: Oxford University Press, 2015), pp. 44–69.

7   Erik Jones, 'Getting the Story Right: How You Should Choose Between Different Interpretations of the European Crisis (and Why You Should Care)', *Journal of European Integration*, vol. 37, no. 7, October 2015, pp. 817–32.

8   See Waltraud Schelkle, *The Political Economy of Monetary Sovereignty: Understanding the Euro Experiment* (Oxford: Oxford University Press, 2017).

9   Dimitri Vayanos, 'Flight to Quality, Flight to Liquidity, and the Pricing of Risk', National Bureau for Economic Research, NBER Working Paper No. 10,327.

10 This is a central theme in Martin Sandbu, *Europe's Orphan: The Future of the Euro and the Politics of Debt* (Princeton, NJ: Princeton University Press, 2015).

11 Serkan Arslanalp and Takahiro Tsuda, 'Tracking Global Demand for Advanced Economy Sovereign Debt', IMF Working Paper WP/12/284, 2012, pp. 28–30.

12 See Guillermo A. Calvo, 'Capital Flows and Capital Market Crises: The Simple Economics of Sudden Stops', *Journal of Applied Economics*, vol. 1, no. 1, November 1998, pp. 35–54.

13 See European Central Bank, 'Transmission Mechanism of Monetary Policy', https://www.ecb. europa.eu/mopo/intro/transmission/html/index.en.html.

14 See European Central Bank, 'Speech by Mario Draghi, President of the European Central Bank, at the Global Investment Conference in London', 26 July 2012, https://www.ecb. europa.eu/press/key/date/2012/html/sp120726.en.html.

15 See European Central Bank, transcript of Christine Lagarde's press conference, 12 March 2020, https://www.ecb. europa.eu/press/pressconf/2020/html/ecb.is200312~f857a21b6c.en.html.

16 See Federal Constitutional Court, 'Judgment of the Second Senate', 5 May 2020, https://www. bundesverfassungsgericht.de/SharedDocs/Downloads/EN/2020/05/rs20200505_2bvr085915en. pdf?__blob=publicationFile&v=7.

17 European Central Bank, transcript of Christine Lagarde's press conference.

18 *Ibid.*

19 See Matt Clinch, 'ECB's Lagarde Walks Back Comments Which Caused Italian Bond Yields to Spike', CNBC, 12 March 2020, https://www.cnbc. com/2020/03/12/ecbs-lagarde-walks-back-comments-which-caused-italian-bond-yields-to-spike.html.

20 European Central Bank, 'Press Release: ECB Announces €750 Billion Pandemic Emergency Purchase Programme (PEPP)', 18 March 2020, https://www.ecb.europa. eu/press/pr/date/2020/html/ecb. pr200318_1~3949d6f266.en.html.

21 See, for example, Sam Fleming and Davide Ghiglione, 'Support for Eurozone Rescue Deal Sparks Backlash in Italy', *Financial Times*, 10 April 2020, https://www.ft.com/content/f77dad8b-

2827-4719-81da-3afaab1162ed.

22 See Erik Jones, 'Italy, Its Populists and the EU', *Survival*, vol. 60, no. 4, August – September 2018, pp. 113–22.

23 See Rachel A. Epstein, *Banking on Markets: The Transformation of Bank–State Ties in Europe and Beyond* (Oxford: Oxford University Press, 2017); and Rachel A. Epstein and Martin Rhodes, 'International in Life, National in Death? Banking Nationalism on the Road to Banking Union', in James A. Caporaso and Martin Rhodes (eds), *The Political and Economic Dynamics of the Eurozone Crisis* (Oxford: Oxford University Press, 2016), pp. 200–32.

24 See Sandbu, *Europe's Orphan*.

25 See, for example, Lorenzo Codogno, Carlo Favero and Alessandro Missale, 'Yield Spreads on EMU Government Bonds', in Richard Baldwin, Giuseppe Bertola and Paul Seabright (eds), *EMU: Assessing the Impact of the Euro* (London: Blackwell, 2003), pp. 211–40.

26 This point is made by Herman van Rompuy, who was president of the European Council when the negotiations took place. See Herman van Rompuy, *Europa in de Storm: Lessen in Uitdagingen* (Leuven, Belgium: Davidsfonds, 2014).

27 See Fleming and Ghiglione, 'Support for Eurozone Rescue Deal Sparks Backlash in Italy'.

28 See Erik Jones, 'A Feasibility Check on Core Elements Needed for "Orderly" Sovereign Debt Restructuring and/ or Debt Mutualisation in the Euro Area', Economic Governance Support Unit, Directorate-General for Internal Policies of the Union, European Parliament, PE 634.397, May 2019,

https://www.europarl.europa.eu/ RegData/etudes/IDAN/2019/634397/ IPOL_IDA(2019)634397_EN.pdf.

29 See Baldur Thorhallsson and Peadar Kirby, 'Financial Crisis in Iceland and Ireland: Does European Union and Euro Membership Matter?', *Journal of Common Market Studies*, vol. 50, no. 5, September 2012, pp. 801–18.

30 See Shalendra D. Sharma, 'Why Ireland's Luck Ran Out and What this Means for the Eurozone', *International Spectator*, vol. 46, no. 1, March 2011, pp. 115–26.

31 For the legal basis for the public-sector purchase programme, see 'Decision (EU) 2015/774 of the European Central Bank of 4 March 2015 on a Secondary Markets Public Sector Asset Purchase Programme (ECB/215/10)', *Official Journal of the European Union*, 14 May 2015, https://eur-lex.europa.eu/legal-content/EN/TXT/PDF/?uri=CELEX:320 15D0010&from=EN.

32 European Central Bank, transcript of Mario Draghi's press conference, 6 September 2012, https://www.ecb. europa.eu/press/pressconf/2012/html/ is120906.en.html.

33 See Erik Jones, 'Do Central Bankers Dream of Political Union? From Epistemic Community to Common Identity', *Comparative European Politics*, vol. 17, no. 4, March 2019, pp. 530–47.

34 See European Council, 'Conclusions of the President of the European Council Following the Video Conference of the Members of the European Council, 23 April 2020', https://www.consilium.europa.eu/ en/press/press-releases/2020/04/23/ conclusions-by-president-charles-michel-following-the-video-conference-with-members-of-the-

european-council-on-23-april-2020/.

35 See, for example, Francesca Basso, 'Nuovo Mes, l'Eurogruppo trova l'accordo. Operativo da giugno', *Corriere della Sera*, 8 May 2020, https://www.corriere.it/economia/finanza/20_maggio_08/nuovo-mes-l-eurogruppo-trova-l-accordo-operativo-meta-maggio-66911904-9118-11ea-8c7e-3b270f2639b4.shtml.

36 See, for example, Steve Goldstein, 'Here's What the ECB Has Been Buying With the Special Pandemic Asset-purchase Program that It Is Set to Expand', *Market Watch*, 4 June 2020, https://www.marketwatch.com/story/heres-what-the-ecb-has-been-buying-with-the-special-pandemic-asset-purchase-program-that-it-is-set-to-expand-2020-06-02.

37 See, for example, Dhara Ranasinghe and Ritvik Carvalho, '"Quitaly" Indicators Back on Euro Zone Markets' Radar', Reuters, 24 April 2020, https://www.reuters.com/article/us-eurozone-markets-breakup-indicators-g/quitaly-indicators-back-on-euro-zone-markets-radar-idUSKCN2262LT.

38 See 'European Union – French–German Initiative for the European Recovery from the Coronavirus Crisis (Paris, 18 May 20)', France Diplomacy, 18 May 2020, https://www.diplomatie.gouv.fr/en/coming-to-france/coronavirus-advice-for-foreign-nationals-in-france/coronavirus-statements/article/european-union-french-german-initiative-for-the-european-recovery-from-the.

39 On 23 May, the governments of Austria, Denmark, the Netherlands and Sweden issued a 'non-paper'. See 'Non-paper EU Support for Efficient and Sustainable COVID-19 Recovery', https://g8fip1kplyr33r3krz5b97d1-wpengine.netdna-ssl.com/wp-content/uploads/2020/05/Frugal-Four-Non-Paper.pdf.

40 See European Commission, 'The EU Budget Powering the Recovery Plan for Europe', 2020, https://ec.europa.eu/info/files/eu-budget-powering-recovery-plan-europe_en.

41 See Guy Chazan, 'German Stimulus Aims to Kick-start Recovery "With a Ka-boom"', *Financial Times*, 4 June 2020, https://www.ft.com/content/335b5558-41b5-4a1e-a3b9-1440f7602bd8.

42 European Central Bank, transcript of Christine Lagarde's press conference, 4 June 2020, https://www.ecb.europa.eu/press/pressconf/2020/html/ecb.is200604~b479b8cfff.en.html.

43 *Ibid.*

44 See Sandbu, *Europe's Orphan*.

45 See James Madison, 'Federalist No. 10', 1787, available at https://billofrightsinstitute.org/founding-documents/primary-source-documents/the-federalist-papers/federalist-papers-no-10/.

46 See, for example, Barry Eichengreen, 'European Monetary Integration with Benefit of Hindsight', *Journal of Common Market Studies*, vol. 50, no. s1, February 2012, pp. 123–36.

47 See Erik Jones, *The Politics of Economic and Monetary Union* (Lanham, MD: Rowman & Littlefield, 2002).

48 Martin Feldstein, 'EMU and International Conflict', *Foreign Affairs*, vol. 76, no. 6, November/December 1997, pp. 60–73.

49 Madison, 'Federalist No. 10'.

50 See Heisbourg, 'From Wuhan to the World', p. 20.

Virtual Territorial Integrity: The Next International Norm

Michael J. Mazarr

Russia's meddling in the 2016 US election – and related efforts to influence elections and referendums in France, Germany, the United Kingdom and elsewhere – has set off alarm bells about the rise of a new form of great-power competition and Russia's growing efforts to disrupt democratic societies.[1] But these political manipulations are symptomatic of a larger emerging reality: the growing capability of states, and even non-state actors, to reach into the homelands of other countries through electronic, informational and precision kinetic means, bypassing conventional military deterrents to achieve dramatic effects.

Efforts to circumvent armies and reach directly into other societies to destabilise and disrupt them go back to ancient Greece. Sparta was terrified of the risk that Athens could foment a rebellion among Sparta's slave classes. Two thousand years later, the Cold War witnessed the superpowers' mutual efforts to meddle in other societies in service of strategic goals.[2] Yet new tools and techniques, combined with the changing technological and information foundations of modern societies, are creating an unprecedented capacity to conduct virtual societal warfare.

Such a development would undermine one of the most important achievements in international politics and the cornerstone of the post-1945 order: the widely accepted norm of territorial integrity. Gradually over the last

Michael J. Mazarr is a senior political scientist at the RAND Corporation.

Survival | vol. 62 no. 4 | August–September 2020 | pp. 101–118   DOI 10.1080/00396338.2020.1792100

two centuries, and especially since 1945, the world community has come to accept an international legal prohibition on outright territorial aggression. The trend owes as much to strategic factors, such as the advent of nuclear weapons and the post-war US global deterrent role, as to normative ones.[3] And it has never been fully observed or enforced. But given the growing set of international legal compacts enshrining this principle, the major-power statements and practices endorsing it, and the relative infrequency of territorial aggression, the norm has become strikingly salient over the last 70 years.[4] The advent of virtual societal aggression threatens to devastate this progress, creating mechanisms by which rivals routinely intervene in one another's territories in ways that skirt existing legal constraints and generate serious risks of escalation. Virtual societal warfare could place homelands in a constant state of siege.

Controlling this burgeoning mode of aggression by creating a new norm of virtual territorial integrity thus stands as one of the most important priorities in sustaining a shared international order. But the task will be complex and challenging. Such aggression takes myriad forms, many of which are difficult to detect, let alone attribute to an attacker. Furthermore, the United States has arguably been the world's most elaborate and consistent practitioner of societal interventions since 1945. Washington has routinely sought to alter the domestic political, social and economic context of target states through clandestine operations, coups, economic sanctions (general and targeted), support for democracy-promoting organisations in overturning repressive regimes and more.

US officials have long resisted any effort to impose meaningful limits on such activities, initially on account of perceived Cold War necessities and more recently because they have become a major tool in the American project of promoting liberal values. But the rapid growth in the techniques and technologies of societal aggression is highlighting a choice the United States can no longer escape: if it wants to encourage norms that prevent episodes like the 2016 election interference, it will have to accept significant constraints on many comparable activities of its own. Finding less intrusive ways of promoting liberal values is a small price to pay for constraining a dangerous trend toward virtual attacks on homelands.

The territorial-integrity norm

Over the last two centuries and particularly since 1945, a principle of international law and politics has emerged that creates a powerful normative barrier to major territorial aggression. Often termed the 'territorial-integrity norm', it embodies the essence of the Westphalian bargain, whereby sovereign states are entitled to govern their own internal affairs.[5] The norm underwrites international stability by rendering illegal and unacceptable a violent mechanism of state interest- and power-seeking that was common, and widely accepted from a normative standpoint, as recently as the nineteenth century. It also reflects arguably fundamental human instincts toward territoriality.[6]

This norm of territorial sovereignty and non-aggression has become deeply embedded in the political and legal charters that undergird the post-war order. Its roots lie in US president Woodrow Wilson's Fourteen Points and the Covenant of the League of Nations, but the norm blossomed in the United Nations Charter, multiple UN declarations, the charters of regional organisations from the European Union to the Organization of American States and the Arab League, and centrepiece agreements such as the Helsinki Final Act.[7] Partly as a result, as the political scientist Mark Zacher has explained, there have been 'very few cases of coercive boundary change' since 1950. 'The decline of successful wars of territorial aggrandizement', he added, 'is palpable'.[8] Most major uses of force (in Afghanistan, Georgia, Iraq and Libya) have not sought to make permanent territorial changes, but rather to enforce political rules or norms. A significant exception is Russia's aggression in Ukraine, and in particular its claimed annexation of Crimea. But broadly speaking, the incidence of outright territorial aggression has become vanishingly small. This achievement, often taken for granted, must count as one of the most important in modern international relations.

This result cannot be attributed entirely to the norm alone. Other factors include the deterrent role of nuclear weapons, the global US military posture and commitment to deterring large-scale conflict, and the declining relevance of territory as a route to prosperity. Nevertheless, the norm has become a baseline expectation of responsible states. Major cases of territorial aggression – from Serbia's regional ambitions in the 1980s and 1990s to Saddam Hussein's attack on Kuwait in 1990 to Russia's invasion of eastern

Ukraine in 2014 – have prompted significant resistance from the international community, including economic, political and military punishments. States that wantonly violate the norm also face severe consequences in terms of their international status and prestige.

Emerging doctrines of societal warfare

Scholars have worried for years about a growing risk to the territorial-sovereignty norm from great-power rivalry and conflict, partly fuelled by a more multipolar international system, which could produce fresh bouts of military adventurism.[9] But the biggest risk to the territorial-integrity norm may not be direct military challenges, but rather indirect ones, including virtual societal warfare designed to achieve many of the goals of traditional territorial aggression while sidestepping its key risks.

In Russia and China, publications by military leaders as well as official statements of national-security strategy have recognised blurring boundaries between military and civilian tools of conflict. Many of these analyses seek to understand the trend as much as they purport to advocate it. For example, the prevalence of a Russian doctrine of hybrid warfare, as opposed to a growing concern in Russia about the risks posed by asymmetric, non-military tools of aggression, has been somewhat exaggerated.[10] Still, a number of official statements and papers by Russian leaders, including Chief of the General Staff of Russian Armed Forces and First Deputy Defence Minister Valery Gerasimov, have conjured the spectre of comprehensive disruptions of stability in political, informational, economic and other domains, designed to crush the will and social cohesion of an adversary.[11]

Probably the clearest and most elaborate early statement of this doctrine can be found in the 1999 Chinese publication *Unrestricted Warfare*.[12] In this monograph, two Chinese colonels argued for a future in which warfare would transcend traditional boundaries, battlefields would have no limits and anyone could be a soldier. This new model of warfare involved the synchronisation of multiple effects – political, economic, diplomatic and informational – to support the overall campaign. Such activities strive toward the accomplishment of limited objectives, they stressed, and employ the least possible amount of force.

Such integrated campaigns can set the stage for conventional military operations. Yet increasingly they are viewed as a substitute for conventional war, as ways to undermine an adversary without ever crossing that threshold. Russian military officials and defence experts have increased their emphasis on the role of information warfare or 'information confrontation', which has

> the goal of inflicting damage to information systems, processes, and resources, as well as to critically important structures and other structures; undermining political, economic, and social systems; carrying out mass psychological campaigns against the population of a State in order to destabilize society and the government; as well as forcing a State to make decisions in the interests of their opponents.[13]

A Chinese information-warfare specialist has similarly argued that 'the objective of war in the information age is to destroy the enemy's will to launch a war or wage a war'; to do so, it 'attacks the will of the nation, the morale of the troops, and the resolve of the commanders'.[14]

China has built on these ideas with more official and formal operational concepts of 'system confrontation' and 'system destruction' warfare. As a 2018 RAND Corporation report explains, this approach is based on the view that

> war is no longer a contest between particular units, arms, services, or even specific weapons platforms of competing adversaries, but rather a contest among numerous adversarial operational systems. This mode of fighting is unique to modern warfare, as are the battlefields on which conflict is waged. This is referred to as systems confrontation. Systems confrontation is waged not only in the traditional physical domains of land, sea, and air, but also in outer space, nonphysical cyberspace, electromagnetic, and even psychological domains.[15]

This concept embodies a holistic approach to conflict, employing a wide range of tools and techniques to paralyse enemy operations and decision-making deep into its homeland.

New forms of territorial aggression involve the manipulation of information, indirect means of influencing social and economic activity and, in the most extreme cases, targeting individuals or groups for physical harm applied remotely. Perhaps the best-known and most deeply studied of these techniques is the use of direct cyber attacks on the information systems, physical infrastructure, business community, civil society or other elements of the target society. Russia's attacks on Ukraine before and after the 2014 incursion, its earlier cyber offensives against Latvia, and North Korea's attack on Sony are good examples. But they represent only the tip of the iceberg of the potential damage cyber attacks can do to societies, including large-scale physical destruction in the event of attacks on power grids or transportation systems, but also more persistent, lower-level actions to gradually erode an opponent's ability to wage war effectively.[16]

Attacks on the Internet of Things are commonplace

The rapidly expanding 'Internet of Things' presents unprecedented new opportunities for mischief involving information disruption. Projected to include anywhere from 20 to 50 billion devices, the Internet of Things is the interlinked network of smart systems ranging from self-driving cars to home thermostats, smart refrigerators and toilets, voice-activated speakers, home-security systems and more.[17] It represents the next phase of information networks: the real-time interconnection of billions of devices talking to one another, often in automated ways. Attacks on this network have already become commonplace.[18] One major recent example was the Mirai botnet, which used networked devices such as digital cameras, routers and home digital video-recording systems to generate a massive distributed denial-of-service attack.[19]

A second and parallel category of virtual societal warfare, reflected in Russian election meddling, involves turbocharged versions of classic propaganda and disinformation, using highly targeted campaigns through social media as well as traditional broadcasting and advertising.[20] Such efforts have been mounted to increase social tensions in the target society by exacerbating polarisation and hatred, and harassing and intimidating individuals or groups critical of the aggressor. Autocratic states are employing these techniques to project influence into other societies, instrumentalising ethnic-diaspora and foreign media outlets, and directly suppressing unwelcome messages.[21]

Aggressors pursuing virtual societal warfare can use these and other capabilities to empower and inspire targeted social groups within the target country. Aided by the micro-targeting advertising capabilities of social media and the globalised interconnection of societies, societal aggressors now have an unprecedented ability to find and support proxy groups, including violent extremists who undertake terrorist campaigns. This tactic can involve anything from direct financial assistance to social-media campaigns to promises of political backing. Examples include Moscow's reaching out to ethnic Russians in the Baltics, its support for extreme political parties (especially right-wing nationalists), Beijing's building ties with the Chinese diaspora throughout Southeast Asia, the Islamic State's seeking out of radicalised Muslims in Europe and indeed Washington's backing of pro-Western interests in Ukraine. Societal aggressors are already pursuing such societal manipulation in part through the large-scale use of corruption and bribery.[22]

Such means of virtual aggression are beginning to morph into a third category of such attacks: direct harassment, and in some cases active harm, of individuals generated through information manipulation. Russia and China have already engaged in web-based trolling against human-rights activists abroad. They have attacked opponents through cyber means, choking off their access to funds or disrupting their social-media presences. Increasingly, the Internet of Things and algorithmic decision-making processes will allow bad actors with cyber capabilities to physically harm or even kill their targets – by changing the results of a medical test or diagnosis, flooding smart watches and smart toilets with invalid biophysical data, spiking the temperature of a house in the middle of the night or even manipulating home-speaker systems.

Over time, these types of aggression are likely to be complemented by more directly physical ones that still seek to blur attribution and evade, rather than directly confront, traditional military protections of territorial integrity.[23] Drones and autonomous systems, deployed on a massive scale, could be used for classic military aggression that violated traditional notions of territorial integrity. But technological advances may allow the covert, tailored, non-attributable use of swarming civilian drones or precisely targeted micro-drones in more novel and surgical ways, including assassination.

Another complementary form of physical aggression could involve engineered biological agents in highly targeted attacks. Biological attacks immediately imperilling large numbers of people en masse would run afoul of the Biological Weapons Convention. But a more surgical attack might merely blight a leading crop in the target country, wiping out parts of its agricultural sector and threatening its food security, or infect an individual with a genetically engineered virus tailored to his or her genetic signature.[24]

Such combinations reflect a kind of conflict that challenges the definitions and boundaries of what is traditionally considered national security.[25] Clever and capable aggressors may soon favour virtual means to achieve offensive gains, reserving traditional military force for self-defence or for providing cover for virtual territorial aggression.

The perils of virtual warfare

Campaigns like this could pose serious dangers to the United States and to international stability. A combination of large-scale cyber attacks, very limited and potentially non-attributable harassment with micro-drones or other minimal kinetic means, and massive disinformation campaigns could theoretically cause chaos in a target society – especially if it is already economically weak or politically polarised.

Imagine a context, some years from now, in which Russia has become even more infuriated about Western sanctions and provocations, and has undertaken a more pointed campaign of disruption and intimidation. Its disinformation efforts remain in high gear, with increasingly effective artificial-intelligence-driven automated accounts on Twitter and Facebook conducting micro-targeted manipulation efforts, and far more sophisticated social-media messaging cascading through democratic societies. Russian exiles, American analysts and Eastern European government officials who speak out against Russia face brutal onslaughts of digital intimidation, leading to or perhaps coordinated with direct physical attacks by local extremist groups. A few anti-Russian activists fall victim to strange diseases. More broadly, Americans who visit websites critical of Russia receive emails or even text messages suggesting that such behaviour is not in their best interests and, drawing on troves of data, threaten them and their families in shockingly precise ways. At the same time, large numbers of US service members find their identities stolen, their finances left in ruins and their reputations smeared with invented allegations published online. American companies perceived as too supportive of Western sanctions fall victim to cyber intrusions and attacks, including theft of intellectual property, and public-sector transportation and public-safety systems experience constant malfunctions. On certain symbolically important dates, large swaths of the Internet of Things misbehave in odd ways. Tens of thousands of smart refrigerators might place massive, simultaneous orders for milk. Wi-Fi-enabled home and smoke alarms could begin going off uncontrollably. Thermostats might raise the temperatures of thousands of homes to intolerable levels – or lower them by 20 degrees in the middle of summer, resulting in mass electricity failures.

In such attacks lie an implicit threat that whoever is behind them could increase their volume and intensity any time they desire. This implicit threat would derive in part from the basic characteristics of virtual societal warfare that distinguish it from traditional military operations. One is range and reach: virtual campaigns can intrude into any society, and often into precisely determined corners of that society. A second characteristic is plummeting unit cost: unlike an F-35 *Lightning* II fighter or an M1 *Abrams* tank, a single digital tool can be replicated by the millions almost for free. Thirdly, virtual attacks are at least partly covert, in some cases are entirely non-attributable and in others allow the aggressor to maintain at least a veneer of deniability. Finally, virtual societal warfare is inherently experimental and rapidly iterative: aggressors are constantly testing new approaches (such as social-media recruitment tactics), evaluating the results and sharpening their technique – all in a matter of weeks, days or sometimes even hours.

In the extreme case, Americans and other targets could lose any real sense that their government was capable of protecting their prosperity, their well-being, even their lives. Were people to lose faith in their governments' efficacy, those governments might, for instance, undertake fraught and further destabilising campaigns of retribution to reaffirm their ability to protect their homelands. The US reaction to 9/11 offers a worrisome preview. Especially if societal warfare began causing actual deaths, the targeted country could easily decide that it was 'under attack' in a manner that justified a military answer. Such escalation could happen quickly or gradually, with an initial response of heightened warning levels and increased global posturing, sparking local confrontations and accidental clashes.

A constant series of virtual attacks could also create an atmosphere of ongoing conflict that undermined the potential for cooperation in areas of shared interests, such as climate and trade. The coming decade looks set to be a period of growing rivalry among major powers in any case, with Russia and China flexing their muscles and demanding a greater say in international rule-making and enforcement, especially in their neighbourhoods. It will be difficult enough to avoid arms races, confrontations over regional issues, recurrent crises or outright military conflict. An overlay of ongoing virtual conflict would inflame an already perilous set of relationships and could set the stage for debilitating insecurity and conflict.

Even the bitter US–Soviet stand-off during the Cold War was moderated by the consensus – at least after the advent of detente – that neither side sought to threaten the existence of the other, and by the availability of nuclear deterrence as the ultimate safeguard of territorial integrity. Each side could remain largely pragmatic and cautious, and view losses in third countries as significant but not vital. The shared perception of a limited but meaningful 'live and let live' dynamic made for a degree of stability in the bilateral relationship. Virtual territorial aggression now threatens to upend that constraint by signalling that other major powers will no longer respect the old limits, and that homelands are no longer secure. This dynamic needs to be arrested before it destroys the broad international equilibrium that has prevailed since the middle of the Cold War.

A virtual territorial-integrity norm

The rising potential for dangerous virtual warfare points to the need for leading countries to develop an agreement parallel to the existing territorial-integrity norm – a virtual territorial-integrity principle that can set limits on non-traditional aggression toward other societies. The effort to build such a norm will be a much more complex endeavour than the one that produced the prohibition on physical violation of territorial integrity. As an initial step, explicit endorsements of such a principle should be added to the UN Charter, and to the charters of regional organisations and multilateral political processes. For example, the mandate of Article 2, Section 4 of the UN Charter that all member states refrain from 'the threat or use of force against the territorial integrity or political independence of any state, or in any other manner inconsistent with the Purposes of the United Nations' could be amended to make clear that the prohibition applies to categories of non-physical aggression including large-scale, destructive manipulation of information networks. References in the charter to 'sovereignty' could be clarified to indicate that it entails virtual as well as territorial claims of sovereign independence.

It goes almost without saying that these amendments would have to be carefully crafted. Most states would not be willing to surrender all forms of espionage, the right to broadcast their positions on major issues or the ability to interact in some ways with citizens of other societies. But a virtual territorial-aggression norm could plausibly prohibit several especially aggressive forms of action, such as cyber attacks on physical infrastructure, interference in electoral processes and active informational campaigns designed to exacerbate social divisions. Drafters could cast them as general statements of intent to make them widely acceptable. While such provisions could be subjectively interpreted, they could still establish a norm whereby national informational and political, as well as physical, boundaries were more firmly recognised and respected, and therefore more susceptible to gaining enforceability.

This concept is akin to – but not the same as – that of a norm governing cyber aggression, the dialogue on which has been under way for some years.[26] Not all forms of virtual aggression use information channels, and the range of cyber aggression is broadening to include techniques not captured by traditional proposals for norms governing behaviour in the information realm. A virtual territorial-aggression norm comes at the problem from a different angle, grounded in geostrategic and sovereign considerations rather than focusing on the use of a specific tool. Even so, the dialogue on cyber norms has ground to a halt for reasons that will obstruct any virtual territorial-aggression norm – in particular, a stark disagreement on what actually constitutes sovereign aggression.[27] Aggression in the virtual world can be much more ambiguous and deniable than purely physical forms of aggression. It is more difficult to identify and punish violators. In some cases, it is also hard to materially distinguish virtual tactics from customary clandestine operations.

The bigger challenge may be the restraint the United States will have to accept on its democracy-promotion efforts as part of any authoritative norm on virtual societal warfare. Washington cannot credibly demand that Russia cease election meddling or China stop cyber industrial espionage while claiming the right to sponsor and openly support pro-Western democracy protesters in Russia and China. Many American officials will reject such comparisons, contending that one category represents an effort to harm the United States and the other a programme of advancing liberal values.[28] But others do not see it that way, and view democracy promotion as just as big a threat to stability as Americans see election meddling. Disputes over such political and ideological issues have played a significant role, for example, in derailing the major United Nations process for discussing potential norms on information security.[29]

These challenges partly account for the difficulty the United States and Russia have had in developing any agreed vision for constraints on information aggression, which is one component of virtual warfare.[30] But the time has come for the US to consider necessary compromises and lead the charge for a formal recognition of a virtual territorial-aggression norm. There is some degree of mutual interest. Based on its own threat perceptions, Russia has indicated a strong and to some extent sincere interest in achieving such restraints, albeit one based on its own version of what the norms would look like. The alternative is a rising campaign of reciprocal homeland aggression that threatens the fabric of world politics and risks spilling over into large-scale conventional warfare of serious destructiveness.

One way forward, which would help address conflicts over constraining liberal-values promotion, would be a general distinction drawing on that in the UN's development of the 'responsibility to protect'. The more controversial aspects of the responsibility to protect involve the third pillar, which speaks to coercive application of the norms. The first pillar, by contrast, merely establishes states' obligations to protect human rights and is therefore 'firmly based on existing international law'.[31] The second pillar reflects a more voluntary approach, whereby the UN and its member states are bound to offer direct support and capacity-building to states that are trying, of their own accord, to avoid such violations.

Analogously, the United States could agree to formal and informal norms governing virtual aggression and interference that restrict it to official support in response to direct appeals for help in democracy and human-rights promotion from legitimate authorities. It would surrender the right to initiate intentional and official action to meddle in other societies. If a democracy were wobbling and asked for economic aid, or if a country in the transition to democracy asked for help with capacity-building and training, US assistance would be fully acceptable under such a concept. This approach could actually encourage more effective policies. Most fruitful

The US would surrender the right to meddle

democratic transitions are home-grown, and the United States would sacrifice little by limiting itself to supporting legitimate transitional actors seeking a helping hand rather than undermining established autocracies. Information tends to flow into these societies largely independently of formal US efforts in any case, and the inspiration for systemic change in autocratic systems frequently stems from basic material factors. Accepting constraints on direct US government support for interventionist policies will not prevent change in these societies.

Approaching the issue from the standpoint of territorial integrity could also potentially provide ways for the United States and Russia to transcend some of their differences over the basis for limits on information-based aggression. As Alex Grigsby has noted, Russia has favoured a new 'cyber arms-control treaty that would, among other things, bar states from developing cyber weapons or using cyber means to interfere in the internal affairs of states'.[32] The United States has countered that 'existing international law' provides a sufficient foundation for such restrictions. The dispute turns in part on the difference between treaties and norms. When the focus shifts from a specific tool to the reach of existing UN Charter constraints on territorial aggression, explicit clarifications of the charter and other formal as well as informal restrictions could offer a promising pathway. Both Russia and China have emphasised concepts of sovereignty as the basis for limits on virtual territorial aggression, and norms grounded in prohibitions on sovereign violations could be more palatable.

These balances, of course, will be extremely difficult to strike in practice. Russia and China are likely to push for very expansive definitions of what counts as societal meddling from the liberal-values-promotion perspective. If accepted, such definitions could force democracies into a position of restricting the free speech of their citizens. It is possible that there simply may not be enough room for agreement on the scope of unacceptable activities to support a meaningful norm.

Any effort to overcome current differences over the basis for new norms will prove challenging. At least on the cyber element, all sides are firmly dug into seemingly incompatible positions. The US view – opposed by Russia and China – is that cyber norms can flow from existing international law, including the law of armed force.[33] The concept of territorial sovereignty has also developed international legal foundations, and even the broader strategy suggested here could end up producing a circular result: violations of territorial sovereignty would be defined as illegitimate uses of armed force, and the approach would land back in the same arguments about the role of international law. Nonetheless, approaching the issue as an extension of the well-established principle of territorial non-aggression – rather than trying to get agreement that a new class of non-kinetic weapons constitutes a use of armed force – could create more ground for compromise.

Those compromises, however, would almost certainly elevate the principle of sovereignty in ways that Russia and China have favoured. This outcome will impose limits on US actions that some will find uncomfortable – activities such as intrusive forms of democracy promotion, as well as drone strikes and disruptive cyber attacks aimed at countries undertaking threatening military programmes.[34] But the growing risks of virtual territorial aggression make such painful trade-offs increasingly essential if the United States and other advanced democracies are to avoid a future of growing homeland vulnerabilities and threats to their citizens. There could, in fact, be a side benefit – forcing the United States and others to resist the temptation to meddle in other societies in ways that frequently do not work or produce unintended consequences.

*   *   *

A stronger norm prohibiting various forms of virtual territorial aggression will not safeguard advanced democracies on its own. Like the existing norm against physical aggression, it must be combined with strong capabilities for deterrence and defence, such as investments in information security and countermeasures against drones. But as in the realm of large-scale warfare, global norms can play a critical role in supporting self-defence measures by defining the range of acceptable behaviour and threatening aggressors with isolation and punishment. Among value-sharing democracies, such norms can help to socialise a taken-for-granted assumption about international conduct, one which can underwrite collective action against violators.

A set of norms governing virtual aggression will only emerge over time. The most plausible way forward might be to start with a handful of the most easily identified mutual accommodations. These could include large-scale, highly destructive cyber attacks and efforts to destabilise society-wide information networks; targeted hostile actions against individuals in other societies; and manipulation of foreign political processes through large-scale information campaigns, intentional programmes to discredit candidates or direct intervention (including financial support for political parties). A first, critical step would be for the United States and others to formally recognise the risks of virtual aggression and make a firm commitment to building norms in this area.

A basic tension has arisen between the post-war, US-led order's liberal ambitions and the emerging multilateral counterweight's refusal and inability to accommodate them. In the eyes of China, Russia and many other states, using techniques of virtual aggression to promote liberal values constitutes an unwarranted extension of the post-war order. Agreeing to limits on unsolicited political intervention in other societies is not the same as abandoning the goal of promoting liberal values, which can be accomplished by means other than election interference and propaganda. If the United States and its like-minded Western allies are unwilling to compromise on this issue, they may end up degrading the very order they are trying to sustain.

Notes

1 See US Senate Select Committee on Intelligence, 'Report on Russian Active Measures Campaigns and Interference in the 2016 US Election', vols 1, 2 and 3, https://www.intelligence. senate.gov/publications/report-select-committee-intelligence-united-states-senate-russian-active-measures.

2 See, for example, Linda Robinson et al., *Modern Political Warfare: Current Practices and Possible Responses* (Santa Monica, CA: RAND Corporation, 2018), chapter two.

3 See John Mueller, 'War Has Almost Ceased to Exist: An Assessment', *Political Science Quarterly*, vol. 124, no. 2, June 2009, pp. 297–321.

4 See Thomas S. Szayna et al., *What Are the Trends in Armed Conflicts, and What Do They Mean for US Defense Policy?* (Santa Monica, CA: RAND Corporation, 2017).

5 See Mark W. Zacher, 'The Territorial Integrity Norm: International Boundaries and the Use of Force', *International Organization*, vol. 55, no. 2, Spring 2001, pp. 215–50.

6 See Dominic D.P. Johnson and Monica Duffy Toft, 'Grounds for War: The Evolution of Territorial Conflict', *International Security*, vol. 38, no. 3, Winter 2013/14, pp. 7–38.

7 For a discussion of the general principles surrounding these charters, see Dieter Grimm, *Sovereignty: The Origin and Future of a Political and Legal Concept*, trans. Belinda Cooper (New York: Columbia University Press, 2015), pp. 77–98. Another very useful discussion of the principle of sovereignty as an internalised norm can be found in Ian Hurd, 'Legitimacy and Authority in International Politics', *International Organization*, vol. 53, no. 2, Spring 1999, pp. 393–9.

8 Zacher, 'The Territorial Integrity Norm'.

9 One example is Graham Allison's argument about the 'Thucydides Trap', a modernised version of power-transition theory as applied to the competition between the United States and China. See *Destined for War: Can America and China Escape Thucydides's Trap?* (Boston, MA: Houghton Mifflin Harcourt, 2017).

10 See Mark Galeotti, 'I'm Sorry for Creating the "Gerasimov Doctrine"', *Foreign Policy*, 5 March 2018, https://foreignpolicy.com/2018/03/05/im-sorry-for-creating-the-gerasimov-doctrine/; Mark Galeotti, 'The Mythical "Gerasimov Doctrine" and the Language of Threat', *Critical Studies on Security*, vol. 7, no. 2, February 2018, pp. 157–61; and

Michael Kofman, 'Russian Hybrid Warfare and Other Dark Arts', *War on the Rocks*, 11 March 2016, https://warontherocks.com/2016/03/russian-hybrid-warfare-and-other-dark-arts/.

11 See Andrew E. Kramer, 'Russian General Pitches "Information" Operations as a Form of War', *New York Times*, 2 March 2019, https://www.nytimes.com/2019/03/02/world/europe/russia-hybrid-war-gerasimov.html.

12 Qiao Liang and Wang Xiangsui, *Unrestricted Warfare* (Beijing: PLA Literature and Arts Publishing House, 1999), https://www.c4i.org/unre-stricted.pdf.

13 See Alexander D. Chekov et al., 'War of the Future: A View from Russia', *Survival*, vol. 61, no. 6, December 2019–January 2020, pp. 35–6.

14 Quoted in John P. Carlin and Garrett M. Graff, *Dawn of the Code War: America's Battle Against Russia, China, and the Rising Global Cyber Threat* (New York: PublicAffairs, 2018), p. 149.

15 Jeffrey Engstrom, *Systems Confrontation and System Destruction Warfare: How the Chinese People's Liberation Army Seeks to Wage Modern Warfare* (Santa Monica, CA: RAND Corporation, 2018), p. ix.

16 See Richard A. Clarke and Robert Knake, *Cyber War: The Next Threat to National Security and What to Do About It* (New York: Ecco, 2011).

17 See Liat Clark, 'By 2020, Everything from Food to Clothes Will Be Connected to the Internet', *Wired*, 11 October 2017, https://www.wired.co.uk/article/niall-murphy-evrythng-internet-of-things-shopping-products.

18 See, for example, Ohad Amir, 'Cyber Threats to IoT in 2020', *TechRadar*, 20 November 2019, https://www.techradar.com/news/cyber-threats-to-iot-in-2020; Lily Hay Newman, 'A Long-awaited IoT Crisis Is Here, and Many Devices Aren't Ready', *Wired*, 9 April 2018; Danny Palmer, 'Cybersecurity: These Are the Internet of Things Devices that Are Most Targeted by Hackers', ZDNet, 12 June 2019, https://www.zdnet.com/article/cybersecurity-these-are-the-internet-of-things-devices-that-are-most-targeted-by-hackers/; and Adam Piore, 'We're Surrounded by Billions of Internet-connected Devices. Can We Trust Them?', *Newsweek*, 24 October 2019, https://www.newsweek.com/2019/11/01/trust-internet-things-hacks-vulnerabilities-1467540.html.

19 See Dave Lewis, 'The DDoS Attack Against Dyn One Year Later', *Forbes*, 23 October 2017, https://www.forbes.com/sites/davelewis/2017/10/23/the-ddos-attack-against-dyn-one-year-later/#47bf2eb1ae9c.

20 See, for example, Michael J. Mazarr et al., *Hostile Social Manipulation: Present Realities and Emerging Trends* (Santa Monica, CA: RAND Corporation, 2019).

21 For a powerful recent survey of the ways in which China is pursuing this agenda, see Sarah Cook, 'Beijing's Global Megaphone', Freedom House Special Report, January 2020.

22 See Philip Zelikow et al., 'The Rise of Strategic Corruption', *Foreign Affairs*, vol. 99, no. 4, July–August 2020.

23 Both types of threat are described in detail in Benjamin Wittes and Gabriella Blum, *The Future of Violence: Robots and Germs, Hackers and Drones – Confronting A New Age of Threat* (New York: Basic Books, 2015).

24 See National Academies of Sciences, Engineering, and Medicine, *Biodefense in the Age of Synthetic Biology* (Washington DC: National Academies Press, 2018).

25 See Lucas Kello, 'The Meaning of the Cyber Revolution: Perils to Theory and Statecraft', *International Security*, vol. 38, no. 2, Fall 2013, p. 8.

26 The literature on cyber norms is extensive. See, for example, Sergei Boeke and Dennis Broeders, 'The Demilitarisation of Cyber Conflict', *Survival*, vol. 60, no. 6, December 2018–January 2019, pp. 73–90; Martha Finnemore, 'Cultivating International Cyber Norms', in Kristin M. Lord and Travis Sharp (eds), *America's Cyber Future: Security and Prosperity in the Information Age* (Washington DC: Center for a New American Security, 2011); and Tim Maurer, Ariel Levite and George Perkovich, 'Towards a Global Norm Against Manipulating the Integrity of Financial Data', Lawfare, 28 March 2017, http://carnegieendowment. org/2017/03/28/towards-global-norm-againstmanipulating-integrity-of-financialdata-pub-68485.

27 On the general challenges of cyber norms and political interference, see Samuel Charap and Ivan Timofeev, 'Can Washington and Moscow Agree to Limit Political Interference?', *War on the Rocks*, 13 June 2019; Joseph S. Nye, 'Can Cyberwarfare Be Regulated?', *Strategist*, Australian Strategic Policy Institute, 3 October 2019; and Siddharth Venkataramakrishnan, 'Experts Struggle to Set Red Lines for Cyber Warfare', *Financial Times*, 30 September 2019.

28 This argument is made powerfully, for example, by Joshua Geltzer and Jake Sullivan, 'How to Prevent the Next Election Disaster', *Politico*, 22 January 2019, https://www.politico. com/magazine/story/2019/01/22/ prevent-election-disaster-224032.

29 See Anders Henriksen, 'The End of the Road for the UN GGE Process: The Future Regulation of Cyberspace', *Journal of Cybersecurity*, vol. 5, no. 1, 2019.

30 See Alex Grigsby, 'Russia, US Offer Competing Vision of Cyber Norms to the UN', Defense One, 29 October 2018, https://www. defenseone.com/politics/2018/10/ russia-us-offer-competing-vision-cyber-norms-un/152382/?oref=d-river.

31 Edward C. Luck, 'The United Nations and the Responsibility to Protect', Stanley Foundation Policy Analysis Brief, August 2008, p. 4.

32 Alex Grigsby, 'The End of Cyber Norms', *Survival*, vol. 59, no. 6, December 2017–January 2018, pp. 110–11.

33 For an analysis of such international legal issues, see Michael N. Schmitt, 'Cyber Operations and the Jud Ad Bellum Revisited', *Villanova Law Review*, vol. 56, no. 3, 2011, https:// digitalcommons.law.villanova.edu/ vlr/vol56/iss3/10.

34 A study commissioned by NATO's Cooperative Cyber Defence Centre of Excellence concluded that the alleged US cyber attack on Iran's nuclear programme was an illegal violation of UN non-aggression norms. See Kim Zetter, 'Legal Experts: Stuxnet Attack on Iran Was Illegal "Act of Force"', *Wired*, 25 March 2013, https://www.wired. com/2013/03/stuxnet-act-of-force/.

Towards a New Model for US–Russian Relations

Thomas Graham and Dmitri Trenin

To date, Russian and American experts disturbed by the sorry state of US–Russian relations have sought ways to repair them, embracing old and inadequate models of cooperation or balance. The task, however, is to rethink them. We need to move beyond the current adversarial relationship, which runs too great a risk of accidental collision escalating to nuclear catastrophe, to one that promotes global stability, restrains competition within safe parameters and encourages needed cooperation against transnational threats. To do that, the new model must take into account the complexity of today's world, the gaping power asymmetries between the two countries, the inevitability of competition and the reality that US–Russian relations have ceased to be the central axis of global affairs.

The models now being advanced fall short on one or more counts. A reset deals only with immediate irritants rather than fundamental causes. Strategic partnership is based on two patently false expectations: on the US side, that Russia will accept American leadership, which it won't; and on Russia's side, that the United States will respect it as an equal, which it isn't. A balance-of-power model sounds more realistic, but falters over the power asymmetries and the diverging world views between the two countries, as well as among the other centres of power. In this respect, today's polycentric world replicates the conditions of the early twentieth century that overturned the European balance-of-power system of the

Thomas Graham is a Distinguished Fellow at the Council on Foreign Relations. **Dmitri Trenin** is the Director of the Carnegie Moscow Center.

Survival | vol. 62 no. 4 | August–September 2020 | pp. 119–134   DOI 10.1080/00396338.2020.1792101

nineteenth century and precipitated two cataclysmic world wars. Detente 2.0 may acknowledge irreconcilable world views, but it fails to accommodate current global power dynamics, with China displacing Russia as America's top strategic rival.

Most importantly, all of these models fail to encompass the complexity and inherent tension of today's world, which is marked by globalism and diversity, interconnectedness and fragmentation, and new patterns of diffusion and concentration of power, and unsettled by technological leaps, values conflicts, crass inequality and hyper-competitiveness. The COVID-19 crisis vividly demonstrates that no state on its own, no matter how powerful and advanced, can master global challenges. Yet the nation-state has reasserted its primacy over all other institutions. Common dangers do not lead easily to cooperation among nations, nor do they banish conflicts or erase differences.[1]

Amid the enormous flux, one pattern still holds true: the United States and Russia are, and will long remain, pillars of the global order. They are among the few truly sovereign states in the world today – that is, states that are resistant to outside interference and able to conduct independent foreign policies in pursuit of national interests. Throughout history, it has been the powerful sovereign states – often called great powers – that have determined the character of international order. That is still the case, despite greater sensitivities about the rights of smaller states and the rise of various non-state actors and supranational institutions.

Moreover, even among sovereign powers, Russia and the United States play a special role. They remain the world's two leading nuclear powers, together holding over 90% of the world's nuclear warheads. They alone have the power to destroy any country, including each other, and end civilisation as we know it, in 30 minutes. They are also the two countries with the largest natural endowments, better positioned to survive extreme global disorder because they can pretend to something close to self-sufficiency. And, although China is rising to their level, they remain the only two powers – by virtue of geographical location or strategic reach – that can affect the entire territory of the Eurasian supercontinent, which along with North America constitutes the core of the modern world. In this light, we cannot abandon the search for a new model of US–Russian relations.

The permanence of differentness

Countries, like individuals, have character, a set of ideas and drives grounded in geography, historical experience and sociopolitical traditions that remain more or less constant, while manifesting themselves in different ways over time. Fundamental change occurs, but only slowly over generations, the drama of revolutions and other social upheavals notwithstanding. The Russian Federation today bears a strong resemblance to tsarist Russia in governing practices and foreign-policy concerns, despite three revolutions at the beginning and one at the end of the twentieth century. Similarly, the United States today, in spite of the never-ending process of social and cultural adaptation, is governed on the basis of an institutional arrangement and a set of ideas established in its founding documents more than two centuries ago.

As great powers, Russia and the United States share certain attributes, but their unique national experiences imbue them with different essences. Each country, for example, holds an abiding faith in its exceptional nature, the United States priding itself on being a paragon of democratic virtue, while Russia presents itself as a champion of justice. Each country has a grand mission, the United States to spread the benefits of democracy and freedom worldwide, Russia to defend the promise of national sovereignty and, by extension, a world of diverse values. Each advocates a world order based on a set of principles: Americans, a rules-based order reflecting their own 'universal' values; Russians, an order grounded in international law freely negotiated by sovereign states. Neither country is prepared to accept any infringement on its own sovereignty, the United States because it sees itself as the shining city on the hill, Russia because its identity is based on the idea of being no one's vassal or follower.

America, a young country among the world's great powers, is ahistorical and forward-looking, infused with optimism that the arc of history bends towards its values of freedom and democracy. Its history is one of rapid, unbroken expansion across a continent and the elimination of any significant threat to its security from a neighbouring power. In this secure continental position, it ventured abroad in search not of lands to conquer but of resources and markets to feed its robust economy, thus spreading its values, which undergirded its power and prosperity at home. Spared the devastation that afflicted other great powers during two world wars in the twentieth century, it emerged as the richest and most powerful country, the leader of the so-called Free World against the global threat of communism during the Cold War. And with the collapse of the Soviet Union in 1991, it stood alone as the uncontested world leader, fancying itself, in the words of then-secretary of state Madeleine Albright, as 'the indispensable nation' that stood taller and saw farther into the future. America's is an unmatched story in the modern era of growth and success.

Russia, by contrast, is informed by a millennial history marked by long cycles of rise, decline and renewal, and a constant struggle to survive and preserve its unique identity in an unforgiving climate and harsh geopolitical setting. This history has fed a realist, even tragic, view of world affairs. Throughout, Russia has faced the vexing challenge of defending a large, sparsely settled country on a vast territory with few formidable physical barriers abutting powerful neighbours or unstable lands. It has repeatedly suffered invasions — by the Mongols and the Poles, by Napoleon Bonaparte and Adolf Hitler — that posed existential threats. It has experienced periodic state collapse, leading to seemingly great discontinuities between Kievan Rus, Muscovy, Imperial Russia, the Soviet Union and the contemporary Russian Federation. Yet each 'new' incarnation of Russia has sought to restore what its leaders and people revered as the true, bedrock Russia. This inherently vulnerable Russia has historically sought security in strategic depth, buffer zones and tight internal control with a capacity for mobilisation. As it grew more powerful than its immediate neighbours did, this outward pressure over time produced the largest country in the world, a geopolitical advance overland unparalleled in modern history.

To others, this expansionary Russia has often appeared not to acknowledge any limits. Yet, with rare exception, Russia has not aspired to rule the world or recreate the world in its own image. Medieval rhetoric of Russia as the 'Third Rome' was more an assertion of holiness than a pretence to universal empire on a Roman or Byzantine model. The Bolsheviks did create the Third International to extend the sway of communism worldwide, but for them Russia was little more than the match that would ignite a world revolution; it was not to be the centre of international communism. Tellingly, Russia's greatest and most revered victories, both of which came at unimaginable sacrifice, are its triumphs over Napoleonic France in 1814 and the defeat of Nazi Germany in 1945, each of which saved Europe from domination by a single power. In the Russian mind, those triumphs were more about restoring order and exacting justice than extending Russia's writ.

Russia has generally eschewed a universalist ideology and based its approach to the outside world in a stern realpolitik, informed by state interests and power relationships. That was true even of the Soviet Union, which, after a brief flirtation with world revolution, reverted under Stalin to the centuries-old tradition that sought to protect Russia's uniqueness while assuring that it had equal rights with the mightiest powers on the planet. Ideology morphed into a general framework for describing the

Russia has eschewed universalist ideology

world to the Soviet population, an instrument of control in the countries of the socialist camp, and often an irritating ritual that decision-makers had to go through to justify actions driven mainly by realpolitik. Those few cases where ideology trumped national interests, such as the Soviet intervention in Afghanistan in the late 1970s, led to overstretch that contributed to the final demise of the Soviet Union.

Unlike Russia, the United States has been driven by a universalist ideology, manifested in its desire to change the world through the expansion of democracy. The only question has been how. One school advocates a focus on building a model democracy, which other countries would seek to emulate. The second, which has dominated American foreign-policy thinking since the Second World War, supports an activist, missionary-like approach, spreading democracy in the name of advancing human welfare worldwide. The United States did so mostly through peaceful suasion and targeted assistance, though it was willing to use force to defend countries (even authoritarian ones) against communist forces during the Cold War. With the end of that period, the United States began to use force more frequently to promote democracy, which also meant establishing friendly regimes dependent on the United States. That approach reached its apogee

— and its nadir — with the George W. Bush administration in Iraq and Afghanistan. Nevertheless, the promotion of democratic values has been inextricably linked with the spread of US influence and has played a central role in defining America's approach to the outside world.

As a corollary, the United States has eschewed realpolitik, insisting that its actions abroad are not a narrow pursuit of parochial national advantage, but rather an effort to extend benefits to other countries and improve global conditions overall. This approach began in earnest with Woodrow Wilson, who as president brought the country into the First World War with the goal of making the world 'safe for democracy'. It gives American foreign policy a deeply moralistic, absolutist cast that divides the world into good and evil regimes, rejecting compromise with the latter as acts of appeasement. Outsiders have denounced this posture as hypocritical, especially given the great benefit the United States gained from its policies during the past century. Yet no American president has been able to sustain elite and public support for a foreign policy that appeared to hew close to realpolitik.

President Donald Trump, to be sure, has made a radical break with this tradition. 'America First' is a value-free, transactional approach to the outside world that unashamedly makes no claim to be working for the betterment of humankind as a whole as it pursues narrowly defined national interests. Whether his break is also a turning point in America's mission or merely a temporary detour remains to be seen. But the weight of history and tradition would suggest that the latter is more likely, and indeed outside the White House much of Trump's own administration has resisted his world view and sought to defend the traditional foundations of American foreign policy.

Russian President Vladimir Putin, meanwhile, represents a return to the mainstream of Russian foreign-policy theory and practice, breaking with the first post-Soviet decade, which in retrospect was an aberration. Then, for the first time in history, Russia sought to integrate itself into institutions that it would not control. It was close to accepting another country's – namely, the United States' – leadership. This attempt, however, failed, after which Russia returned to a more traditional role of a lone major power. Today's Russia is squarely focused on its own interests as defined by the Kremlin.

Geography, historical experience and sociopolitical tradition have thus created a fundamental clash between the United States and Russia that lies behind all the concrete episodes of conflict. In its purest expression, the United States, as a great power, has sought to remake the world in its image, while Russia, as a great power, has struggled to preserve its sovereign standing and independence. America's universalist democratic ideology tilts towards unipolarity (even Trump wants America to dominate the world, if not through leadership of a multilateral order, then through American domination of each and every bilateral relationship). Russia, by contrast, has worked since the 1814–15 Congress of Vienna for a multipolar world, in which a concert of great powers, with equal rights and a veto on joint decisions, manages world affairs. America's continuing quest for primacy inevitably runs up against Russia's assertion of its independence and demand for equality.

The new model of US–Russia relations

The confrontation between the United States and Russia today is thus systemic. It is not a product of misunderstandings or a mismatch between leading personalities on the two sides. But this antagonistic relationship is markedly different from that of the Cold War. It is no longer an all-out, zero-sum, existential game for geopolitical and ideological dominance. Neither is it the main axis of world politics.

The confrontation is dangerous nonetheless. Washington sees Russia's effort to reassert itself as a great power with global influence, including its thinly veiled attempts to influence US domestic politics, as intolerable disruptions of its, and its allies', post-Cold War project to extend the liberal world order across the globe. Moscow, for its part, sees America's robust use of its multidimensional power as a challenge to Russia's domestic political stability and a threat to the country's external security. In these circumstances, the risk of an inadvertent collision escalating to an armed conflict, potentially with the use of nuclear weapons, is uncomfortably high. Coexistence remains an imperative today, as it was during the Cold War.

This situation is unlikely to change soon. A fresh Russian attempt to reconcile with the United States on Washington's terms is as difficult to imagine as Washington's changing its intensely negative view of Putin and his policies, notwithstanding Trump's apparent affinity for Putin on a personal level. Even Putin's eventual departure will not likely change the situation. The view that US policies are inimical to the national interests of Russia is by now well established among the principal stakeholders of the Russian state. So, forget strategic partnership. What is possible is reducing the current high-intensity confrontation to a medium-intensity rivalry, which characterised US–Russian relations before the onset of the Cold War. In the longer term, competition conducted with a measure of mutual restraint, leavened by cooperation on some transnational challenges, should be the realistic goal for both Washington and Moscow.[2]

This new normal would bear some resemblance to the detente of the 1970s, but the existing polycentric, interconnected world and the rise of China have changed the stakes and counsel a new diplomatic style. Polycentrism creates a context in which the competition, no matter how serious or sustained, is no longer zero-sum. Each country needs to take into account its relations with other global and regional centres of power. This fosters a natural restraint that can be reinforced by bilateral agreements.

If the competition is no longer bipolar, the diplomacy can no longer be solely, or even primarily, bilateral. Bilateral relations need to be embedded in a multilateral framework. Since the end of the Cold War, the two countries have participated in what we might call ad hoc coalitions of the necessary to deal with concrete problems – the Contact Group for Balkan conflicts, the Minsk Group for Nagorno-Karabakh, the Six-Party Talks on North Korea and the P5+1 on Iran, for example. Looking forward, these coalitions need to become routine and extended to include discussion of strategic issues and regional architecture. Although the Chinese now reject the idea, a China–Russia–US dialogue on strategic stability is necessary, supplemented perhaps with the addition of France and the United Kingdom. The recent American–Russian–Saudi negotiations to stabilise global oil markets should become a permanent feature of interaction among the energy superpowers.

Other coalitions are thinkable and practical – for instance, with Germany and France on European security, separately with Israel and Turkey on the

Middle East, with India on Eurasian security and with Japan on Northeast Asia. These small, multilateral strategic dialogues mitigate the negative consequences of US–Russian asymmetries, enrich the discussions and are more likely to result in ideas that can be implemented in practice because the critical countries on a given issue are engaged from the beginning.

Many of these dialogues are not ripe for official discourse at this point. They are best pursued unofficially in expert channels, ideally with official support. This approach would foster a kind of private–public partnership for managing US–Russian relations and help generate the public support necessary for the long-term success of any initiative. The result would be a web of multilateral fora, official and unofficial, that would stabilise US–Russian relations and restrain competition.

Immediate tasks

To move towards this new model, Washington and Moscow need to take immediate steps to ratchet down the confrontation, to create safer conditions for the continuing rivalry and to act on the urgent need for cooperation in a few areas, such as the fight against COVID-19. Three steps are critical.

Firstly, the two countries have to restore normal diplomatic relations, restarting regular discussions on the full range of issues on the diplomatic agenda. Engagement does not necessarily mean cooperation. On the contrary, tough competition will continue. Nor is re-engagement a reward for bad behaviour – in particular, in Ukraine – as many Americans will object: it is a matter of national security. It will enable each side to develop a better understanding of the goals, interests and red lines of the other side, and thereby reduce the risk of unintended conflict. It is simply not prudent for two countries with the destructive power of the United States and Russia to lack normal diplomatic dialogue.[3]

The second necessary step is extending for five years the New Strategic Arms Reduction Treaty (START), due to expire in February 2021, and launching a sustained discussion on strategic stability. The treaty has serious limitations – it is bilateral in a strategic world that has already become multipolar, it does not cover many of the new high-tech weapons systems that are coming on stream, and it does not cover space and the cyber domain or tactical nuclear weapons. However, it provides for a monitoring and verification system that allows insight into each country's nuclear arsenal and helps build predictability. After the demise of the Anti-Ballistic Missile Treaty in 2002 and of the Intermediate-Range Nuclear Forces Treaty in 2019, it makes no sense to add another measure of uncertainty to an already complex, confusing equation by letting the last remaining major arms-control agreement lapse.[4]

That last issue relates to the third immediate task: resolving the issue of foreign interference in domestic politics. The intensity of the issue on the American side might ease if November's presidential election yields a clear victory for one or the other candidate, which thereby could not be credibly attributed to Russian meddling. But the issue will not go away. Resolution will likely require expanding the issue to interference broadly construed as extending beyond the disruption and abuse of computer networks and manipulation of public opinion through social media, to measures that the United States has routinely practised in the post-Cold War years to promote democracy in Russia. These include, for example, direct support and encouragement for political activists and groups opposed to the Kremlin.[5] The Russian leadership sees these long-standing US policies as attempts at regime change. Any resolution of this issue will likely not entail an agreement not to interfere, but rather one on what interference is tolerable in an interconnected world that makes it unavoidable.[6]

As for the obvious area for immediate cooperation – the COVID-19 pandemic – expectations should be restrained. The pandemic is not the basis for a reset in relations, as some leading Russians have suggested; it is not the twenty-first-century equivalent of the struggle against Hitler in dimension or existential threat.[7] Cooperation in developing a vaccine will be encumbered by memories of Cold War biological-warfare programmes. Renewed American concern about Russian disinformation, and Russian complaints about biased Western reporting, will also hamper cooperation without strong leadership, which Trump cannot deliver in a politically polarised country he himself nurtures. In any event, multilateral cooperation is a more urgent need than bilateral US–Russian collaboration.

Long-term challenges

Progress on these immediate tasks will facilitate productive discussion of other issues on which the United States and Russia are major players with at times overlapping, at times competing, interests, but which can only be resolved multilaterally. Over the long term, the challenge for the two countries is to foster durable frameworks for responsible competition on key global issues and in strategic regions – Europe, the Middle East, East and South Asia, and the Arctic.

At the top of the list is a complex set of issues that bear on strategic stability: nuclear, biological and chemical weapons; advanced conventional weapons; and space-based and cyber weapons. The task is to prevent nuclear war through reliable strategic deterrence between the nuclear powers and by retarding the spread of weapons of mass destruction. Ultimately, we will need to elaborate a new concept for strategic stability for an increasingly multipolar world, in which the United States and Russia remain the primary players, China is rapidly enhancing its capabilities, and a number of mid-level and regional powers – including France, India, Iran, Israel, North Korea, Pakistan and the UK – have the capability to disrupt stability. Separate agreements or understandings on space and cyberspace should complement any on nuclear weapons.

As a matter of self-preservation, both Washington and Moscow should have a keen interest in preserving strategic stability. The first step, as already noted, is extending New START for five years and commencing sustained strategic-stability talks. They could also usefully clarify nuclear doctrine to assure one another that they are not lowering the nuclear threshold. And they should continue to cooperate to constrain the nuclear ambitions of North Korea and Iran. But their efforts alone will not suffice. Eventually they will need to persuade China to join strategic-stability talks, which Beijing currently refuses to do. The rapidly sharpening Sino-American rivalry makes a China–US military-security dialogue ever more urgent. As a near-term alternative, Washington and Moscow should include these matters – strategic stability, space and cyberspace – in their bilateral security discussions with Beijing, while continuing to work with it on North Korea, Iran and other proliferation concerns.

Beyond the strategic realm, the regional security architecture and regimes along Russia's entire periphery are ideally suited to multilateral approaches. Starting with the Arctic, the task is twofold. Firstly, constructive work must continue within the Arctic Council (Canada, Denmark, Finland, Iceland, Norway, Russia, Sweden and the United States) on protecting the Arctic's delicate ecology, while responsibly opening the region up for more intensive commercial development of its abundant resources and maritime trade routes under conditions of rapid warming. Secondly, the great-power competition that could turn the region into one of perilous geopolitical rivalry – a matter that lies outside the purview of the Arctic Council – must be restrained.

It is hard to see how either the United States or Russia would benefit from unbridled military competition in the High North. To encourage restraint, Washington and Moscow should be more transparent about their own military operations in the Arctic. They should also work with the other littoral states (Canada, Denmark and Norway) on further confidence-building measures to restrain competition between the US/NATO and Russian militaries, and on ways to deal with China's and other outside maritime powers' mounting interests. That all these countries are NATO members, save for Russia, does not necessarily put Moscow at a disadvantage. Canada's legal position on the Northwest Passage, for example, is similar to Russia's on the Northern Sea Route, also known as the Northeast Passage. And Russia would likely have greater influence in the small multilateral format than it would in a larger one that included China, Japan and a number of other European states.

Europe poses a much greater challenge. Creating a durable security regime, which is in the interest of both Russia and the United States, will require settlement of the frozen and ongoing conflicts in the former Soviet space and the Balkans, agreement on the limits of NATO and European Union expansion, and restraint in military operations along the NATO–Russia border. Accomplishing this will take years. In the meantime, the United States and Russia could see to it that their moves do not exacerbate the current situation. Both parties need to exercise restraint in deployments in Europe of destabilising weapons systems, such as intermediate-range missiles, whether nuclear-tipped or not. Other steps should include abstaining from holding large-scale or provocative military activities close to the NATO–Russia border. The now nearly defunct NATO–Russia Council should be turned into a mechanism for deconfliction. And Americans in particular need to keep in mind that, from the Russian perspective, moves to include Ukraine or Georgia in NATO would spark a new major crisis with a high risk of a military collision.

European countries will obviously have to be key participants in this discussion, but the EU is unlikely to develop sufficient cohesion to act as an independent strategic player in foreign and security policy. That will put great responsibility on Moscow and Washington to develop the broad security framework, but they cannot succeed by talking over other countries' heads. Two key European states, France and Germany, at a minimum have to be engaged in these discussions. This is, in effect, the way the Ukraine crisis is being managed, even if the

The US and Russia cannot create a condominium

United States is not formally part of the Normandy contact group (France, Germany, Russia and Ukraine) charged with resolving the conflict in eastern Ukraine. A French–German–Russian–US quadrilateral format, augmented by one or two other countries, could also be used to facilitate resolution of other outstanding conflicts, as well as to explore the larger strategic issue of a comprehensive security regime. The fact that in 2019 these countries managed to act in unison to deal with a political crisis in Moldova demonstrates that this is not a pious wish.

The broader Middle East presents a challenge of a different order of complexity. The task is to stabilise a region characterised by sectarian and inter-state conflict, weak governments and internal disorder, and extremist forces. It is difficult to envision a set of agreed institutional arrangements among the key regional powers – Egypt, Iran, Israel, Saudi Arabia and Turkey – that would serve as the foundation of a security regime. Rather, peace and security will have to arise through the delicate manipulation of an ever-shifting balance of power. The United States and Russia, as the two most important outside powers, have critical roles to play, but they cannot create a condominium. They should focus their efforts on ensuring that no one country can achieve sufficient power to dominate the others. This will require restraining Iran's nuclear programme under an international accord, and discouraging other regional players' nuclear ambitions while helping develop mutual restraint in the Persian Gulf. US–Russian support for building mutual understanding across the Gulf, in a format that includes the regional players, could be particularly useful.

In addition, Moscow and Washington share an interest in countering terrorists and extremists in the region. An American–Israeli–Russian dialogue could foster counter-terrorism cooperation in the Middle East and North Africa. Meanwhile, to prevent Afghanistan from again becoming a haven for international terrorists as the United States withdraws, Russia and the US should continue their bilateral talks, while replacing the current 6+2 (China, Iran, Pakistan, Tajikistan, Turkmenistan and Uzbekistan plus Russia and the United States) talks on Afghanistan with some arrangement that draws in other key players – Iran and perhaps Turkey as well as China, India and Pakistan – into efforts to stabilise the country.

Finally, East and South Asia are the geopolitical centre of the most important bilateral relationship of the twenty-first century, that between the United States and China, whose burgeoning rivalry extends across the globe. The task is to accommodate the inexorable rise of China in a way that does not lead to a direct US–China confrontation or otherwise destabilise the region while bolstering the strategic autonomy of other key regional powers, as well as India and Russia at a minimum. Washington will not be able to restore the Cold War-era triangular relationship with Beijing and Moscow, this time pointed at China. Russia will not align with the United States against China, rightfully regarding partnership with Beijing as one of its most valuable post-Cold War achievements.

One way for Russia to encourage equilibrium in its relations with China without alienating it is to develop relations with other key players, such as India, Japan and Europe. Moscow actively promotes multilateral platforms that include China, such as the BRICS (Brazil, Russia, India, China, South Africa), the Shanghai Cooperation Organisation (China, India, Pakistan, Russia and four Central Asian states) and RIC (Russia, India and

China). There is also room for US–Russian triangles with India and Japan, and eventually even a China–Russia–US dialogue. One thing the United States would be strategically wise to do is to facilitate full normalisation of Russo-Japanese relations.[8] As the United States continues to develop the quadrilateral dialogue with Australia, India and Japan, both Russia and the US will engage with Association of Southeast Asian Nations (ASEAN) countries. Such a web of multilateral fora would encourage greater security and stability in East and South Asia.

* * *

Since the eruption of the Ukraine crisis in 2014 and the collapse of US–Russian relations into confrontation, many observers have looked for ways to return them to a more constructive track. Periodic Russian attempts, inspired by the Second World War experience, to create grand coalitions with the United States against terrorism in 2001 and 2015, and to fight the COVID-19 pandemic in 2020, were doomed to fail. The United States is used to building coalitions of its own, and leading others. In any event, the threats in all those cases, while horrible, were not existential. The idea of improving US–Russian relations by means of cooperating on climate change and other environmental issues is equally delusional. The issues themselves are subject to fierce debate within both countries, and even if they were to cooperate, that would be too shallow a base for improving relations in general. Their ongoing cooperation in space, for instance, has not prevented or even tempered the current US–Russian confrontation.

The hard truth is that the aspirations for partnership that the two sides harboured at the end of the Cold War have evaporated irretrievably. The future is going to feature a mixed relationship of competition and cooperation, with the balance heavily tilted towards competition and much of the cooperation aimed at managing it. The challenge is to prevent the rivalry from devolving into acute confrontation with the associated risk of nuclear cataclysm. In other words, the United States and Russia need to cooperate not to become friends, but to make their competition safer: a compelling and realistic incentive. The methods of managing great-power rivalry in the past 200 years — through balance-of-power mechanisms and, for brief periods, detente — are inadequate for the complexity of today's world and the reality of substantial asymmetry between the United States and Russia. What might work is what we could call responsible great-power rivalry, grounded in enlightened restraint, leavened with collaboration on a narrow range of issues, and moderated by trilateral and multilateral formats. That is the new model for US–Russian relations.

Notes

1   See generally Graham Allison, 'The New Spheres of Influence: Sharing the Globe with Other Great Powers', *Foreign Affairs*, vol. 99, no. 2, March–April 2020, pp. 30–40.

2   See Thomas Graham, 'Let Russia Be Russia: The Case for a More Pragmatic Approach to Moscow', *Foreign Affairs*, vol. 98, no. 6, November–December 2019, pp. 134–46.

3   See, for instance, Seyom Brown, 'The New Nuclear MADness', *Survival*, vol. 62, no. 1, February–March 2020, pp. 63–88.

4   See Alexey Arbatov, 'Mad Momentum Redux? The Rise and Fall of Nuclear Arms Control', *Survival*, vol. 61, no. 3, June–July 2019, pp. 7–38.

5   See, for example, Henrik Breitenbauch and Niels Byrjalsen, 'Subversion, Statecraft and Liberal Democracy', *Survival*, vol. 61, no. 4, August–September 2019, pp. 31–41.

6   See Michael J. Mazarr, 'Virtual Territorial Integrity: The Next International Norm', *Survival*, vol. 62, no. 4, August–September 2020, pp. 101–18.

7   See Nikolas K. Gvosdev, 'Don't Bet on Reset: US–Russian Relations in the Wake of the Coronavirus', Russia Matters, 22 April 2020, https://www.russiamatters.org/analysis/dont-bet-reset-us-russian-relations-wake-coronavirus.

8   See Olga Puzanova, 'Contemplating a Russia–Japan Rapprochement', *Survival*, vol. 62, no. 1, February–March 2020, pp. 149–56.

Deterrence and the NPT: Compatible and Reinforcing

Gregory F. Giles

The Nuclear Non-Proliferation Treaty (NPT) has now been in force for 50 years. The upcoming Treaty Review Conference, postponed due to the COVID-19 pandemic, will likely see intensified debate about the relationship between disarmament and deterrence. At issue are rising demands from some non-nuclear-weapons states for more substantial disarmament progress while other state parties place greater reliance on nuclear deterrence in a changing security environment. Largely absent from the debate is the nature of the relationship between deterrence and the NPT. Clearly this issue is crucial to the purpose and viability of the treaty.

Nuclear deterrence, of course, pre-dated the NPT and its influence was widely, if warily, acknowledged during treaty negotiations. It was particularly troubling to certain officials and analysts in the late 1950s that the further spread of nuclear weapons would be destabilising and make it more difficult for the United States, the United Kingdom and the Soviet Union to achieve nuclear disarmament. Frank Aiken, Ireland's minister of external affairs and a driving force behind the NPT, noted that 'the danger now exists that an increase in the number of states possessing nuclear weapons may occur, aggravating international tension and the difficulty of maintaining world peace, and thus rendering more difficult the attainment of general disarmament agreement'.[1]

Gregory F. Giles is a senior director at Science Applications International Corporation (SAIC) and advises the US government on deterrence and non-proliferation issues. The views expressed here are his own and do not necessarily reflect the official policy or position of SAIC, Lawrence Livermore National Laboratory, the Department of the Air Force or the US government.

Survival | vol. 62 no. 4 | August–September 2020 | pp. 135–156   DOI 10.1080/00396338.2020.1792125

Aiken introduced a series of resolutions in the United Nations General Assembly between 1958 and 1961, the so-called Irish Resolutions, which evolved into the 'guiding concept' for the NPT.[2] In essence, states possessing nuclear weapons would undertake not to relinquish control over them or transmit information about their manufacture to states not possessing them, and states not possessing nuclear weapons would undertake not to manufacture or otherwise acquire control of such weapons. Aiken's call to limit the dispersion of nuclear weapons did not find universal support. Canada, for example, agreed in 1958 with the notion of discouraging the indiscriminate transfer of nuclear weapons to nations that did not possess them, but otherwise held that nuclear-weapons transfer 'should not be prohibited completely until appropriate disarmament measures had been agreed upon'.[3] By this time, the US had embraced nuclear weapons to offset and deter preponderant Soviet conventional forces on NATO's doorstep. US nuclear weapons were forward-deployed on the soil of NATO allies and, in the event of imminent war, could be mated with various delivery systems operated by those allies. Among them, Canada believed in the strategy of nuclear deterrence, and in 1958 decided to equip its forces in Europe with nuclear-capable surface-to-surface rockets.[4]

In arriving at the Irish Resolutions, Aiken was pragmatic. He recognised the fact that the nuclear powers' defence 'now depended upon nuclear weapons'.[5] Hence, the 1960 Irish Resolution draft 'did not call for immediate surrender or destruction of nuclear weapons', and did not oppose the nuclear powers retaining them as long as they were kept in the possession and under the control of their own forces.[6] Publicly, Aiken acknowledged that keeping nuclear weapons on the territory of allies was 'regrettable' but 'necessary' in an atmosphere of distrust.[7] Privately, however, he was supportive of nuclear deterrence. According to a declassified October 1958 US State Department cable, 'Aiken said he thoroughly realized [the] deterrent value of atomic arsenal over Soviet conventional forces but pointed out under his resolution [the] US, UK and France could continue to build up stockpiles and even test if they so desired; [the] only prohibition against [the] US would be giving bombs to non-nuclear powers'.[8]

After meeting with Aiken in November 1958, Henry Cabot Lodge, Jr, the US ambassador to the UN, reported to the secretary of state that 'while [Aiken] believes international disarmament may in the long run be impossible, he holds that some form of cooperation on armaments control is possible and he believes this could lead to a "Pax Atomica" and enduring stability. He believes [the] US and USSR recognize they have little to gain from nuclear war and, thus, stability can be ensured if nuclear weapons are stabilized, i.e., [via] agreement on nontransfer.'[9] Thus, Aiken recognised the stabilising effect of nuclear deterrence – including the stationing of US nuclear weapons in the territory of its allies as long as they remained under US control – and studiously avoided positions that could undermine it. In honouring the content and intent of the Irish Resolutions, the NPT similarly did not preclude nuclear and extended deterrence.

In a widely praised history of the NPT, Egyptian diplomat Mohamed Shaker similarly acknowledged the importance of nuclear deterrence to national security:

> The role that nuclear weapons has also come to play as an instrument of foreign policy and deterrence has marked the post-World War II era. In such an atmosphere, nations have followed different courses to ensure their security. Some have found that the best way to ensure their own security was to acquire the lethal weapons themselves. Others have joined military alliances whereby they enjoy a sort of guarantee of nuclear protection by the major nuclear ally. Some have even signed bilateral agreements for defense purposes with the nuclear ally. For the majority of nations, the non-aligned, security has generally been sought through efforts to achieve nuclear disarmament and arms control measures including the non-use or threat of use of nuclear weapons.[10]

Shaker further observed that the concept of nuclear deterrence had come to play 'a crucial role in preventing the use or threat of use of nuclear weapons in military interventions'.[11] He later warned, however, that 'no matter how effective and stable the nuclear deterrent may appear to some, general confidence has never been placed in it'.[12] Shaker seemed to be ascribing a democratisation

standard to deterrence, implying that its legitimacy was somehow dependent on how many states subscribed to it. This is a misguided benchmark.
Most states do not face a nuclear-armed foe, and those that do find world
opinion of little practical value to their self-defence. Shaker also asserted that
'the Irish Resolution was based on the assumption that the nuclear-weapon-
States themselves were going to disarm in the foreseeable future'.[13] Yet Aiken
himself was under no such illusions. However reluctantly, NPT framers and
scholars alike have been unable to refute the contribution of nuclear weapons
to deterring great-power conflict and to international stability.

American and Russian interest in the NPT

Both the US and Soviet Union warmed to the notion of a non-proliferation
treaty largely because of deterrence calculations. For them, nuclear deterrence
could be simplified and bolstered to the extent that it remained largely a bipolar
affair. By the mid-1950s, US concern over potential proliferation was already
manifest at the highest levels. In a May 1954 meeting of the National Security
Council, US president Dwight D. Eisenhower despaired over the prospect
that small countries might soon have their own nuclear weapons.[14] The following year, Eisenhower appointed Harold Stassen as a special consultant on
disarmament. Stassen first raised the notion of a pledge by all non-nuclear
states not to manufacture nuclear weapons with his Soviet counterpart,
Valerian Zorin, in 1957, a year before the first Irish Resolution was promulgat-
ed.[15] In July 1958, John Foster Dulles, Eisenhower's secretary of state, candidly
shared with French president Charles de Gaulle the US view that nuclear proliferation would destabilise both the deterrence-based international system
and the Western alliance while complicating arms-control negotiations with
the Soviets. Hence, the US was discouraging additional independent nuclear
forces even at the risk of souring relations with key allies.[16]

Underlying Dulles's apprehension was a statistical danger in proliferation. RAND Corporation strategist Fred C. Iklé explained it in 1960:

> According to the 'statistical theory' the probability of a global thermonuclear
> war increases as the number of nuclear powers increases because: (a) the
> larger the number of these powers, the greater the probability that nuclear

weapons will be used in some conflict (both because of more opportunities and a greater chance of irresponsibility); and (b) if nuclear weapons are used in conflict, the risk of its expanding into a global war is greater than if the conflict remained non-nuclear.

The counterargument, which should be weighed against this proposition, is that the diffusion of nuclear capabilities might make the involvement of major powers in local conflicts appear to be more risky and hence render it less likely … Intuitively, one would probably give more weight to the 'statistical theory' than to this counterargument, but the case is not as clear-cut and well-proven as it might seem at first blush.[17]

As Iklé implied and Shaker observed, there was a general tendency to accept proliferation's statistical danger at face value but 'there was really no profound analysis of the danger'.[18]

Nevertheless, the concept of statistical risk permeated US thinking well into the 1960s. For instance, the highly influential Gilpatric Committee, formed to advise US president Lyndon B. Johnson on how to respond to China's 1964 nuclear test, concluded in January 1965 that 'the spread of nuclear weapons poses an increasingly grave threat to the security of the United States. New nuclear capabilities, however primitive and regardless of whether they are held by nations currently friendly to the United States, will add complexity and instability to the deterrence balance between the United States and the Soviet Union.'[19] The following year, Robert McNamara, the secretary of defense, opined that 'the danger of nuclear war increases – I'd say geometrically – with the increase in the number of nations possessing independent nuclear forces'.[20]

The US unabashedly held a double standard with respect to nuclear deterrence and nuclear proliferation. In his 1969 testimony in support of US ratification of the NPT, John S. Foster, Jr, the Pentagon's director of defence research and engineering, declared that

we have based our nuclear weapon policy on the concept of deterrence. With the unrest that exists in many areas of the world today, we must deal with the prospect that some additional nation may in the future desire a nuclear deterrent. In the event of such proliferation, the consequences of an accident or a miscalculation by an aggressive state could be so tragic as to far outweigh the possible stability from their possession. Consequently, I believe that nuclear weapons are a unique kind that must remain subject to unique controls.[21]

In short, while nuclear deterrence had steadied superpower relations, the US had doubts about its stabilising effect in a regional context.

The Soviets, ever wary of nuclear weapons falling into the hands of West Germany, likewise accepted at face value the statistical danger of proliferation. Responding to the Irish Resolution of 1961, a senior Soviet official observed, 'It does not seem necessary … to dwell on the acute danger to peace which could be created by an increase in the number of Powers possessing nuclear weapons'.[22] In his remarks to the Supreme Soviet in 1965, Soviet foreign minister Andrei Gromyko warned that 'an increase in the number of nuclear countries producing and possessing nuclear weapons is accompanied by a growing danger of the outbreak of war using such weapons'.[23] Gromyko further cautioned that proliferation would undo the strategic balance between the Soviet Union and the US, adding new and unpredictable variables to the equation.[24]

Once the US was able to reassure the Soviet Union in late 1966 that West Germany would not attain control over US nuclear weapons, the two superpowers, as the lead negotiators of the NPT, were able to agree quickly on the treaty's core undertakings.[25] In August 1967, each country tabled an identical treaty draft containing the Article I commitment by nuclear-weapons states not to transfer to any recipient whatsoever nuclear weapons or control over them directly or indirectly, and not in any way to help non-nuclear-weapons states to manufacture or otherwise acquire nuclear weapons or control over them. The identical drafts also featured the Article II commitment by non-nuclear-weapons states not to receive nuclear weapons or accept direct or indirect control over them; not to manufacture or otherwise acquire nuclear weapons; and not to seek or receive any assistance in the manufacture of nuclear weapons or other nuclear explosive devices. These draft articles remained unaltered through the UN General Assembly vote approving the NPT in June 1968.[26]

Had it not been for the American and Soviet recognition that deterrence would become vastly more complicated if nuclear weapons spread widely, it is doubtful that the NPT would exist. Indeed, one might argue that the NPT came about mainly to protect nuclear deterrence. The US and the Soviet Union consented to the Article VI disarmament provision of the NPT only after they had mutually agreed to the deterrence-enhancing core provisions of Articles I and II,[27] and in belated recognition that some balance of obligations would be needed to persuade non-nuclear-weapons states to accede to the treaty.[28]

Nuclear deterrence as reinforcement for the NPT

It is self-evident that in allowing certain states to continue possessing nuclear weapons, the NPT accepts deterrence as the chief purpose for such weapons. This proposition has not been directly challenged. There has been an indirect challenge, however. In 1994, pursuant to a UN General Assembly resolution, the UN secretary-general requested the International Court of Justice (ICJ) to provide an advisory opinion on the 'legality of the threat or use of nuclear weapons'.[29] While not a specific legal test of nuclear deterrence, the subject did weigh on the judges' minds. Following a 7–7 tie vote that had to be broken by the ICJ president, the court concluded in 1996 that 'the threat or use of nuclear weapons would generally be contrary to the rules of international law applicable in armed conflict, and in particular the principles and rules of humanitarian law; however … the Court cannot conclude definitively whether the threat or use of nuclear weapons would be lawful or unlawful'.[30] The court found it could not 'ignore the practice referred to as "policy of deterrence," to which an appreciable section of the international community adhered for many years'.[31] Indeed, as Judge Shigeru Oda of Japan wrote in his dissenting opinion: 'The doctrine, or strategy, of nuclear deterrence, however it may be judged and criticized from different angles and in different ways, was made a basis for the NPT regime which has been legitimized by international law, both conventional and customary, during the past few decades.'[32] The upshot is that deterrence lies at the heart of the NPT and cannot be delegitimised without dismantling the foundation of the treaty.

In negotiating the NPT, the US established the principle that 'the treaty deals only with what is prohibited, not with what is permitted'.[33] The US shared this interpretation in advance with the USSR and key non-nuclear-weapons-states negotiators, who raised no objections. In this regard, besides the practice of nuclear deterrence, it is useful to review what else the NPT covers and permits:

- The NPT deals only with nuclear weapons, be they offensive, such as gravity bombs or missile warheads, or defensive, such as atomic demolition munitions or nuclear warheads for use atop anti-ballistic missiles. The treaty does not apply to nuclear-weapon delivery systems or nuclear propulsion.[34]
- The NPT allows continuing modernisation of nuclear weapons by nuclear-weapons states.[35]
- The NPT neither imposes a freeze on the production of nuclear weapons by the nuclear-weapons states, nor prescribes the destruction of their existing stockpiles.[36]
- The NPT allows nuclear-weapons assistance between nuclear-weapons states.[37]
- The NPT allows nuclear-weapons assistance to flow from a non-nuclear-weapons state to a nuclear-weapons state.[38]
- The NPT allows a nuclear-weapons state to transit nuclear weapons through, and base nuclear weapons on, the territories of a non-nuclear-weapons state.[39]
- The NPT allows the transfer of nuclear-delivery vehicles or systems and control over them to any recipient, so long as such transfer does not involve nuclear bombs or warheads.[40]
- The NPT allows consultations and planning between nuclear-weapons-state and non-nuclear-weapons-state allies so long as no transfer of nuclear weapons or control over them results.[41]

For all its permissiveness, particularly in allowing the nuclear-weapons state parties to modernise their nuclear forces, Shaker observed that 'the

Treaty as it finally materialized is in concert with the non-proliferation concept as formulated in the "Irish Resolution," which had envisaged that only "States not possessing nuclear weapons would undertake not to manufacture or otherwise acquire control of (nuclear) weapons"'.[42] He also acknowledged that 'the Treaty goes beyond the "Irish Resolution" in prohibiting the transfer of nuclear weapons between [nuclear-weapons states], which was not envisaged in 1961'.[43]

During the NPT negotiations, the Nigerian delegation asked, 'how could the deterrent value of nuclear weapons justly be denied to those renouncing the weapons themselves?'[44] For Nigeria, the answer lay in some form of nuclear umbrella for the NPT signatories until such time as nuclear weapons were eliminated from the world's arsenals. The country proposed 'an international deterrence system'.[45] It foundered because the superpowers were not prepared to take on greater security commitments than their existing alliances, and some non-nuclear-weapons states were just as reluctant to subscribe to any arrangement that might compromise their non-aligned status. Even so, there was a sufficiently strong desire among non-nuclear-weapons states for so-called positive security assurances that the Soviet Union, UK and US issued separate but equivalent offers of help in the event of nuclear threat or attack. These assurances are incorporated into UN Security Council Resolution (UNSCR) 255, adopted in June 1968, just before the NPT was opened for signature.

The essence of UNSCR 255 is that the threat of nuclear use against a non-nuclear-weapons state party to the NPT would create a situation in which the Security Council – as a practical matter, its nuclear-weapons-state permanent members – would have to act immediately in accordance with their obligations under the UN Charter. UNSCR 255 also reaffirms that non-nuclear-weapons states thus threatened retain the inherent right under Article 51 of the UN Charter of individual and collective self-defence, until the Security Council takes the necessary measures to restore international peace and security.[46]

While ancillary to the NPT, UNSCR 255 highlights the way in which deterrence was instrumental to the creation and operation of the treaty. Shaker noted that the resolution's prospect of quick assistance outside the Security

Council pursuant to Article 51 encouraged countries such as Belgium, Japan, the Netherlands and West Germany to accede to the NPT by satisfactorily ensuring that the NPT would not interfere with extended deterrence.[47] Certainly in the US view, sponsorship of UNSCR 255 by three permanent nuclear-weapons-state members of the Security Council introduced a 'powerful element of deterrence against nuclear aggression or the threat of such aggression'.[48] The principal intended beneficiaries were countries threatened by China, which was not a party to the NPT nor a permanent member of the Security Council at the time the treaty was opened for signature in 1968.[49]

Much has changed since then. For example, UNSCR 255 was updated and extended in 1995 with UNSCR 984, adding France and China. This was an important gain for the NPT and for deterrence of nuclear threats or use. More recently, however, the return of great-power competition has cast doubt on unified action by the five permanent nuclear-weapons-state members of the Security Council (P5). Nevertheless, we cannot a priori rule out situations in which the P5 find common cause in resisting a nuclear threat to the peace. Credible threats of nuclear use by North Korea, for example, might precipitate it. In any event, unified action by the P5 is not required for UNSCRs 255 and 984 to be of deterrent value, as they permit individual states to provide or support immediate assistance to a non-nuclear-weapons state party to the NPT that is threatened by, or attacked with, nuclear weapons, and to guarantee the inherent right of individual and collective self-defence.

Broad NPT consensus behind deterrence

It bears recalling that it was not only the US and the Soviet Union that sought to safeguard nuclear deterrence via the NPT; a number of America's allies in Europe and Asia were also keen to ensure that the treaty would protect existing extended-deterrence arrangements, particularly in light of US–Soviet strategic nuclear parity and China's nuclear rise. Recent scholarship reveals that assurances to Italy, Japan, the Netherlands and West Germany that the NPT would not preclude allied nuclear sharing and consultation were pivotal to their accession to the treaty and forswearing of nuclear weapons. This negotiating history disproves recent Russian allegations that NATO nuclear sharing violates the NPT.

According to Andreas Lutsch, 'West German security was based on nuclear deterrence'.[50] To West German officials, NATO's primary function was to provide durable US nuclear protection to the Federal Republic. West German leaders thus had to be reassured that the NPT prohibition on the indirect transfer of nuclear weapons did not apply to US nuclear weapons reportedly deployed on West German soil. In confirming this, Johnson remarked that West Germany insisted on a two-key system, whereby Bonn was assured that Washington would have to engage with it on the deployment of nuclear weapons in West Germany and their use, and that US–allied nuclear consultations had to be protected in any non-proliferation treaty.[51] West German officials 'ascribed central importance' to US public and private assurances of the permissibility of nuclear sharing under the NPT in their decision to accede to the treaty. Indeed, in signing the NPT, West Germany noted that it was doing so with the understanding that the NATO nuclear alliance was guaranteeing its security.

The US was similarly the main guarantor of Italy's external security, as Leopoldo Nuti observes, but Rome harboured some doubt as to the credibility of extended deterrence in an era of US–Soviet strategic nuclear parity.[52] Fearing political marginalisation, Italy concluded that only those countries that had access to nuclear weapons would have influence over NATO decision-making. Between 1955 and 1959, Italy therefore reportedly accepted the deployment of US nuclear weapons on its soil and welcomed the US proposal for a multilateral nuclear force (MLF) within NATO.[53] Like West Germany, Italy sought assurances that a non-proliferation treaty would not impede NATO nuclear sharing. Indeed, Italy and West Germany quietly agreed to coordinate their opposition to any non-proliferation treaty that would constrain NATO nuclear sharing. Italy was a major opponent of the NPT for years, until these concerns were satisfactorily addressed.

Elmar Hellendoorn has shed light on the inner workings of the Dutch foreign ministry with respect to negotiations on the NPT in the mid-1960s. For the ministry's directorate responsible for NATO nuclear affairs, US nuclear weapons were a means of deterring the Soviet Union, and nuclear sharing within NATO a way to foster Alliance unity and cohesion. Nevertheless, there were those in the ministry who did not fully trust US extended deterrence and sought to preserve a European nuclear option whereby, should a federated European super-state emerge, the US could bow out of the proposed MLF, leaving an independent West European nuclear force in its place. Max van der Stoel, the Dutch under-secretary of state for foreign affairs in the mid-1960s, was wary of French and German dominance of such a state, however. He inspired a Dutch effort within NATO to foreclose the possibility that the US veto on the use of nuclear weapons might be surrendered to a European super-state. Ironically, this brought the Netherlands closer to the Soviets' sceptical view on nuclear sharing, much to the dismay of the US. In time, however, Washington itself abandoned the MLF proposal, alleviating Dutch worries and clearing the way for the NPT.[54]

As Yoko Iwama has explained, Japan was crestfallen by China's 1964 nuclear test, which took place during the Tokyo Olympics no less.[55] China's nuclear ascent prompted Eisaku Sato, the Japanese prime minister, to seek and receive assurances from Johnson in January 1965 that the US would extend its nuclear deterrent to Japan. The following year, concrete deliberations on Japan's policy toward the NPT began. Among the Ministry of Foreign Affairs' top concerns was whether the prospective treaty would prevent the deployment of US nuclear weapons on Japanese soil, should it become necessary to deter China. Japan was also concerned that the NPT not impede nuclear consultations with the US. In short, despite Johnson's pledge, the NPT was seen as placing the Japan–US Security Treaty potentially at risk. At this point, Tokyo was not a direct participant in the negotiations, and was watching very closely how NATO nuclear-basing and -sharing arrangements were to be reconciled with the treaty. Provided the NPT did not ban the deployment of nuclear weapons or nuclear consultation, the Japanese concluded that the treaty would sufficiently safeguard Japan's national security. Elements within the foreign ministry remained opposed to the NPT, however, fearing the loss of Japan's nuclear option and diplomatic bargaining power. These elements reached out to West Germany, going so far as to propose coordinated opposition to the treaty and, potentially, cooperation in the development of nuclear weapons. West Germany's eventual decision to join the NPT and US confirmation of the extended-deterrence guarantee to Japan played a central role in overcoming opposition within the foreign ministry to sign and ratify the treaty.

NATO nuclear sharing

It is clear that protecting NATO nuclear-sharing arrangements within a non-proliferation treaty was essential not only to NATO members, but also to other states counting on US extended deterrence. Stassen had originally characterised the very concept of NATO nuclear sharing as a means of checking the proliferation of nuclear weapons in Western Europe.[56] Giving NATO members a say and role in Alliance nuclear matters could reassure them that they did not need to develop nuclear weapons of their own. Non-aligned states had their doubts about such sharing, however, and in 1965 drove the passage of UN General Assembly Resolution 2028 (XX), which established, among other things, the principle that a non-proliferation treaty should be 'devoid of any loop-holes which might permit nuclear or non-nuclear Powers to proliferate, directly or indirectly, nuclear weapons in any form'.[57] Ultimately, though, the non-aligned states were content to let the US and the Soviet Union subsequently resolve the issue of nuclear sharing on their own.[58] The Soviet Union and its Warsaw Pact allies were adamantly opposed to NATO nuclear-sharing arrangements out of fear that they would lead to a nuclear-armed West Germany, and because the Soviets wanted to sow political division within the Western Alliance.[59]

The US explained during the NPT negotiations that 'no proposal which the United States had considered in NATO would place control of nuclear weapons, or information on their manufacture, in the hands of any non-nuclear country'.[60] Canada, a participant in the negotiations, concurred, stating that it considered NATO nuclear-sharing arrangements to be consistent with the Irish Resolutions in that they were designed as alternatives to national nuclear-weapons programmes; Italy and the UK, the other NATO members involved in the NPT negotiations, shared that view.[61] The US also emphasised the security imperative behind such sharing: 'so long as hundreds of Soviet nuclear-tipped rockets are arrayed against Europe, effective European participation in strategic deterrence should be provided'.[62]

The US was able to reassure the Soviet Union that it would retain complete control over its nuclear weapons in Europe, laying to rest the MLF and with it scenarios of an eventual European nuclear force involving West Germany. In return, Moscow dropped its objections to NATO's existing nuclear-sharing arrangements.[63] Shaker commended the nuclear-sharing compromise as 'in fact in line with the Irish Resolution', rightly concluding that 'there was no prospect of success for a non-proliferation treaty without settling the problem of nuclear sharing within NATO to the satisfaction of the two blocs facing each other in Europe'.[64]

Given the vital importance of nuclear sharing to NATO security, the nature and durability of Moscow's acquiescence was a major Western consideration in weighing accession to the NPT. In US Senate ratification hearings on the military implications of the NPT in early 1969, the question was raised whether the Soviets might at some future date interpret the NPT's prohibition against the transfer of nuclear weapons to non-nuclear-weapons states to cover their participation in NATO nuclear decisions. In response, Gerard C. Smith, director of the Arms Control and Disarmament Agency, offered the US interpretation that the NPT did 'not deal with allied consultations and planning on nuclear defense so long as no transfer of nuclear weapons or control over them results', and that it does 'not deal with arrangements for deployment of nuclear weapons within allied territory'.[65] Smith cast these interpretations as 'an integral part of the legislative history of this treaty fully known to the Soviets, and which have not been contradicted by the Soviets'.[66]

This representation reflected a predetermined Soviet–American dispensation that allowed the Soviets to save face for what amounted to a major concession.[67] William Foster, the chief US NPT negotiator, was instructed to tell his Soviet counterpart Alexei Roshchin that if the Soviet Union disagreed with the US interpretations on NATO nuclear sharing, the United States would have to reconsider its support for the NPT. Dean Rusk, the US secretary of state, later made the same points to Gromyko.[68] US officials agreed not to require explicit Soviet agreement with the US interpretation, and to treat the mere absence of Soviet objection as consent. Adrian Fisher, one of the lead US negotiators of the NPT, offered details of this compromise in his Senate testimony:

> In the course of the negotiations we advised the Soviets that [NATO nuclear sharing] would be raised … in the context of Senate consideration of the

treaty, and we told them the answer we were going to give and said that this is the way we proposed to do it. If they would object they would bear the responsibility. They have not indicated acquiescence or agreement because they can't be asked to agree about certain arrangements that we keep secret ... They have been told that this would be made public in the context of this very hearing ... and that if they were to object they would bear the responsibility for the consequences that would happen. We have received no objection.[69]

NATO non-nuclear-weapons states had also wanted the clarifications on the permissibility of nuclear sharing publicly disclosed during the hearings, apparently so as to make them politically binding. West Germany, for one, would have preferred explicit assurances from the Soviets that they accepted the American interpretation, but the US discouraged Bonn from seeking them.[70]

The silence from Moscow was deafening. Shaker observed that Moscow did not challenge the US interpretation even when the Soviet instrument of ratification was being signed in November 1969 (some nine months after the US Senate hearings) at the Presidium of the Supreme Soviet, during which Gromyko spoke.[71] The NPT drafting process further supports Soviet acceptance of NATO nuclear sharing. In particular, the Soviet Union agreed to drop from the final treaty more specific language from its draft of September 1965, which would have explicitly prohibited non-nuclear-weapons states from seeking to acquire control over the emplacement and use of nuclear weapons for units of their armed forces 'even if such units or personnel are under the command of a military alliance'.[72] On the broader issue of nuclear-weapons deployment on the territories of non-nuclear-weapons states, Shaker noted that 'the Treaty, in fact, does not deal with common arrangements for deployment of nuclear weapons within allied territory', and that 'deployment was not prohibited in any of the previous drafts'.[73] Indeed, at the first NPT Review Conference in 1975, Moscow opposed efforts by a number of non-nuclear-weapons states to seek the withdrawal of nuclear-weapons delivery systems from their respective territories, explaining that such an effort would be counterproductive for East–West relations.[74]

Recent Russian allegations that NATO nuclear-sharing arrangements violate the NPT thus appear to be baseless attempts by Russian President Vladimir Putin's government to undermine NATO political unity in the wake of its aggression against Ukraine and illegal annexation of Crimea. As Rose Gottemoeller, then deputy secretary-general of NATO, remarked in 2019, NATO nuclear-sharing arrangements were settled with Moscow decades ago: 'There is no cause for complaint.'[75] Perhaps Moscow would do well also to recall Smith's cautionary observation in 1969: 'The Soviets know that if they should take an official position in opposition to [nuclear-sharing arrangements], very serious problems would arise.'[76] The US made it clear during the NPT negotiations that it could not abide an NPT without NATO nuclear sharing, and that the NPT remains in Moscow's interest.

Disarmament and deterrence

Heading into the NPT negotiations, the US and the Soviet Union clearly were not seeking a disarmament agreement. Even the most basic of arms-control pacts, the nuclear-test ban, had proven fraught enough at the time. Both Washington and Moscow believed that trying to saddle the NPT with disarmament measures would inevitably hold up agreement, and the moment to curtail the spread of nuclear weapons would be lost. Moreover, they could hardly have been expected to commit to reaching agreement on disarmament when it would be impossible to predict the exact nature and results of the requisite negotiations. Washington and Moscow were of the view, however, that the NPT would help create favourable conditions for the eventual achievement of nuclear, as well as general, disarmament.[77] Under a compromise brokered by Mexico, all NPT state parties therefore undertook in Article VI 'to pursue negotiations in good faith' toward such measures. The Mexican solution met with a lukewarm reception by other non-nuclear-weapons states, and Article VI has remained a constant source of friction in the global nuclear order.[78]

Article VI is silent on nuclear deterrence. Since the NPT allows that which it does not explicitly prohibit, the treaty can be construed as implicitly recognising that nuclear deterrence will continue to operate on the path to nuclear disarmament. This interpretation is consistent with other moves by the US and the Soviet Union during the NPT negotiations to resist efforts to impugn or constrain nuclear deterrence. For example, Romania introduced a proposal for preamble language acknowledging that 'the danger of nuclear war can only be eliminated by the cessation of the manufacture of nuclear weapons'.[79] The proposal was not accepted. At the first NPT Review Conference, efforts by the non-nuclear-weapons states to impose nuclear disarmament on the nuclear-weapons states were rejected by the latter and their allies, in part because they were seen as interfering with US–Soviet relations.[80] Then, as now, a number of nuclear- and non-nuclear-weapons states alike were relying on deterrence, however paradoxically, to reduce the risks of nuclear war to tolerable levels.

In the future, nuclear deterrence must be sustained alongside disarmament if states that rely on the former for their security are to move toward the latter. This entails managing the complexities of deterrence as nuclear weapons are reduced to very low numbers and eventually to zero.[81] Even in the event of actual disarmament, a latent type of nuclear deterrence will likely operate in the form of one state's ability to reconstitute a nuclear force quickly if another state has surreptitiously done so. This kind of deterrence calculus is not theoretical. It took hold over a decade ago, when the George W. Bush administration concluded that it could step up its dismantlement of non-deployed nuclear weapons once it had in place an ability to remanufacture nuclear weapons quickly if the need arose.[82]

*   *   *

The NPT's disarmament provisions do not impede deterrence. The relationship between nuclear deterrence and the NPT is, and always has been, symbiotic. Deterrence, particularly in the form of a nuclear umbrella extended by the US over its allies, keeps additional states from seeking their own nuclear weapons to confront existential threats. By globally limiting the spread of nuclear weapons, the NPT helps to keep major-power deterrence stable. For these reasons, the NPT was designed not to impinge on the practice of nuclear deterrence by the nuclear-weapons states pending disarmament, and those states have committed themselves to upholding the treaty regime. It is incumbent on all those who rely on deterrence for their security to make this symbiotic relationship more explicit in their NPT diplomacy. Likewise, it behoves those who value the NPT to recognise that delegitimising nuclear deterrence risks the very foundation of the NPT.

Notes

1   Mohamed I. Shaker, *The Nuclear Nonproliferation Treaty: Origin and Implementation, 1959–1979* (London: Oceana Publications Inc., 1980), p. 4.

2   *Ibid.*, p. 24.

3   *Ibid.*, p. 7.

4   See Don Munton, 'Canada's Affair with Nuclear Weapons: Building, Debating, Acquiring, Retiring', in John Baylis and Yoko Iwama (eds), *Joining the Non-proliferation Treaty: Deterrence, Non-proliferation and the American Alliance* (London: Routledge, 2019), p. 115.

5   Quoted in Shaker, *The Nuclear Nonproliferation Treaty*, p. 19.

6   *Ibid.*

7   Frank Aiken, 'Can We Limit the Nuclear Club?', *Bulletin of the Atomic Scientists*, vol. 17, no. 7, September 1961, p. 265.

8   'Document 04. US Delegation to the United Nations Telegram DELGA 108', 7 October 1958, available at the National Security Archive, https://nsarchive2.gwu.edu//dc.html?doc=5017513-Document-04-U-S-Delegation-to-the-United-Nations. Although France did not test its first nuclear device until 1960, by 1958 steps were well under way to build the *force de frappe*, and de Gaulle's return to power that year left little room for doubt about his nuclear intentions.

9   'Document 13. US Mission to the United Nations Telegram DELGA 340 to State Department, "Disarmament"', 3 November 1958, available at the National Security Archive, https://nsarchive2.gwu.edu//dc.html?doc=5017523-Document-13-U-S-Mission-to-the-United-Nations.

10 Shaker, *The Nuclear Nonproliferation Treaty*, p. 472.

11 *Ibid.*, p. 479.

12 *Ibid.*, p. 644.

13 *Ibid.*, p. 31.

14 See Shane Maddock, 'The Fourth Country Problem: Eisenhower's Nuclear Nonproliferation Policy', *Presidential Studies Quarterly*, vol. 28, no. 3, Summer 1998, p. 553.

15 *Ibid.*, pp. 558–60.

16 *Ibid.*, p. 562.

17 Fred Charles Iklé, 'Nth Countries and Disarmament', *Bulletin of the Atomic Scientists*, vol. 16, no. 10, December 1960, p. 391. The seminal article on this problem in the NATO context is Albert Wohlstetter, 'Nuclear Sharing: Nato and the N+1 Country', *Foreign Affairs*, vol. 39, no. 3, April 1961, pp. 355–87. On the counter-argument, the classic treatment is Kenneth N. Waltz, 'The Spread of Nuclear Weapons: More May Be Better', *Adelphi Paper* 171 (London: International Institute for Strategic Studies, 1981).

18 Shaker, *The Nuclear Nonproliferation Treaty*, pp. 28–9.

19 'A Report to the President by the

Committee on Nuclear Proliferation' (also known as the 'Gilpatric Report'), 21 January 1965, available at the National Security Archive, https://nsarchive2.gwu.edu//NSAEBB/NSAEBB1/nhch7_1.htm.

20 Mason Willrich, *Non-proliferation Treaty: Framework for Nuclear Arms Control* (Charlottesville, VA: Michie Company, 1969), p. 38.

21 US Senate Committee on Armed Services, *Hearings Before the Committee on Armed Services, United States Senate, Ninety-first Congress, First Session on Military Implications of the Treaty on the Nonproliferation of Nuclear Weapons, February 27 and 28, 1969* (Washington DC: US Government Printing Office, 1969), 27 and 28 February 1969, p. 15, https://books.google.com/books?id=0SM3AQAAIAAJ&printsec=frontcover&source=gbs_ge_summary_r&cad=0#v=onepage&q&f=false. Hereafter referred to as *Military Implications of the NPT*.

22 Evgeny M. Chossudovsky, 'The Origins of the Treaty on the Non-proliferation of Nuclear Weapons: Ireland's Initiative in the United Nations (1958–1961)', *Irish Studies in International Affairs*, vol. 3, no. 2, 1990, p. 123.

23 Hal Brands, 'Non-proliferation and the Dynamics of the Middle Cold War: The Superpowers, the MLF, and the NPT', *Cold War History*, vol. 7, no. 3, August 2007, p. 403.

24 *Ibid.*

25 See George Bunn, *Arms Control by Committee: Managing the Negotiations with the Russians* (Stanford, CA: Stanford University Press, 1992), pp. 77–80, in which the author cites a White House meeting between Johnson and Gromyko as the 'turning point'. Bunn was the first chief counsel of the US Arms Control and Disarmament Agency (1961–69) and one of the lead negotiators of the NPT.

26 International safeguards against the diversion of peaceful nuclear activities to weapons purposes remained contentious, largely over Soviet insistence that the International Atomic Energy Agency also administer safeguards for the European Atomic Energy Community (Euratom). Hence, the identical draft treaties of August 1967 contained only a placeholder for Article III international controls. See Shaker, *The Nuclear Nonproliferation Treaty*, pp. 106–8.

27 The August 1967 identical draft treaties contained only preamble language on disarmament, not a treaty article. Disarmament was not included as Article VI in identical US and Soviet treaty drafts until January 1968. See Shaker, *NPT Origin and Implementation*, pp. 114, 558.

28 *Ibid.*, pp. 266, 566-7, 588.

29 The vote hardly represented a sweeping anti-deterrence mandate; it passed 78–43 with 38 countries abstaining and 26 not voting. See Newell L. Highsmith, 'On the Legality of Nuclear Deterrence', *Livermore Papers on Global Security*, no. 6, Lawrence Livermore National Laboratory, Center for Global Security Cooperation, April 2019, p. 10, https://cgsr.llnl.gov/content/assets/docs/CGSR_LivermorePaper6.pdf.

30 *Ibid.*, p. 1.

31 *Ibid.*, p. 15.

32 *Ibid.*, p. 35 n. 70.

33 Shaker, *The Nuclear Nonproliferation Treaty*, p. 234.

34 Willrich, *Non-proliferation Treaty*, p. 69.

35 Shaker, *The Nuclear Nonproliferation Treaty*, pp. 214, 241, 249.

36 *Ibid.*, p. 249.

37 According to Shaker, this was intended to enable continued US assistance to the UK on the design, development and fabrication of nuclear weapons through the provision of technology, non-nuclear components of weapons and unfabricated nuclear material. Shaker, *The Nuclear Nonproliferation Treaty*, p. 260.

38 *Ibid.*, p. 261.

39 *Ibid.*, pp. 246–7.

40 *Ibid.*, pp. 202–3.

41 *Ibid.*, p. 239.

42 *Ibid.*, p. 254.

43 *Ibid.*, p. 261.

44 *Ibid.*, p. 524.

45 United Nations General Assembly, Preparatory Committee for the Conference of Non-Nuclear-Weapon States, 'Security Guarantees in the Context of Measures to Prevent the Spread of Nuclear Weapons: Paper by the Rapporteur', A/CONF.35/PC/L.14, 12 September 1967, p. 13, https://s3.amazonaws.com/unoda-web/documents/library/conf/A-CONF35-PC-L14.pdf.

46 Shaker, *The Nuclear Nonproliferation Treaty*, Appendix 4, pp. 968–9.

47 *Ibid.*, pp. 517, 542. See also United Nations General Assembly, 'Non-proliferation of Nuclear Weapons: Report of the Preparatory Committee for the Conference of Non-Nuclear-Weapon States', A/6817, 19 September 1967, Annex IV, p. 6, https://undocs.org/A/6817.

48 Shaker, *The Nuclear Nonproliferation Treaty*, p. 546.

49 Willrich, *Non-proliferation Treaty*, pp. 172–3, 180. France also was not an NPT signatory but was a nuclear-weapons state and permanent Security Council member; it abstained from UNSCR 255.

50 Andreas Lutsch, 'Problem Solved? The German Nuclear Question and West Germany's Accession to the NPT (1967–1975)', in Baylis and Iwama (eds), *Joining the Non-proliferation Treaty*.

51 Shaker, *The Nuclear Nonproliferation Treaty*, p. 233 n. 121.

52 See Leopoldo Nuti, '"A Turning Point in Postwar Foreign Policy": Italy and the NPT Negotiations, 1967–1969', in Roland Popp, Liviu Horovitz and Andreas Wenger (eds), *Negotiating the Nuclear Non-proliferation Treaty: Origins of the Nuclear Order* (London: Routledge, 2017); and Leopoldo Nuti, 'Extended Deterrence and National Ambitions: Italy's Nuclear Policy, 1955–1962', *Journal of Strategic Studies*, vol. 39, no. 4, April 2016, p. 577.

53 Much has been written on the ill-fated MLF. Shaker deals with it extensively in *The Nuclear Nonproliferation Treaty*, pp. 129–89.

54 See Elmar Hellendoorn, 'The Birth of a Nuclear Non-proliferation Policy: The Netherlands and the NPT Negotiations, 1965–1966', in Popp, Horovitz and Wenger (eds), *Negotiating the Nuclear Non-proliferation Treaty*.

55 See Yoko Iwama, 'The Japanese Ministry of Foreign Affairs and the Decision to Join the Non-proliferation Treaty', in Baylis and Iwama (eds),

Joining the Non-proliferation Treaty.

56 Maddock, 'The Fourth Country Problem', p. 558.

57 Shaker, *The Nuclear Nonproliferation Treaty*, Appendix 2, p. 935.

58 *Ibid.*, pp. 226–7, 230.

59 *Ibid.*, p. 164.

60 *Ibid.*, p. 50.

61 *Ibid.*, p. 158.

62 *Ibid.*, p. 165.

63 *Ibid.*, p. 233.

64 *Ibid.*, pp. 129, 232.

65 *Military Implications of the NPT*, p. 122.

66 *Ibid.*

67 The Soviet Union was under considerable pressure from Warsaw Pact members not to relent on potential West German access to nuclear weapons. See Douglas Selvage, 'The Warsaw Pact and Nuclear Nonproliferation, 1963–1965', Working Paper No. 32, Cold War International History Project, Woodrow Wilson International Center for Scholars, April 2001, https://www.wilsoncenter.org/sites/default/files/working_paper_no._32_repaired.pdf.

68 Bunn, *Arms Control by Committee*, p. 80.

69 US Senate Committee on Foreign Relations, *Hearings Before the Committee on Foreign Relations, United States Senate, Ninetieth Congress, Second Session on Executive H, Treaty on the Nonproliferation of Nuclear Weapons, July 10, 11, 12 and 17, 1968* (Washington DC: US Government Priting Office, 1968), p. 364, https://babel.hathitrust.org/cgi/pt?id=uiug.30112038152960&view=1up&seq=7.

70 Lutsch, 'Problem Solved?', p. 99.

71 Shaker, *The Nuclear Nonproliferation Treaty*, p. 247.

72 Willrich, *Non-proliferation Treaty*, pp. 75–6. See also Shaker, *The Nuclear Nonproliferation Treaty*, Appendix 3B, p. 941.

73 Shaker, *The Nuclear Nonproliferation Treaty*, p. 240.

74 *Ibid.*, p. 247.

75 'NATO Nuclear Policy in a Post-INF World', speech by NATO deputy secretary-general Rose Gottemoeller at the University of Oslo, 9 September 2019, https://www.nato.int/cps/en/natohq/opinions_168602.htm. See also William Alberque, 'The NPT and the Origins of NATO's Nuclear Sharing Arrangements', Études de l'Ifri Proliferation Papers, no. 57, Institute Français de Relations Internationales, Security Studies Center, February 2017, https://www.ifri.org/sites/default/files/atoms/files/alberque_npt_origins_nato_nuclear_2017.pdf.

76 *Military Implications of the NPT*, p. 122.

77 Shaker, *The Nuclear Nonproliferation Treaty*, p. 566.

78 *Ibid.*, p. 567.

79 *Ibid.*, pp. 574–7.

80 *Ibid.*, p. 601.

81 See, for example, James M. Acton, *Deterrence During Disarmament: Deep Nuclear Reductions and International Security*, Adelphi 417 (Abingdon: Routledge for the IISS, 2011).

82 See Christopher A. Ford, 'Learning to Speak Disarmament in the Language of Security', New Paradigms Forum, 29 September 2009, http://www.newparadigmsforum.com/NPFtestsite/?m=200909.

Opportunistic Aggression in the Twenty-first Century

Hal Brands and Evan Braden Montgomery

In 415 BCE, after six years of peace, the second phase of the Peloponnesian War began when Athens launched a military expedition to Sicily. That expedition, however, suddenly allowed Sparta to impose a heavy toll on its long-time adversary. As its forces confronted a deteriorating situation on the ground, Athens opted to dispatch additional troops rather than accept defeat, which convinced Sparta to invade Attica and sever its rival's overland supply lines. In the words of Thucydides, 'what chiefly encouraged the Spartans to act with energy was their belief that Athens, with two wars on her hands – one against them and one against the Sicilians – would be now easier to crush'.[1]

Two centuries later, during the Second Punic War, Rome faced a similar situation. Following a series of battlefield setbacks at the hands of the Carthaginians, the Romans unexpectedly found themselves defending their eastern flank against the Macedonians. According to Polybius's account, when news of Rome's loss at Lake Trasimene reached Greece, an adviser to King Philip V of Macedonia encouraged the ambitious young ruler to exploit the situation: 'This is the moment to strike a blow, when

Hal Brands is the Henry Kissinger Distinguished Professor of Global Affairs at Johns Hopkins University's Paul H. Nitze School of Advanced International Studies and a scholar at the American Enterprise Institute. He is also a columnist for Bloomberg Opinion and is currently writing a book on how history can inform America's approach to competition with China and Russia. **Evan Braden Montgomery** is a senior fellow and the director of research and studies at the Center for Strategic and Budgetary Assessments. He is the author of *In the Hegemon's Shadow: Leading States and the Rise of Regional Powers* (Cornell University Press, 2016).

Survival | vol. 62 no. 4 | August–September 2020 | pp. 157–182   DOI 10.1080/00396338.2020.1792129

the Romans have suffered a disastrous defeat.'[2] After the calamitous Battle of Cannae, Philip V not only formed an alliance with Hannibal Barca, the famed Carthaginian general, but also saw an opening to expand into Roman client states in nearby Illyria. Despite the ongoing threat from Carthaginian forces on the Italian peninsula, the possibility that Macedonia could extend its influence over the Balkans and undercut Rome's position in the region led to a conflict that continued for a decade and ended without any significant Roman gains.[3]

As these examples show, opportunistic aggression – one of the most dreaded but least examined strategic problems confronting the United States today – has a long lineage. Great powers commonly find themselves saddled with commitments that exceed their available resources.[4] The extreme version of this situation – the nightmare scenario – is facing two or more wars simultaneously. With this danger in mind, American defence planners have long sought to ensure that the United States has the capability to wage more than one conflict at a time. Today, however, in recognition of its resource limitations and a deteriorating security environment, the United States has adopted a defence strategy focused on defeating a single major power – either China or Russia – rather than two lesser threats at once.[5] This means that the US military might be overtaxed and perhaps even overwhelmed should it have to deal with more than one military challenge. And because an overstretched superpower is a tempting target, the United States must reckon with the possibility of opportunistic aggression: an adversary attempting to change the status quo while Washington is preoccupied. In a particularly grave scenario, one major power might exploit a conflict between the United States and another major power to wage a war for regional dominance in Eastern Europe or the Western Pacific.[6]

Despite the ominous salience of this scenario, opportunistic aggression occupies an uneasy place in US defence strategy. On the one hand, the need to prevent or respond to this threat has been an article of faith among defence planners for decades. Consequently, it has had a significant influence on the size, shape and posture of the US armed forces. On the other hand, there has been relatively little scholarly work that explores how frequently it arises and what forms it can take.[7] Because the United States has now adopted a one-war strategy, the fortunes of that strategy will hinge, in part, on the likelihood of opportunistic aggression. If it is a genuine threat, a one-war strategy could create dangerous, even disastrous, vulnerabilities. If not, the risks of a one-war strategy are probably modest.

In fact, opportunistic aggression is not a phantom menace conjured up by overanxious defence planners.[8] It has occurred many times, from antiquity to the Cold War, and in many forms, sometimes with devastating consequences. There are also several plausible pathways by which opportunistic aggression against the United States and its interests could arise today. The canonical scenario – one enemy launching a major war while America is already fighting another enemy – cannot be discounted given America's geopolitical circumstances. But opportunistic aggression encompasses a spectrum of options, from coalition war fighting to proxy conflict to cut-throat diplomacy. It can unfold without a shot being fired; it can change the geopolitical status quo without a second war being started. These subtler aspects of the phenomenon are not as well understood, but they also have the potential to create big problems for an overstretched superpower.

> *Opportunistic aggression can change the status quo*

Moreover, there is no silver bullet for dealing with the threat of opportunistic aggression. The surest way would be to spend more money on the defence capabilities that would allow Washington to reliably deter or wage more than one conflict at a time, but that seems infeasible given resource constraints that could get much tighter as a result of the fiscal fallout from COVID-19. That reality may tempt American officials to consider a variety of poor man's options, from cutting deals with adversaries to threatening asymmetric escalation in a second war. Yet if some of these options look appealing on paper, they could prove difficult or dangerous to execute. The United States may or may not decide to make the military investments required to significantly buy down the risk associated with opportunistic aggression. But policymakers should not fool themselves into thinking that there are easy, low-cost alternatives to keeping that threat at bay.

An overview of opportunistic aggression

Opportunistic aggression commonly means the use of force by a challenger when its enemy is already fighting another war. The logic underpinning this danger is straightforward: if deterrence is a function of the perceived capability and perceived willingness of a defender to uphold the status quo, then involvement in a confrontation with one adversary raises the risk of deterrence failure vis-à-vis another. All things equal, a state that is fighting one war will have fewer forces available to fight a second. It should also prefer to avoid an additional conflict so that it can concentrate on winning the first. This dynamic creates an opening for a new challenger to strike.[9]

The possibility of opportunistic aggression looms whenever a state faces two or more competitors, which is not uncommon for most major powers. Continental powers such as Imperial Germany, the Austro-Hungarian Empire, tsarist Russia and the Soviet Union each had to wrestle with concurrent rivalries, which created difficult trade-offs and even had fatal consequences in some cases, especially when states went on the offensive in ill-advised attempts to address multiple threats on their own terms.[10] Opportunistic aggression seems to be a particular bane of global maritime powers. These states often face multiple rivals and have a variety of economic interests and security commitments across multiple regions. During its long period of global dominance, for example, the United Kingdom contended with numerous existing and potential rivals, such as Germany, France, Japan, Russia and the United States, not to mention frequent conflicts with local actors along the imperial periphery.[11]

The prospect of opportunistic aggression has also created recurring dilemmas for the United States. From the late 1940s through the early 1970s, Washington faced challenges from both the Soviet Union and the People's Republic of China. Throughout the Cold War, moreover, it undertook military engagements in places such as Korea and Vietnam, which risked creating openings for the Soviet Union. As a result, avoiding opportunistic aggression was a prominent objective in US defence strategy. During the 1960s, the Kennedy and Johnson administrations committed (rhetorically, at least) to building a two-and-a-half (2.5) war capability that would allow Washington to fight wars against the Soviet Union, Communist China and one smaller power simultaneously, thereby decreasing the ability of one communist rival to exploit an American showdown with another. Even after the 2.5-war standard was rendered unnecessary by the US–China rapprochement, the United States maintained a 1.5-war standard so that it could fight a minor conflict somewhere in the world without tempting the Soviet Union to attack in Europe or elsewhere.[12]

After the Cold War, the concept of opportunistic aggression became even more central to US defence strategy. Although the United States no longer faced a rival superpower, it confronted challenges from three rogue powers – Iran, Iraq and North Korea – across two distant theatres. US officials feared that a conflict on the Korean Peninsula might incentivise Iran or Iraq to expand in the Middle East, or that a conflict in the Middle East might tempt North Korea to lash out at its neighbours in Northeast Asia.[13] For more than two decades, the United States maintained a force designed to handle two major regional contingencies simultaneously or nearly simultaneously. As the 1997 Quadrennial Defense Review explained, 'maintaining this core capability is central to deterring opportunism – that is, to avoiding a situation in which an aggressor in one region might be tempted to take advantage when US forces are heavily committed elsewhere'.[14]

The two-war construct was premised on the idea that the United States would be squaring off against relatively weak rivals. The current security environment is more dangerous, however, and the risk of opportunistic aggression appears to be on the rise, for three reasons. Firstly, the number of serious challengers has increased. Today, the United States is planning for potential conflicts against five different actors (China, Iran, North Korea, Russia and major terrorist organisations) across at least three different theatres. Secondly, the strength of individual competitors has increased. China and Russia are far more capable militarily than any of the rogue states that the United States sought to contain after the Cold War.[15] Thirdly, the level of coordination between US rivals has grown. China and Russia have forged a diplomatic partnership that features heightened military cooperation and raises the possibility that they might work together during a confrontation with the United States.[16] For these reasons, it is important that American strategists begin to think more carefully, and with greater nuance, about the possibility of opportunistic aggression.

The history of opportunistic aggression

Opportunistic aggression has not been a rare or trivial occurrence. In fact, it has been the cause of important wars and the source of serious great-power defeats. Opportunistic aggression comes in a wide variety of forms that go beyond our conventional understanding of the concept. And although some, such as conflict initiation and conflict intervention, entail the use of force, others, such as assertive bargaining and military build-ups, do not.

The type of opportunistic aggression that captures the most rapt attention of strategists and planners is overt military action. The most straightforward mode is conflict initiation: an opportunistic aggressor starts a war that is largely independent of whatever war its target is already fighting, for instance by seizing undefended territory, settling a local score, carving out a sphere of influence or inflicting a direct blow against the target. That puts the defender in the position of fighting on two fronts unless it chooses to accept an immediate loss on one of them. Whether conflict initiation entails directly attacking a preoccupied foe or assaulting its overseas interests, the aggressor is exploiting a window of opportunity to alter the status quo.

During the Napoleonic Wars, the fact that Britain had its hands full encouraged other states to pursue their interests at its expense. In 1812, with issues such as commerce restrictions and naval impressment heightening Anglo-American tensions, the United States displayed a limited tolerance for negotiations and was quick to settle these disputes by force, due in part to Britain's ongoing conflict against France. In fact, Washington opted for war – partially in hopes of achieving revisionist ambitions such as the conquest of Canada – only shortly before learning that London had conceded the main source of their quarrel by repealing its restrictions on neutral trade.[17] Britain had little desire to fight the United States given its heavy commitments against Napoleon Bonaparte. In London, the War of 1812 was 'seen as a stab in England's back, treacherously delivered during a desperate crusade against the tyrant of Europe'.[18]

The first half of the twentieth century also saw opportunistic conflict initiation, with enormous consequences for regional and global stability. In multiple cases, Japan – a revisionist state that aspired to dominate the Asia-Pacific region – was the perpetrator. In 1914, Tokyo recognised that the outbreak of war in Europe would 'upset the whole balance of power in East Asia' and leave Japan 'free to pursue its ambitions almost without check'.[19] Shortly after the conflict began, it occupied German-leased territory in China and seized German colonies in the South Pacific. Twenty-five years later, when the Second World War again threw the European continent into chaos, Japan saw another opportunity to create a vast sphere of influence. Indeed, one of the main debates among Japanese cabinet members was whether to exploit the opportunity created by the defeat of the Netherlands, the fall of France and the anticipated collapse of the UK to advance into Southeast Asia, or instead to take advantage of the unanticipated German attack against the Soviet Union to expand north out of Manchuria.[20] Tokyo chose the former option, although it also hoped to attack a beleaguered Soviet Union at a later date, much like a 'jackal state' that was 'ready to jump in for the choice pickings of a kill made by others'.[21]

Starting a separate war is not the only mode of opportunistic aggression. Rather than initiating a new campaign, an aggressor might opt for conflict intervention.[22] For instance, an opportunistic aggressor could turn a bilateral war into a coalition war by allying with its rival's opponent to augment that opponent's strength, thus inflicting a sharp blow on a shared enemy. Alternatively, an opportunistic aggressor could turn a bilateral war into a proxy war by employing low-profile methods to extend a conflict's duration, heighten its intensity and increase the toll it takes on an adversary.

In 1585, for example, England openly agreed to supply money and troops to Dutch rebels fighting for independence against its rival, Spain, which helped them hold out against what was then the world's strongest power.[23] In 1778, France formally sided with American revolutionaries in their war for independence from Great Britain, providing money and supplies as well as troops and naval power. In helping the Americans prevail, Paris inflicted payback on London for its earlier defeat in the Seven Years War, secured or regained imperial territories, and weakened England so that it could not support France's continental rivals.[24] And in June 1940, Italy opportunistically invaded France one month after Germany did. 'The hand that held the dagger has struck it into the back of its neighbor', Franklin Roosevelt remarked.[25]

As for less overt cases of intervention, the second half of the twentieth century saw numerous instances of superpower proxy wars. The Soviets intervened covertly in Korea, sending pilots and fighter aircraft to bolster North Korea's air defences.[26] Moscow also provided lethal anti-aircraft weapons and other support to North Vietnam to raise the cost of US intervention in Southeast Asia. Moscow's reasoning, Richard Nixon lamented, was that 'the war in Vietnam costs the Soviet Union only a small amount of money and costs the US a great many lives'.[27] Washington later took revenge by supporting Afghan guerrillas after the Kremlin stumbled into its own version of Vietnam, inflicting high costs on an overextended Soviet Union.[28]

Other forms of aggressive opportunism can alter the status quo or impose costs without firing a shot. In the near term, a state's involvement in a war can reduce its leverage and leave it with little choice but to accept harsh demands from third parties watching from the sidelines. After Germany's initial victories in 1939 and 1940 defeated or pressured European powers with colonial holdings in Asia, British and American leaders feared that Japan would exploit the situation to press diplomatic demands. Indeed, Tokyo pushed the Dutch to provide critical raw materials from Southeast Asia. It also insisted that the UK and Vichy France close the Burma Road that was used to supply the Chinese nationalists in their war against the Japanese.[29] Not least, Tokyo demanded that the Vichy regime give it access to air bases in Indochina and allow transit of Japanese troops through that territory. Although Vichy officials agreed, Japan attacked French forces in northern Indochina and eventually invaded southern Indochina as well.

Over the long term, a state's engagement in a protracted conflict can also enable its rival to shift the balance of power (or make the existing balance of power more expensive to sustain) through determined military modernisation. With the United States embroiled in Vietnam, the Soviet Union undertook a significant conventional build-up in Europe as well as a rapid build-up of its strategic nuclear forces.[30] 'While we have been heavily engaged in Southeast Asia', then-secretary of defense Melvin Laird commented in 1971, 'the Soviet Union has built a military momentum relative to the US in virtually all aspects of military strength'.[31] More recently, as the United States became preoccupied with wars in Afghanistan and Iraq,

China accelerated a massive modernisation effort designed to coerce its neighbours and counter US intervention. 'China is reshaping the military order in Asia', a Pentagon official remarked in 2008, 'and it is doing so at our expense'.[32] In both cases, the costs of war – in money, materiel, personnel and attention – created a window of opportunity for a competitor to alter the military balance.

Future opportunistic aggression against the US

Although opportunistic aggression has been a genuine problem in the past, predicting when, where and how it might occur in the future is difficult. For one thing, a revisionist power's decision to engage in or forgo aggression will be based on more than whether its rival is preoccupied: just because a window of opportunity opens, a state will not necessarily jump through it.[33] If the United States were already suffering losses in a conflict, a revisionist spectator would see an increase in its relative power without ever taking any risks. Any decision to go to war, by any rival, would presumably reflect a variety of geopolitical and domestic calculations, some of which have little to do with perceptions of American distraction. Nevertheless, Washington's geopolitical situation does create an inherent risk of opportunistic aggression, and by working through the various possibilities we can get a better sense of where the danger really lies.

To start, although American planners have worried for decades about simultaneous conflicts with two minor powers, Washington should probably worry more today about a contingency involving at least one of its great-power rivals given the capabilities they can bring to bear and the damage they could inflict on the US-led international system. Theoretically, this could occur in a variety of ways. One major power might opt for aggression while the United States is busy dealing with another, which has the potential to become a worst-case scenario if Russia and China launch large-scale wars simultaneously or fight together as allies. Alternatively, a major power could make a move while the United States is focused on North Korea or Iran. Lastly, a major power might play the role of a catalyst rather than the opportunist; that is, a fight with Russia or China might open the door to aggression by North Korea or Iran.

Several factors could influence what specific forms these threats take and whether they arise at all. For example, opportunistic conflict initiation should depend in part on Washington's perceived willingness and ability to redirect its forces from one fight to another, especially since it does not presently have the resources to wage two wars at once. If the Pentagon can quickly win the first conflict and pivot to the second, that should enhance the deterrence of potential opportunists. By contrast, a slow victory or stalemate would keep US forces busy and make opportunistic aggression more attractive. At the same time, if the stakes are comparatively low in the first war, Washington might be willing to cut its losses and tackle the second, which should help keep opportunists on guard. But if the stakes are high in the first contingency, the United States might feel forced to fight on despite competing demands, which makes opportunism more likely.

A slow victory would keep US forces busy

In addition, opportunistic conflict intervention should be contingent on geographic constraints, which will affect the amount and type of support that one aggressor could provide to another. Specifically, a revisionist state would have a limited capacity to openly assist another actor and operate together as a coalition if these potential allies were located far apart, especially since most US rivals have been emphasising military capabilities designed to project force in their own neighbourhoods rather than into other regions. An opportunist should also be reluctant to support another state if the risk of retaliation outstrips the estimated reward of bloodletting, which suggests that deniable or ambiguous methods of assistance would make this type of intervention more attractive.

These considerations offer several broad takeaways. Firstly, there are some threats that strategists and planners can probably afford to worry less about, even if they should not be dismissed entirely. For instance, there are reasons to doubt that a major power would actually start a second war while the United States is fighting a minor power – that Russia would use a US conflict with Iran to make a land grab in the Baltic region, or that China would exploit it to invade Taiwan. In these cases, the opportunistic power might well anticipate a rapid US victory over the smaller power, while the comparatively low stakes of the initial conflict suggest that Washington might simply choose to shift its focus if confronted with a bigger, more important fight.

The obvious caveat here involves a situation in which a major-power aggressor believes that it only needs a very brief window of opportunity to achieve its gains. Russia, for instance, might assess that it could overpower limited NATO forces or simply seize a relatively small chunk of lightly defended territory in the Baltic region before the US could react, severely testing and perhaps discrediting NATO's Article V guarantee.[34] Many US analysts deem this scenario plausible given the balance of military power in key areas. But even if an opportunistic great power calculated that a brief delay in the American response would be sufficient to accomplish a limited military objective that delivered a big strategic pay-off, it would still be taking a major risk on its ability to win quickly and decisively. This might make such a gamble less attractive.[35]

The likelihood of confronting a great-power coalition is even lower. To be sure, both Russia and China would have strong incentives to aid one another in a contest with the United States. Although their relationship is still marked by tensions and high levels of mistrust, neither Moscow nor Beijing would wish to see its fellow authoritarian power defeated by Washington for fear that the US would then focus more of its energies on the remaining challenger.[36] Both powers might also be tempted to turn a major war into a 'Suez moment' for the United States – a decisive defeat that would undermine its prestige and power for years, creating openings for more ambitious authoritarian revisionism.[37] But even though Russia and China have conducted combined exercises in various locales, distance dictates that they can probably fight together only in Northeast Asia.[38] Moreover, even if Russia had an opportunity to assist China in a conflict against the United States and Japan in the East China Sea, it might not want to advance the strategic cause of a contiguous rising power with expansionist ambitions, especially one that would no longer need to divide its attention. While Russia would not want China to decisively lose a war with the United States, it might not want it to decisively win one, either.

Secondly, some threats strategists and planners fear are very real. The possibility of dual great-power wars – say, a Chinese assault on Taiwan followed by a Russian attack in the Baltic region – is more plausible than many sceptics might accept. Not only does Washington lack the capabilities to win both fights at once, or even to win a single fight quickly, but a loss in either scenario could shatter key US alliances.[39] That is, the speed of victory would probably be low while the interests at stake would undoubtedly be high. A window of opportunity for a second power would open once it recognised that Washington was not in a position to shift focus and conduct another campaign. Given the geopolitical rewards that a victory over a distracted United States would bring, this possibility might look quite attractive to revisionist leaders in Moscow or Beijing. If Russian President Vladimir Putin wished to fracture NATO and push the Alliance back from Russia's borders, he would never have a better chance than during a Sino-American war that brings the US military to the very limit.

This risk might be even higher than currently assessed due to Russia's or China's ability to shift the geopolitical status quo by taking relatively limited military actions. A 1914-style offensive would not be required for Russia to seize Narva or otherwise commit aggression in the Baltics, perhaps by ambiguous means, or for China to violently assert itself against one of its neighbours in the South China Sea.[40] Both countries could pursue such goals via limited actions of relatively short duration, meant to create new realities that would be disproportionately expensive and deadly for America and its allies to reverse. If the calculation is that Beijing or Moscow needs only a short period of time to violently revise the status quo in its near abroad, then the intense American preoccupation created by a war with the other authoritarian power would provide an alluring opportunity.[41]

The prospect of a minor power starting a war while the United States is fighting a major power is also a serious one, even if it is somewhat less dangerous than a dual great-power war scenario. Because the US would be embroiled in a high-stakes conflict with a low probability of quick success, a minor power would have increased freedom of action to take advantage. If Iran sought to initiate a coercive military campaign against the Gulf

Cooperation Council countries, for example, the optimal time would be when the United States was deeply committed elsewhere.

Great-power intervention in a US war against a minor power is also plausible. Major powers are unlikely to side directly with minor powers to create the threat of a coalition war, due to geographic constraints as well as a risk–reward disparity. The added damage they could inflict on the United States probably would not outweigh the costs they would suffer compared to those of remaining on the sidelines and watching Washington fight. Russia could send some aircraft and naval combatants into a US–Iran war in the Middle East, for instance, but those capabilities probably would not change the ultimate outcome. (If China intervened in a US–North Korea war, it would likely be to preserve a geographical buffer on its borders and not to help Pyongyang win.[42]) Nevertheless, a major power might see a US conflict with Iran or North Korea as a low-cost chance to bleed the US by providing its opponent with weapons or other assets it could use to increase the price America

Russia and China might aid each other

would pay, especially if they were not so advanced that their origins would be obvious. The more the United States suffers today in a war against Iran or North Korea, the thinking might go, the harder it will be for the US to thwart Russian or Chinese ambitions in the future. The efforts need not be covert, merely low-profile enough that the United States does not feel compelled to respond. During the Korean War, for instance, American officials strongly suspected that Soviet pilots were flying combat missions, but they chose not to make an issue of it for fear of worsening tensions and potentially provoking an expanded war at a time of US vulnerability.[43]

Thirdly, there are a number of credible scenarios that warrant more attention than they are getting. For instance, although Russia and China might not band together in a coalition, they might still aid each other in a conflict with the United States on a more discreet and limited basis. For instance, either country could quietly provide arms or intelligence to the other, or it could employ hard-to-attribute, non-kinetic measures such as cyber attacks and disinformation campaigns to hinder the mobilisation and deployment of American forces.[44] Either major power could also undertake subtle military moves – such as massing forces near a potential hotspot – to give the United States pause by demonstrating that it would be vulnerable in other areas if it fully committed to the first theatre.[45] If the goal were simply to prevent the United States from winning decisively, or to increase the costs it suffers from a great-power contest, Moscow and Beijing would have options.

At the same time, the United States should be on guard for major-power efforts to alter the status quo without firing a shot. Precisely because a US war against Russia or China would so consume America's combat power and so test America's global position, it would create extremely high incentives for the United States and its allies to ensure that another conflict did not erupt at the same time. That, in turn, would create opportunities for revisionists on the sidelines, Russia and China most of all, to posture for advantage. Beijing and Moscow have so far been hesitant actually to use force against the United States and its allies. In this light, blackmail, whether obvious or subtle, could be very appealing in a crisis.[46]

Russia might seek as the price of its neutrality concessions from the West on Ukraine, the security architecture of Eastern Europe or the resolution of the civil war in Syria. It could punctuate those demands by posturing forces that would enable it to take stronger action if Washington and its allies refused. China could perceive similar openings amid a US–Russian showdown. It might demand economic or political concessions from Taiwan designed to limit that island's sovereignty, assuming that the United States would not be able to intervene in a crisis. It might also push wavering allies such as the Philippines to realign more tightly with China or demand that the US recognise its de facto territorial gains in the South China Sea.

America could also induce Russia or China to undertake below-the-threshold or grey-zone provocations.[47] Pressure short of outright violence against American allies and partners in Southeast Asia, or the intensification of Russian activities in Ukraine, would not run much risk of war or even a serious diplomatic showdown with an overtaxed United States.[48] But they would represent a form of coercive diplomacy by shifting facts on the ground and essentially daring an overcommitted superpower to respond. China arguably intensified its grey-zone activities in the South China Sea when the US Navy was temporarily sidelined by coronavirus, offering a preview of what may well come if the American military is consumed by another great-power conflict.[49]

Finally, US involvement in any war, but especially one with a great power, could create an opening for other states to enhance their military capabilities. Although a short, sharp war with Russia in Eastern Europe might not create as robust an opportunity for a Chinese build-up as the years of American involvement in Iraq and Afghanistan, heavy losses in personnel and materiel might enlarge China's scope for modernising its forces and shifting the balance of power in the Western Pacific and beyond.[50] A regional power could also attempt to exploit American involvement in a serious conflict with a major power by rapidly making military improvements Washington would otherwise more forcefully resist. A poor US showing in a war with China, for example, might provide the breakout time Iran needs to become a threshold nuclear state, or for North Korea to conduct the additional missile and nuclear tests needed to refine its intercontinental attack capabilities.[51]

The potential permutations of opportunistic aggression are numerous, and not all scenarios are equally likely or consequential. Moreover, opportunistic aggression does not happen in a vacuum. Its occurrence would hinge heavily on factors independent of whether American forces were already engaged elsewhere.[52] But there are several plausible scenarios in which a United States committed on one front might find itself menaced by an opportunistic adversary, with potentially severe consequences for American interests and security.

Averting opportunistic aggression

There are six possible strategies for averting opportunistic aggression, several of which overextended great-powers have adopted in the past. The first two – spending more and asymmetric escalation – offer military solutions. The second two – securing the flank and sharing burdens – aim to reduce the number of threats a great power confronts. The last two – holding the ring and driving a wedge – are intended to prevent hostile actors from banding together. All of these approaches, while offering some appeal, face stiff challenges today.

Consider the military solutions. Spending more involves improving the ability to respond to multiple crises. This was the approach the UK took by adopting the two-power naval standard in 1889, a policy meant to ensure that a war against France would not deplete British naval power to the point that the British Empire would be vulnerable to Russian aggression. After the Cold War, the United States spent enough to afford it a credible deterrent against two adversaries at once. The present-day equivalent of this strategy would be for the United States to return to a 1.5-war or two-war standard, so it could handle two significant conflicts simultaneously. Yet this solution would get very expensive very quickly. Britain's two-power standard became harder to maintain in the face of Germany's naval build-up.[53] Even during the post-Cold War era, there were concerns about whether America's two-war standard was realistic. The challenges to a 'spend' strategy are even greater today. Developing an authentic 1.5-war strategy would likely require sustained increases in military spending over the next five to ten years, at a time when defence budgets seem likely to decline, perhaps significantly. Building a force that can defeat challenges from China and Russia simultaneously would be harder still.[54]

> *A nuclear threat may not be credible*

The other military strategy, asymmetric escalation, is also problematic. This approach involves compensating for conventional military vulnerability by threatening dramatic escalation. The United States could rely on its nuclear deterrent to hold aggressors at bay while it was engaged in a major conventional fight elsewhere. It could also threaten strategic cyber attacks against an opportunistic aggressor's critical infrastructure or military capabilities. Options short of nuclear escalation, however, might not inflict enough pain to compel an aggressor to back down. A Russian leader who is willing to roll the dice in the Baltics might also tolerate enormous hardship to avoid defeat.[55] The liabilities of nuclear escalation are equally severe: a threat to wage nuclear war over Taiwan or Latvia may not be credible, given that America would be risking a potentially cataclysmic nuclear exchange to avoid the loss of a relatively small amount of territory far from its borders.

Among approaches that prescribe reducing threats and burdens, securing the flank entails limiting the number of opponents by reaching agreements with potential adversaries. During the 1890s and early 1900s, an overstretched UK appeased the United States, allied with Japan and settled outstanding disputes with France and Russia to focus on Germany. In the 1970s, Israel dramatically lowered the possibility of another multi-front war by making peace with Egypt. Revisionist powers have also pursued this strategy: in 1939, Germany sealed the Molotov–Ribbentrop Pact with the Soviet Union and secured Moscow's benign neutrality, setting the stage for the invasion of Poland and later France.

Today, securing the flank might entail seeking a detente with Russia that allowed the United States to concentrate on China, or pursuing a rapprochement with North Korea or Iran to permit more intense focus on great-power competition.[56] In either case, though, this strategy would probably sacrifice interests that once seemed important enough to defend. Decreasing tensions with Russia could require the United States to accept Moscow's manipulation of Western political processes and its coercion of Eastern European neighbours. Setting aside differences with North Korea could mean allowing it to develop nuclear and missile forces unopposed. And easing tensions with Iran might entail acquiescing to its provocations across the Middle East. Not only would these efforts weaken US partnerships in the regions where they were implemented, but they could also have a cascading effect on Washington's credibility across its alliance portfolio.[57] Put differently, this strategy would suddenly treat commitments as independent after many decades of American officials insisting that they were interdependent.

Another option is sharing burdens: encouraging local actors to take more responsibility for their own and regional security so they can deter opportunism and help hold the line if deterrence fails. During the late nineteenth century, when the demands of imperial defence and the provision of public goods were scattering Britain's forces across the globe, policymakers in London pushed the dominions to take more strategic responsibility.[58] Following Vietnam, the United States shared burdens in an even more comprehensive way. The Nixon Doctrine declared that Asian allies and partners menaced by internal aggression must face those threats largely by themselves. Simultaneously, a 'regional sheriffs' policy outsourced security commitments in key regions to friendly actors such as Israel and Iran.[59]

In the contemporary context, the United States could give its NATO allies more responsibility for deterring and checking Russian aggression.[60] In the Asia-Pacific, the US could prod its security partners to bolster their capacity to resist an assault by China. And in the Middle East, Washington might exhort local states to take the lead in deterring expansionist behaviour by Iran. Although the United States would undoubtedly help its allies and partners with intelligence, arms sales and other enablers prior to or during a crisis, it would rely on its friends for geopolitical initiative and combat power. An increased reliance on other states, however, could erode US influence and create capability limitations and collective-action problems that increase the probability of deterrence failure. While Europe's economic power dwarfs Russia's, for instance, European states would still struggle to meet the Russian geopolitical threat without strong US leadership, which catalyses collective action and unifies states with vastly differing threat perceptions.[61] Bereft of customarily strong US support, local states might simply accommodate revisionist powers. Emboldened revisionist powers themselves also might push harder.

Finally, there are the strategies for dividing or otherwise neutralising potential pairs of aggressors. Holding the ring entails making common cause with a potential opportunist's enemy to reduce the prospect of intervention. The Anglo-Japanese alliance of the early twentieth century is a classic example. During the Russo-Japanese war, the alliance dissuaded France from coming into the conflict on behalf of its ally Russia for fear of triggering a war with the UK. Tokyo was thus able to fight and defeat a single enemy. Yet such a strategy has two principal liabilities. Firstly, finding new friends might create new enemies. The British worried that allying with Japan might lead to conflict with the United States; Washington was indeed displeased with the pact and insisted on its abrogation in the 1920s. Secondly, capable new allies are in short supply because the US alliance system is already so extensive, and most unaligned states are not powerful or close enough to affect Russian or Chinese calculations. One option would be to deepen the US relationship with India so that China might face a threat on its western flank.[62] But India appears reluctant to join a containment effort against China, and would perforce be unwilling to join the United States in a war against China.

Driving a wedge involves fracturing potential coalitions by setting two potential opponents against each other.[63] In the late eighteenth and early nineteenth centuries, Napoleon's success in conquering most of Europe reflected his ability to avoid multi-front wars by using threats and bribes to divide the coalitions confronting him. During the Cold War, the US employed a two-phase wedge strategy vis-à-vis the Sino-Soviet alliance: first exerting maximum pressure on Beijing to increase its dependence on Moscow and thereby straining the relationship, and then, after the Sino-Soviet split, building a relationship with China to confront the Kremlin with the prospect of a two-front war.[64] The obvious target for a contemporary wedge strategy would again be the Russia–China partnership, in which there are frictions due to increasing asymmetries in strength and influence. The United States could try to play one off the other, but it could take years for the tensions between two rivals to disrupt an emerging coalition.[65] US efforts to pressure China so that it demanded more resources from the Soviet Union eventually worked, but it took well over a decade and a series of nuclear crises. It is not clear, moreover, that Washington can overcome the shared threat perceptions and common ambitions driving Russia and China together anytime soon.[66] Finally, when a wedge strategy involves concessions to a hostile power, it risks discomfiting the allies that the hostile power threatens.

*   *   *

The United States is in a quandary. The threat of opportunistic aggression is baked into Washington's position as a global power confronting multiple threats. History reminds us that this phenomenon is no illusion, and that it can be quite dangerous. America's present rivals have a variety of plausible options, from fighting dual wars to exploiting American vulnerabilities for coercive advantage. There is no easy solution or clearly dominant strategy for mitigating the challenge.

In theory, the US could reduce the danger by selectively employing a variety of the available options: modestly increasing military spending; de-escalating confrontations with regional powers without conceding key interests; delegating some responsibility to allies and partners; building better relations with India; and subtly working to increase the strains between Russia and China. Yet that would require a strategic clarity and focus that are utterly lacking in US leadership right now. Moreover, if post-COVID-19 reductions in defence spending are as severe as some analysts forecast, even a hybrid approach may not be possible.[67] It also would run the risk that the United States might do just enough to convince itself that it is responding to the problem, without actually doing enough to solve it.

A necessary first step is simply to acknowledge the stark choice the United States faces. Spending significantly more on defence in the coming years, as a way of developing the capabilities and force structure needed to buy down the risk of opportunistic aggression, currently seems infeasible. Yet the alternative may be to pursue strategies that are far riskier than they first appear. Reasonable observers can debate which approach is preferable and how to weigh the respective costs and dangers. US officials, however, should not deceive themselves into thinking that the threat of opportunistic aggression is negligible or that there is a cheap, nifty way of eliminating it. That would delay the inevitable reckoning until the moment when the danger finally materialises – a course that would prove the most perilous of all.

Notes

1   Thucydides, *History of the Peloponnesian War*, trans. Rex Warner (New York: Penguin, 1972), Book VII, p. 487. See also Paul A. Rahe, 'The Primacy of Greece: Athens and Sparta', in James Lacey (ed.), *Great Strategic Rivalries: From the Classical World to the Cold War* (New York: Oxford University Press, 2016), p. 76.

2   Polybius, *Rise of the Roman Empire*, trans. Ian Scott-Kilvert (London: Penguin, 1979), Book V, p. 101.

3   See R.M. Errington, 'Rome and Greece to 205 B.C.', in A.E. Astin et al. (eds), *The Cambridge History of the Ancient World, Volume 8: Rome and the Mediterranean to 133 BC*, 2nd ed. (Cambridge: Cambridge University Press, 1989).

4   This situation is often called

the 'Lippmann gap'. See Walter Lippmann, *US Foreign Policy: Shield of the Republic* (Boston, MA: Little, Brown & Co., 1943), pp. 7–8; and Samuel Huntington, 'Coping with the Lippmann Gap', *Foreign Affairs*, vol. 66, no. 3, Winter 1987–88, pp. 453–77.

5   See Hal Brands and Evan Braden Montgomery, 'One War Is Not Enough: Strategy and Force Planning for Great Power Competition', *Texas National Security Review*, vol. 3, no. 2, Spring 2020, https://tnsr.org/2020/03/one-war-is-not-enough-strategy-and-force-planning-for-great-power-competition/; and Jim Mitre, 'A Eulogy for the Two-war Construct', *Washington Quarterly*, vol. 41, no. 4, Winter 2019, pp. 7–30.

6   See National Defense Strategy Commission, 'Providing for the Common Defense: The Assessments and Recommendations of the National Defense Strategy Commission', November 2018, https://www.usip.org/publications/2018/11/providing-common-defense.

7   There are partial exceptions. Stephen Van Evera explains how the deployment of a state's military forces in one theatre can create windows of opportunity for rivals in other theatres. See Stephen Van Evera, *Causes of War: Power and the Roots of Conflict* (Ithaca, NY: Cornell University Press, 1999), chapter four. Randall Schweller, by contrast, has emphasised the role of profit-driven bandwagoning, to include states opportunistically joining ongoing conflicts. Randall L. Schweller, 'Bandwagoning for Profit: Bringing the Revisionist State Back In', *International Security*, vol. 19, no.

1, Summer 1994, pp. 72–107. John Mearsheimer has noted that a state's involvement in a war might create an opening for its rivals to support its adversary. John J. Mearsheimer, *The Tragedy of Great Power Politics* (New York: W.W. Norton, 2001), pp. 154–5. Finally, a recent study by several authors shows that states with multiple rivals are tempting targets for compellent threats because a challenger knows that their resources cannot be concentrated against it. Douglas B. Atkinson, Joshua Jackson and George W. Williford, 'Rivalry, Uncertainty, and Militarized Compellent Threats', *Journal of Global Security Studies*, February 2020, https://academic.oup.com/jogss/advance-article-abstract/doi/10.1093/jogss/ogz079/5735640. This essay offers a more systematic appraisal of opportunistic aggression, one that is historically informed and yields an analytical framework that can be applied to today's rivalries.

8   For a study that plays down the possibility of opportunistic aggression, see Michael Mazarr et al., *What Deters and Why: Exploring Requirements for Effective Deterrence of Interstate Aggression* (Santa Monica, CA: RAND Corporation, 2018).

9   See Geoffrey Blainey, *The Causes of War*, 3rd ed. (New York: The Free Press, 1988). Opportunistic aggression is not the only scenario that could lead a country to face multiple challenges at once. A country could also face two or more unrelated conflicts, as happened when the United States intervened in the Dominican Republic while also escalating in South Vietnam

in the spring of 1965.

10 See A. Wess Mitchell, *The Grand Strategy of the Habsburg Empire* (Princeton, NJ: Princeton University Press, 2018).

11 See Aaron Friedberg, *The Weary Titan: Britain and the Experience of Relative Decline, 1895–1905* (Princeton, NJ: Princeton University Press, 1988); and William R. Thompson, 'Why Rivalries Matter and What Great Power Rivalries Tell Us About World Politics', in William R. Thompson (ed.), *Great Power Rivalries* (Columbia, SC: University of South Carolina Press, 1999), p. 12.

12 See John Lewis Gaddis, *Strategies of Containment: A Critical Appraisal of American National Security Policy During the Cold War* (New York: Oxford University Press, 2005).

13 See National Defense Strategy Commission, 'Providing for the Common Defense'.

14 William S. Cohen, 'Report of the Quadrennial Defense Review', US Department of Defense, May 1997, https://apps.dtic.mil/dtic/tr/fulltext/u2/a326554.pdf. See also Hal Brands, *Making the Unipolar Moment: US Foreign Policy and the Rise of the Post-Cold War World* (Ithaca, NY: Cornell University Press, 2016), pp. 324–5, 331–2.

15 See Chris Dougherty, *Why America Needs a New Way of War* (Washington DC: Center for a New American Security, 2019).

16 See Michael O'Hanlon and Adam Twardowski, 'An Alliance Between Russia and China Is the Next Military Threat', *Hill*, 12 December 2019, https://thehill.com/opinion/national-security/474424-an-alliance-between-russia-and-china-is-the-next-military-threat.

17 See David French, *The British Way in Warfare, 1688–2000* (London: Unwin Hyman, 1990), p. 114; and Jasper M. Trautsch, 'The Causes of the War of 1812: 200 Years of Debate', *Journal of Military History*, vol. 77, no. 1, January 2013, pp. 273–93.

18 Kenneth Bourne, *Britain and the Balance of Power in North America, 1815–1908* (Berkeley, CA: University of California Press, 1967), p. 8.

19 W.G. Beasley, *Japanese Imperialism, 1894–1945* (Oxford: Oxford University Press, 1987), p. 109.

20 The deployment of US naval forces to the Atlantic in support of the undeclared war against Germany also reduced American military strength in the Pacific, contributing to a window of opportunity for Japan. See Van Evera, *Causes of War*, pp. 89–90.

21 S.C.M. Paine, *The Japanese Empire: Grand Strategy from the Meiji Restoration to the Pacific War* (Cambridge: Cambridge University Press, 2017), p. 152.

22 Conflict initiation and conflict intervention could also interact with one another. For instance, one aggressor might intervene in an ongoing conflict to impose costs on a defender, while another aggressor could jump through the window of opportunity created by that intervention to start a second war.

23 See Geoffrey Parker, 'Spain, Her Enemies and the Revolt in the Netherlands, 1559–1648', *Past & Present*, vol. 49, no. 1, November 1970, pp. 72–95.

24 See Mark Grimsley, 'The Franco-

American Alliance During the War for Independence', in Peter R. Mansoor and Williamson Murray (eds), *Grand Strategy and Military Alliances* (Cambridge: Cambridge University Press, 2016).

25 Quoted in Henry Steele Commager, *The Story of the Second World War* (Washington DC: Potomac Books, 2004), p. 89.

26 See Mark O'Neill, 'Soviet Involvement in the Korean War: A New View from the Soviet-era Archives', *OAH Magazine of History*, vol. 14, no. 3, Spring 2000, pp. 20–4.

27 Document 31, 'Memorandum of Conversation Between Nixon and Anatoly Dobrynin, 20 October 1969', in *Soviet–American Relations: The Détente Years, 1969–1972* (Washington DC: US Government Printing Office, 2007), p. 87.

28 See James Scott, *Deciding to Intervene: The Reagan Doctrine and American Foreign Policy* (Durham, NC: Duke University Press, 1996).

29 See Akira Iriye, *The Origins of the Second World War in Asia and the Pacific* (New York: Longman, 1987), pp. 97–101.

30 See Michael McGwire, *Military Objectives in Soviet Foreign Policy* (Washington DC: Brookings Institution Press, 1987), pp. 55–6.

31 Memo, Laird for Nixon, 8 December 1971, in Richard A. Hunt (ed.), *Melvin Laird and the Foundation of the Post-Vietnam Military, 1969–1973*, Documentary Supplement, Secretaries of Defense Historical Series, vol. VII (Washington DC: Historical Office of the Office of the Secretary of Defense, 2016), p. 480, https://history.defense.gov/Portals/70/Documents/secretaryofdefense/Laird%20Document%20Supplement.pdf.

32 Quoted in Brands, *Making the Unipolar Moment*, p. 360.

33 See Richard Ned Lebow, 'Windows of Opportunity: Do States Jump Through Them?', *International Security*, vol. 9, no. 1, Summer 1984, pp. 147–86.

34 See Elbridge Colby, 'Against the Great Powers: Reflections on Balancing Nuclear and Conventional Power', *Texas National Security Review*, vol. 2, no. 1, November 2018, https://tnsr.org/2018/11/against-the-great-powers-reflections-on-balancing-nuclear-and-conventional-power/.

35 Nevertheless, the losses that the United States suffered while fighting a minor power could erode Washington's relative power position and its ability to deter future conflicts with major powers. See Evan Braden Montgomery, 'Primacy and Punishment: US Grand Strategy, Maritime Power, and Military Options to Manage Decline', *Security Studies* (forthcoming).

36 For a good discussion of the relationship, see Richard Ellings and Robert Sutter, *Axis of Authoritarians: Implications of China–Russia Cooperation* (Seattle, WA: National Bureau of Asian Research, 2018).

37 Russia finds it hard enough to compete with an America that is heavily distracted by China; its predicament would be far worse after the United States had defeated Beijing militarily, even in a limited war. See Michael Kofman, 'Raiding and International Brigandry: Russia's Strategy for Great Power Competition', *War*

on the Rocks, 14 June 2018, https://warontherocks.com/2018/06/raiding-and-international-brigandry-russias-strategy-for-great-power-competition/.

38 See, for instance, Associated Press, 'Russia, China Hold Naval Exercises in Baltic', *Military Times*, 25 July 2017, https://www.militarytimes.com/news/2017/07/26/russia-china-hold-naval-exercise-in-baltic/.

39 Some analysts have questioned whether the United States could win even a single great-power war. See Michael J. Mazarr, 'Toward a New Theory of Power Projection', *War on the Rocks*, 15 April 2020, https://warontherocks.com/2020/04/toward-a-new-theory-of-power-projection/; and Robert O. Work and Greg Grant, 'Beating the Americans at Their Own Game: An Offset Strategy with Chinese Characteristics', Center for a New American Security, June 2019.

40 See, for instance, Josh Rubin, 'NATO Fears that This Town Will Be the Epicenter of Conflict with Russia', *Atlantic*, 24 January 2019, https://www.theatlantic.com/international/archive/2019/01/narva-scenario-nato-conflict-russia-estonia/581089/.

41 See Dan Altman, 'By Fait Accompli, Not Coercion: How States Wrest Territory from Their Adversaries', *International Studies Quarterly*, vol. 61, no. 4, December 2017, pp. 881–91.

42 See Oriana Skylar Mastro, 'Why China Won't Rescue North Korea: What to Expect if Things Fall Apart', *Foreign Affairs*, vol. 97, no. 1, January–February 2018, pp. 58–67.

43 See John Lewis Gaddis, *The Cold War: A New History* (New York: Penguin, 2005), p. 60.

44 Both China and Russia have extensive cyber-warfare capabilities. See, for example, Jr Ng, 'China Broadens Cyber Options', *Asian Military Review*, 15 January 2020, https://asianmilitaryreview.com/2020/01/china-broadens-cyber-options/.

45 On the underlying logic of this point, see US Armed Services Committee, 'Testimony of Mara Karlin to the Senate Armed Services Committee Hearing on Recommendations for a Future National Defense Strategy', 30 November 2017, https://www.armed-services.senate.gov/imo/media/doc/Karlin_11-30-17.pdf.

46 See, for example, Michael Green et al., *Countering Coercion in Maritime Asia: The Theory and Practices of Gray Zone Deterrence* (Washington DC: Center for Strategic and International Studies, 2017).

47 One way to reduce this particular risk would be to increase transparency through the use of airborne-surveillance assets. See Thomas G. Mahnken, Travis Sharp and Grace B. Kim, *Deterrence by Detection: A Key Role for Unmanned Aircraft Systems in Great Power Competition* (Washington DC: Center for Strategic and Budgetary Assessments, 2020).

48 The logic of these activities is explained in Michael J. Mazarr, *Mastering the Gray Zone: Understanding a Changing Era of Conflict* (Carlisle Barracks, PA: US Army War College Press, 2015). See also Geraint Hughes, 'War in the Grey Zone: Historical Reflections and Contemporary Implications', *Survival*, vol. 62, no. 3, June–July 2020, pp. 131–58.

49 See Shashank Bengali, 'What the

Coronavirus Hasn't Stopped: Beijing's Buildup in the South China Sea', *Los Angeles Times*, 10 April 2020, https://www.latimes.com/world-nation/story/2020-04-10/coronavirus-doesnt-deter-chinas-aggression-in-south-china-sea.

50 The downward pressure on American defence spending, which effectively augmented the Soviet build-up, did not cease until the end of the 1970s, even though US involvement in Vietnam concluded in 1973. See Brian Auten, *Carter's Conversion: The Hardening of American Defense Policy* (Columbia, MO: University Press of Missouri, 2009).

51 On Iran's 'breakout time', see Agence France-Presse, 'Iran's Nuclear Deal Breaches Mean Breakout Time Could Be Mere Months – Experts', *Times of Israel*, 9 March 2020, https://www.timesofisrael.com/spotlight-returns-to-irans-nuclear-program-amid-ongoing-breaches-of-deal/.

52 See Mazarr et al., *What Deters and Why*.

53 See Paul Kennedy, *Strategy and Diplomacy 1870-1945* (London: George Allen and Unwin, 1983), pp. 129–60.

54 See Brands and Montgomery, 'One War Is Not Enough'; Congressional Budget Office, 'Long-Term Implications of the 2020 Future Years Defense Program', August 2019, https://www.cbo.gov/system/files/2019-08/55500-CBO-2020-FYDP_0.pdf; Mazarr, 'Toward a New Theory of Power Projection'; and National Defense Strategy Commission, 'Providing for the Common Defense'.

55 See Elbridge Colby and David Ochmanek, 'How the United States Could Lose a Great-power War', *Foreign Policy*, 29 October 2019, https://foreignpolicy.com/2019/10/29/united-states-china-russia-great-power-war/.

56 See Robert Blackwill, *Implementing Grand Strategy Toward China: Twenty-two US Policy Prescriptions* (New York: Council on Foreign Relations, 2020).

57 See Hal Brands, Eric Edelman and Thomas Mahnken, *Credibility Matters: Strengthening American Deterrence in an Age of Geopolitical Turmoil* (Washington DC: Center for Strategic and Budgetary Assessments, 2018).

58 See Donald C. Gordon, *The Dominion Partnership in Imperial Defense, 1870–1914* (Baltimore, MD: Johns Hopkins University Press, 1965).

59 See Robert Litwak, *Détente and the Nixon Doctrine: American Foreign Policy and the Pursuit of Stability, 1969-1976* (Cambridge: Cambridge University Press, 1986).

60 See Elbridge Colby, 'How to Win America's Next War', *Foreign Policy*, 5 May 2019, https://foreignpolicy.com/2019/05/05/how-to-win-americas-next-war-china-russia-military-infrastructure/.

61 See Stephanie Pezard et al., *European Relations with Russia: Threat Perceptions, Responses, and Strategies in the Wake of the Ukrainian Crisis* (Santa Monica, CA: RAND Corporation, 2017).

62 See Evan Braden Montgomery, 'Competitive Strategies Against Continental Powers: The Geopolitics of Sino-Indian-American Relations', *Journal of Strategic Studies*, vol. 36, no. 1, February 2013, pp. 76–100.

63 See especially Timothy Crawford, 'Preventing Enemy Coalitions: How Wedge Strategies Shape Power

Politics', *International Security*, vol. 35, no. 4, Spring 2011, pp. 155–89.

[64] See John Lewis Gaddis, *The Long Peace: Inquiries into the History of the Cold War* (Oxford: Oxford University Press, 1987).

[65] For instance, the US could encourage China's neighbours to purchase Russian arms and pursue a trilateral strategic arms-control agenda that holds agreements Russia wants hostage to Chinese intransigence. See Gregory Kulacki, 'China Is Willing to Negotiate on Nuclear Arms, but Not on Trump's Terms', *Defense One*, 30 March 2020, https://www.defenseone.com/ideas/2020/03/china-willing-negotiate-nuclear-arms-not-trumps-terms/164204/; and Paul Stronski and Nicole Ng, 'Cooperation and Competition: Russia and China in Central Asia, the Russian Far East, and the Arctic', Carnegie Endowment for International Peace, 28 February 2018, https://carnegieendowment.org/2018/02/28/cooperation-and-competition-russia-and-china-in-central-asia-russian-far-east-and-arctic-pub-75673. Over the longer term, Washington might put greater pressure on Russia, forcing it to become more dependent on China, which could eventually prove intolerable to Moscow.

[66] See Hal Brands, 'Trump Can't Split Russia from China – Yet', Bloomberg, 31 July 2018, https://www.bloomberg.com/opinion/articles/2018-07-31/trump-can-t-split-russia-from-china-yet.

[67] See Daniel Egel et al., 'Defense Budget Implications of the COVID-19 Pandemic', RAND Blog, 7 April 2020, https://www.rand.org/blog/2020/04/defense-budget-implications-of-the-covid-19-pandemic.html.

The UAE and the War in Yemen: From Surge to Recalibration

Thomas Juneau

The growing assertiveness of Saudi Arabia's foreign policy has been attracting overseas attention, and with good reason. Led by Crown Prince Muhammad bin Salman (MbS), Riyadh has begun to display unprecedented ambition, notably in leading the intervention in Yemen, blockading Qatar, assassinating and coercing dissidents abroad, and imposing sanctions on Canada. The foreign policy of its smaller neighbour, the United Arab Emirates (UAE), has also displayed a steadily growing assertiveness, with important consequences, notably in Egypt, the Horn of Africa, Libya, Qatar and Yemen. The UAE, however, has attracted less attention.

Three main variables have driven the evolution of Emirati foreign policy in recent years: growing economic and military power, an increasingly acute threat perception and changes in leadership. Taken together, ambition, necessity and vision explain why the UAE has responded to changes in its regional environment by shifting towards a more ambitious foreign policy.[1] In 2015, the UAE's foreign-policy goals prompted it to join a Saudi-led intervention in Yemen. Its participation in the conflict has been beneficial to the UAE in various ways, but in 2019 the country's leadership decided that these benefits were coming at too great a cost. It undertook to recalibrate the level and nature of the UAE's involvement in the Yemen conflict,

Thomas Juneau is associate professor at the University of Ottawa's Graduate School of Public and International Affairs, and a former analyst with Canada's Department of National Defence. He is also a non-resident fellow at the Sana'a Center for Strategic Studies. He tweets @thomasjuneau.

Survival | vol. 62 no. 4 | August–September 2020 | pp. 183–208   DOI 10.1080/00396338.2020.1792135

without ceasing its participation altogether. This article explores the causes and consequences of Emirati policy in Yemen, tracking its evolution and considering its future prospects.

Drivers of Emirati assertiveness

The UAE's power has steadily expanded as its growing economy has allowed it to make major investments in its military and other instruments of national power.[2] The Stockholm International Peace Research Institute (SIPRI) estimates that in 2014 (the most recent year for which data is available), the UAE's military spending was $22.8 billion, making it the second-largest military spender in the Middle East and 14th in the world. Strikingly, the country's defence budget increased by 136% from 2006 to 2014.[3] Changes in the regional distribution of power have also had a major impact on the UAE, as the collapse or weakening of traditional powers Egypt, Iraq and Syria has freed up space for ambitious mid-sized states such as the UAE. As Robert Gilpin has argued, an increase in a country's relative power can produce a growing desire to shape its environment.[4]

A more assertive Saudi Arabia has forced its smaller Emirati neighbour to make important reassessments, even as the UAE's threat perceptions have become more acute. The UAE has felt threatened by uprisings against authoritarian regimes in the Arab world since 2010 and the subsequent spread of instability in the region, and especially by the fall of president Hosni Mubarak in Egypt, a close partner. The UAE has watched with growing alarm as the Muslim Brotherhood – supported by the UAE's rival, Qatar – has taken advantage of instability in Egypt and elsewhere to expand its influence. These fears were compounded by a perception of American withdrawal and a feeling of neglect as the administration of Barack Obama sought to distance the United States from its traditional Persian Gulf partners, especially the UAE and Saudi Arabia. The UAE is also concerned with the threat posed by al-Qaeda and its regional franchises, and observed the emergence of the Islamic State (ISIS) with alarm. Finally, the UAE views Iran as a growing and aspiring regional hegemon whose influence can only come at the expense of the UAE's own, and that of its partners.

This growing alarm over regional insecurity is closely linked to domestic anxiety for regime stability. The ideology of the Muslim Brotherhood and the precedent-setting events of the uprisings, in particular, are worrying for the UAE because it fears they undermine monarchical structures and give legitimacy to representative politics, both of which pose an existential threat to the ruling families of the seven emirates that make up the UAE. Emirati leaders want to influence regional trends in part to make themselves safer at home.

The steady rise to power of Mohammed bin Zayed Al Nahyan (MbZ) has also profoundly shaped Emirati foreign policy. After the death of the original ruler of Abu Dhabi and president of the UAE Sheikh Zayed bin Sultan Al Nahyan in 2004, his eldest son Khalifa bin Zayed succeeded him. MbZ, Khalifa's younger half-brother, became Crown prince. Since then, MbZ has steadily accumulated power in Abu Dhabi and in federal decision-making structures, especially after Khalifa suffered a stroke in 2014. His hardline views on Iran and the Muslim Brotherhood, and his preference for close alignment with Saudi Arabia, have profoundly shaped Emirati foreign policy.[5]

Objectives of Emirati foreign policy

Managing the UAE's relationship with Saudi Arabia is a complex undertaking: relations have been tense in the past (the UAE had poor relations with the previous Crown prince and former interior minister Mohammed bin Nayef), and the prospect of a hostile or collapsed Saudi state is the most significant potential threat to Emirati security. MbZ has calculated that today, the UAE is better off bandwagoning with MbS-led Saudi Arabia. For MbZ, this best positions the UAE to understand Saudi thinking and nudge Saudi actions in a direction favourable to the UAE. In Yemen and elsewhere, the UAE has assessed that it is not powerful enough to take a leading role, but it can maximise its influence alongside Saudi Arabia.

This approach means that the UAE has closely tied its fortunes to MbS. MbZ genuinely supports MbS's reforms, especially the economic ones, understanding that their success is vital to the long-term viability of Saudi Arabia, and therefore to Emirati prosperity and security. In this sense, MbZ not only wants but *needs* MbS to succeed. At the same time, MbZ disagrees with many Saudi policies. There are disagreements about the conduct of the war in Yemen; furthermore, the UAE was severely unimpressed with the assassination of Jamal Khashoggi, a dissident Saudi journalist, both for the horrible judgement it demonstrated and for the amateur way in which it was carried out.[6] There has, however, been a decision by both countries to manage these differences. The result has been a close partnership with cooperation reaching unprecedented levels.

Managing relations with Washington is the UAE's other fundamental priority. The UAE believes that the era of American dominance in the Gulf is slowly coming to an end, and views the US as an increasingly erratic partner. The decline in Emirati trust in the US as the extra-regional guarantor of its security began in 2003 with what it viewed as the mistaken invasion and bungled occupation of Iraq. Under president Obama, Saudi Arabia and the UAE perceived the US as retrenching from the region and felt that their interests were being neglected. They were especially fearful that Washington would tilt towards Iran after the 2015 nuclear deal, and that the Obama administration's policy of rebalancing towards Asia would lead the US to further diminish its presence in the Middle East.[7]

The UAE views the US as increasingly erratic

There has been a greater alignment of views between the UAE and the administration of Donald Trump, notably in their shared hostility towards Iran. Nevertheless, after early enthusiasm, disillusion has appeared as Emirati leaders have come to view Trump as erratic and unreliable, and preoccupied with domestic issues. Still, MbZ views him as a pliant president who will not criticise the UAE's actions.[8]

Even though the UAE is concerned with the long-term trend of American retrenchment and unpredictability, the US remains an important partner and security guarantor. The UAE wants to hedge its bets, but remains committed to the partnership. It therefore expends significant resources to gain influence in Washington, notably through aggressive lobbying campaigns. It has largely succeeded in branding itself as the 'foremost US military partner in the Arab world', and has closely aligned its military doctrine and force posture with that of the US.[9]

Beyond these two bilateral relationships, Emirati foreign policy aims at managing threats, chief among them the Muslim Brotherhood, regional uprisings, Qatar, Iran, and groups such as al-Qaeda and ISIS.

Until the end of the first decade of this century, the UAE tolerated the Muslim Brotherhood. There were Brotherhood members and sympathisers among the faculty and students (both local and foreign) of the country's universities, and there were even government ministers affiliated with the movement. The Brotherhood was not a major domestic threat; its following was small and easily monitored. UAE authorities drastically changed their perception after 2010 in the wake of the regional uprisings and the prospect of the movement's growing power, fearing, in particular, its alternative blueprint for state power derived from political Islam and obtained through the ballot box in a non-hereditary system. Domestic repression in the UAE has since been brutal, while opposition to the Brotherhood has become an important driver of UAE foreign policy.

More broadly, countering the spread of revolutionary uprisings and demonstrating their failure have become central objectives of Emirati policy. This, combined with opposition to the Brotherhood, has led the UAE to support 'secular authoritarianism' throughout the region.[10] This helps explain its actions in Tunisia (where it has worked to undermine the country's democratic transition), Libya (where it supports Khalifa Haftar, who opposes a central government that includes elements linked to the Brotherhood) and Egypt (where President Abdel Fattah Al-Sisi overthrew an elected Brotherhood government in 2013, with Emirati support, and has since adopted a hardline stance against the movement).

Countering Qatari influence has become another major priority, especially since 2017. Qatar–UAE relations have ebbed and flowed since the countries' independence in 1971. Tension rose after 2010, with Qatar supporting groups aligned with the Brotherhood, notably in Egypt and Libya, and the UAE supporting groups opposed to organised Islamists (and, in some cases, hardline Salafis). More broadly, there is a competition between these two small but ambitious Gulf powers to position themselves relative to Saudi Arabia and the US. Accumulating tension finally exploded in 2017 when the UAE, along with Saudi Arabia, Bahrain and Egypt, imposed a blockade on Qatar.

Another objective for UAE foreign policy is to deter and roll back what it perceives as growing Iranian influence. There is a long-standing rivalry between the two countries, fuelled originally by Iran's occupation since 1971 of three islands in the Gulf claimed by the UAE. The UAE shares its wariness of Iran with Saudi Arabia, though it tends to be more pragmatic: there is less inflation in Abu Dhabi of the threat Iran poses than there is in Riyadh.[11] There are also internal divisions within the UAE, with Dubai and the other small emirates disagreeing with Abu Dhabi's harder stance and preferring a more pragmatic approach providing for trade with Iran.[12]

Additionally, Emirati foreign policy seeks to counter the threat posed by al-Qaeda, the Islamic State and their regional franchises. A series of failed plots between 2005 and 2007 made it clear for Abu Dhabi and Dubai that al-Qaeda poses a serious threat. The emergence of the Islamic State after 2014 only heightened Emirati fears, particularly because the group attracted recruits and financing from the UAE and some of its neighbours. A number of failed and successful plots in Saudi Arabia exacerbated these fears.

Finally, because the UAE's model of economic development is premised on its position as a logistics hub for regional trade,[13] maritime security is a vital interest, especially in the U-shaped area around the Arabian Peninsula encompassing the Persian Gulf, the Arabian and Oman seas, the Gulf of Aden and the Red Sea. It is through these waters that the UAE exports oil and imports 90% of its food. As the UAE's power has grown and its regional interests have expanded, it has pursued strategic depth in these waters, their ports and the inland areas around them.[14] The country understands that it can best achieve its goals through partnerships: it has increased cooperation with other actors sharing similar interests, notably India in the Arabian Sea and the European Union in the Red Sea on counter-piracy operations.

The UAE has pursued its maritime goals through various means: investments in ports; friendly relations with local actors (states and some substate and non-state actors); and the use of, and in some cases the establishment of, military facilities. Since 2015, for example, Eritrea has hosted a joint

Saudi–UAE military facility in its Red Sea port of Assab, from which the UAE established supply lines to Yemen. The UAE also established bases in two breakaway regions of Somalia (a naval base in Puntland and a military base in Somaliland) and invested in modernising their ports.[15]

Explaining UAE policy in Yemen, 2015–19

The wave of uprisings that spread through the Arab world in early 2011 rapidly reached Yemen, eventually causing its president, Ali Abdullah Saleh, to resign. He was replaced in 2012 by his deputy, Abd Rabbo Mansour Hadi, under a pact brokered by the United Nations. The deal resulted in the establishment of a National Dialogue Conference intended to lead to a new constitution. The process collapsed in 2014, however, and the country tipped into civil war when the Houthis, a rebel group from the country's northwest long dissatisfied with its own economic, political and cultural marginalisation, seized the capital, Sana'a, and rapidly expanded south-wards. Increasingly concerned about the Houthis' incursions across the Saudi border and their ties to Iran, Riyadh agreed in March 2015 to launch an intervention, at President Hadi's request, officially to restore his interna-tionally recognised government and roll back the Houthis. The UAE initially played a lesser role in the coalition, but by summer had become, after Saudi Arabia, its most important member, planning and conducting its operations in a manner largely independent from Saudi Arabia.[16]

The decision to join the war

The UAE's primary objective in Yemen in this first phase was to support Saudi Arabia. A Saudi failure would be a disaster for the UAE as it would weaken Saudi Arabia regionally and damage MbS domestically. For this reason, all UAE decisions in Yemen flow from the broader objective of managing relations with Saudi Arabia.[17] Its support of Saudi Arabia has brought the UAE benefits, such as a foothold in southern Yemen and the ability to shape Saudi decisions. For example, the UAE pressed Saudi Arabia to commit to the Stockholm process, which led to a UN-brokered agreement in 2018 calling for a ceasefire and the withdrawal of forces from the port of Hudaydah.

The main threats to Emirati security converge in Yemen. The local branch of the Muslim Brotherhood, known as Islah, is one of the main actors in the country,[18] and the UAE has sought to weaken it and block its path to an important role in post-war Yemen. This has led to friction with Saudi Arabia, which has had close (though often difficult) relations with Islah and therefore continues to deal with it and see a role for it in post-war Yemen.

More broadly, Emirati policies in Yemen aim to send the forceful message that the revolution which toppled Saleh in 2011 failed. This translates into continued support for the Saleh family and active steps to prevent democratisation.

Qatar played a role in Yemen prior to 2011, notably through its attempts to position itself as a mediator between the central government and the Houthis. Qatar was also originally a member of the Saudi-led coalition in 2015, but left because of its dispute with Saudi Arabia and the UAE. The UAE's main concern is Qatar's long-standing ties to Islah, which is consistent with Doha's support, region-wide, for Brotherhood-aligned groups.[19] The extent of Doha's support is unclear;[20] nevertheless, the UAE wants to ensure that no space opens up for Qatar in Yemen.

Countering Iran's influence in Yemen also forms part of the Emirati calculus. Both the UAE and Saudi Arabia were alarmed by the expansion of Houthi power in 2014–15. Like Saudi Arabia, the UAE views the Houthis as close partners of Iran, but whereas Saudi Arabia inflates Iranian influence over the Houthis, the UAE has a more realistic view that the Houthis are not Iranian puppets, and that ultimately Iran has invested only modest resources in the country.[21] Though the UAE intends its intervention to send a message to Iran – that it opposes the spread of its influence in Arab affairs – it has not intervened in Yemen primarily to counter Iran. The Iranian presence is a concern, but far from the dominant one.[22]

The UAE also has an interest in opposing al-Qaeda in the Arabian Peninsula (AQAP) and, to a lesser extent, the Islamic State in Yemen (ISY).[23] This is not its primary objective, but was still a consideration early on, when AQAP occupied swaths of land in southeast Yemen, and since 2016, as the fighting against the Houthis has stabilised.[24] For the UAE, countering AQAP is an end in itself, but also a means of projecting its influence in southern

Yemen through the local militias it has mobilised to fight AQAP. Moreover, the UAE has successfully positioned itself as the United States' indispensable local partner in counter-terrorism operations. In Yemen, America's own counter-terrorism efforts rely heavily on Emirati forces, who have a presence on the ground and growing intelligence networks. According to media reports, the two countries work closely together with, for example, American forces training Emirati pilots for combat operations in Yemen.[25]

Finally, Houthi expansion in 2014 and 2015 – when the movement took control of a large section of Yemen's western half stretching all the way to Aden and the southern coast – threatened maritime security around the Arabian Peninsula. As a result, a key UAE priority has been to gain influence over ports on the southern and western coasts. UAE interest in developing and consolidating its access to ports elsewhere in the southern Red Sea–Gulf of Aden corridor has also intensified due to a need to support operations in Yemen. The UAE has established bases or facilities on islands in these waters (Soqotra in the Gulf of Aden and Perim near the Bab al-Mandeb Strait) and in Assab in Eritrea.

UAE strategy in Yemen, 2015–19

At the centre of Emirati policy in Yemen has been, from the outset, the poor state of its relationship with President Hadi.[26] Personal relations between MbZ and Hadi are especially abysmal, with MbZ viewing him as incompetent and weak.[27] The UAE particularly opposes Hadi's heavy reliance on Islah. UAE–Hadi relations marginally improved in 2018, partly because of reconciliation efforts by Saudi Arabia, which also tried but failed later that year to broker better ties between the UAE and Islah. The UAE systematically opposes Hadi, as well as security and intelligence organisations within the internationally recognised Yemeni government that support him, such as the National Security Bureau and the Political Security Organization. Meanwhile, the UAE has worked to prop up rivals within the loose coalition around the president.[28]

The UAE's strategy since 2015 has largely been premised on its ties to southern actors, many of which seek independence. This is not out of sympathy for their aspirations, but the product of necessity: southern groups are opposed to Islah for historical reasons, making them natural partners.[29] (Geography also brings them together, since the UAE seeks a presence in the ports on the southern coast.) Following a difficult unification between the People's Democratic Republic of Yemen (commonly known as South Yemen) and the Yemen Arab Republic (North Yemen) in 1990, tensions boiled over in 1994 when a failed uprising in the south was brutally suppressed by the northern-dominated government (notably with help from Islah-affiliated militias, partly explaining ongoing animosity between the group and southern separatists). From 1994 until 2011, southern discontent simmered, but internal bickering prevented the separatist movement from succeeding.[30] During the National Dialogue (2012–14), some southern groups were open to dealing with the Houthis, since both sought autonomy from the centre. With time, however, especially after the Houthis' brutal takeover of Aden in early 2015, most southern groups joined the anti-Houthi camp.

Saudi Arabia initially sought to avoid involvement in southern politics, delegating management of most of the area to the UAE.[31] Long-standing ties between the UAE and southern Yemen – the ruling family of Abu Dhabi, the Al Nahyan, trace their lineage to Ma'rib in central Yemen, for example – have facilitated these links. Some southern leaders also fled to what were then the Trucial States (now the UAE) when Marxists took over what became South Yemen in the 1960s, just as southern leaders fleeing the Houthis since 2014 have sought refuge in the UAE.

The UAE opposes southern independence, at least officially. It could, however, eventually agree to it.[32] In doing so it would become the most influential power in what would be a weak state dependent on external support, giving it a foothold overlooking strategic maritime routes. The UAE also understands that separation would be a complex and violent process, but that it may be the best outcome in comparison to the seemingly impossible task of bringing Yemen together again. In the meantime, the UAE's ambivalence – officially supporting unity but backing separatists – has frustrated local partners.[33]

At the centre of the UAE's strategy is its support for the Southern Transitional Council (STC), an umbrella coalition of southern separatists. In 2017, Hadi fired Aydarus al-Zubaydi, the governor of Aden, and other prominent southern leaders because he viewed them as too close to the UAE. In response, they formed the STC, with UAE support. Headquartered in Aden, the STC brings together southern actors who agree on little besides their desire for autonomy or independence, and their opposition to Hadi and Islah. The UAE initially provided the STC – as a group, and individually to its leaders – with financial and material support. It still hosts many of its leaders, including Zubaydi, in Abu Dhabi and arranges travel on a regular basis to south Yemen. This allows the UAE to control their movements, contributing to the fear among many STC leaders that they are being used by the UAE.[34]

The UAE has also mobilised, trained and equipped southern militias, comprising about 90,000 troops. It had fairly strong command and control over them, with some variation. It largely followed the American model of embedding special forces to advise local militias, supervising the delivery of support (weapons, cash, intelligence) and helping to lead local fighters. The UAE also paid militia members on time, which led to higher morale than among government units.[35]

> *The UAE has mobilised and equipped southern militias*

The most important militia group is the Security Belt in Aden. It was formed in 2016 and consists of about 15,000 fighters, and has emerged as the main provider of security in and around the city.[36] It is commanded by Hani Bin Breik, a Salafist who is also the deputy secretary of the STC. The Security Belt helped expel the Houthis from Aden in 2015 and has since partnered with Emirati and American forces to fight AQAP. It also actively opposes Islah.[37] Its members are technically under the command of the Interior Ministry, but received training and salaries from the UAE and, in practice, were at least partly controlled by Emirati commanders.[38] Its troops are dominated by Salafists, but also include many with tribal and non-ideological backgrounds.

The UAE replicated what it viewed as its successful Security Belt model by building up the Hadrami Elite Forces (HEF) and Shabwa Elite Forces (SEF) in two other southern provinces.[39] Each includes about 3,000–4,000 local troops who were mobilised, trained and equipped by the UAE. They initially helped expel AQAP from Mukalla in 2016, the main port in south-central Yemen. The HEF holds sway in southern Hadhramaut, especially in Mukalla and the interior area, while Islah is influential in the north.[40]

The UAE began developing its presence in Mahra, Yemen's easternmost province, in 2015. This rapidly became a source of friction with Oman, Mahra's eastern neighbour. This tension, grounded in historical border disputes, has been compounded by Oman's reservations about the Saudi–UAE intervention in Yemen. Saudi Arabia and the UAE, for their part, accuse Oman of turning a blind eye to Iranian smuggling of weapons to the Houthis through Mahra, and have generally been irritated by Oman's policy of maintaining cordial ties with Iran and the Houthis.[41] The UAE initially sought to promote STC influence in Mahra, but faced local resistance as fewer Mahris embrace a separatist agenda compared to the rest of the south. The UAE also tried to replicate its Security Belt model, but with limited success, again because of local resistance.[42] Eventually, the UAE agreed to let Saudi Arabia take the leading role in the province, especially since 2017, when Saudi forces entered Mahra and established positions in key locations, such as the Al Ghaydah Airport, along the Omani border and at small ports along the coast. This has led to growing local resentment against the Saudi presence and clashes between locals and Saudi forces.[43]

The island of Soqotra holds a central position in the UAE's strategy of securing maritime channels around the Arabian Peninsula because of its strategic location where the Gulf of Aden meets the Indian Ocean. Since 2015, the UAE has invested in infrastructure on the island and provided humanitarian and development assistance.[44] It also announced in 2017 that it had completed the construction of a military facility, including an airstrip. In early 2018, the Yemeni government and many locals accused the UAE of occupying the island. Saudi mediation led to the withdrawal of some UAE troops and their replacement by Saudi ones. But the UAE maintains a military presence consisting of its own troops and southern separatist troops it backs, who control the airport and main port, as well as ongoing development projects.

On the west coast, UAE interests include the Bab al-Mandeb Strait on the southwestern corner of Yemen and Hudaydah, Yemen's second port after Aden, through which much of the country's humanitarian assistance arrives and which has been under Houthi control since 2015. Emirati strategy in the west has focused on supporting Tareq Saleh and the Amaliqah (Giants) Brigade, over which UAE command and control is not as strong as over southern militias.[45]

The UAE provides support to Tareq Saleh, a nephew of the former president who still leads well-equipped and competent military units previously loyal to his uncle, especially the Republican Guard. Tareq and other members of the Saleh clan, especially Ahmed Ali, the former president's son and heir apparent, also have a poor relationship with Hadi and Islah; the UAE thus views the clan's support as another tool to undermine Islah. The UAE's support of Ahmed Ali and Tareq is probably also predicated on the expectation that they could be national leaders in post-war Yemen – leaders who would be dependent on Emirati support and would symbolise, as relatives of a dictator who ruled for 33 years, the failure of the revolution.

The Giants Brigade, led by southern Salafi commanders and numbering about 15,000, has played a major role in the battle for Hudaydah. Many southern leaders are concerned about what the brigade will do if or when the Houthis are defeated on the west coast; they fear that its return to the south would lead to conflict. There is also much mistrust between Tareq Saleh and the Giants Brigade. The UAE has so far been mostly successful in keeping a lid on these tensions. There is, however, significant potential for long-term problems.

Explaining the shift in UAE policy in 2019

The UAE began a partial withdrawal and redeployment of its forces in Yemen in June 2019. Emirati officials said they would henceforth focus more on counter-terrorism and less on fighting the Houthis. They announced the withdrawal of troops from Hudaydah, effectively abandoning hopes of taking the city from the Houthis.[46] The UAE did not announce the precise number of troops to be withdrawn (or, for that matter, the number of troops that were present as of June 2019), nor the timetable for their withdrawal. The UAE also withdrew most or all of its troops from central areas, such as Ma'rib, and peripheral ones, such as Shabwa, where Saudi Arabia took over some of its patronage networks. The UAE did not, however, abandon its support for most of the southern militias it helped establish, and chose to maintain a presence in several sites in the south that it deems crucial.[47] Indeed, it has continued to institutionalise its influence in the south, which remains central to its regional ambitions. The UAE has also maintained its support for members of the Saleh family, notably Tareq in the west. As of early 2020, the remaining number of Emirati troops in Yemen likely numbered in the low hundreds.

The UAE's ability to revise its assessment of the situation in Yemen and of its role in the war, and then to implement significant policy changes, testifies to the nimbleness of its foreign policy, at least as compared to Saudi Arabia's. Even before its decision in 2019 to recalibrate its mission, the UAE was already more clear-eyed than Saudi Arabia about the mounting criticism in the US Congress and the American media about the Yemen campaign, despite steadfast support from the Trump White House. And while it has been adroit in containing the damage and deflecting negative press coverage towards Saudi Arabia, the UAE has been keenly aware that this public-relations challenge could easily intensify. It eventually decided that the costs of its involvement in Yemen were exceeding the benefits. This is not to say that there were no benefits, but the Emirati leadership increasingly came to believe that this negative cost–benefit ratio was likely to worsen in the future. In response, it shifted resources to ensure that gains could be maximised, while losses were minimised and contained. Abu Dhabi has accepted that there is no prospect for stability in Yemen for the foreseeable future. Instead of prioritising stabilisation through the strengthening of the central government, the UAE has adopted a more pragmatic course. It assesses that peace is unlikely in the short to medium term (and possibly in the long term), and has decided to accept this and position itself to benefit from it.

> *The UAE was more clear-eyed than Saudi Arabia*

This strategy can be compared to Iran's approach in fragile states. Much like Iran does in Iraq, Lebanon, Syria and Yemen, the UAE supports non-state actors in Yemen militarily and politically. In some cases, these actors work at cross purposes with the recognised government, and in other cases in parallel to it. This allows the UAE to pursue its interests (managing ties to Saudi Arabia; countering AQAP, Iran and Islah; securing its presence in ports) while building long-term influence. It does this by keeping its presence relatively modest in size, using special forces to support local partners and subcontracting some of the work to mercenaries. The UAE has thus succeeded in positioning itself, in a short period, as the indispensable power in the south.

Another positive element for Emirati policy in Yemen has been the management of its most important foreign-policy priority, relations with Saudi Arabia. It has managed to avoid serious tension in its relations with its most important neighbour, despite the unpredictability of MbS-led Saudi policy and the existence of real disagreements. That said, Abu Dhabi saw that this delicate balancing act was likely to become increasingly difficult in the future.

Thirdly, the UAE has gained significant experience in Yemen, learning lessons that will benefit its power projection for years to come. The UAE's forces were on the front lines, improving their skills in mounting multiple complex operations, including urban warfare, amphibious landings, reconstruction and precision airstrikes. The country has become increasingly skilled at mobilising, training, equipping and leading non-state militias and exploiting them in the pursuit of its interests, a valuable skill which Iran largely monopolised in the Gulf until recently. The UAE has also learned a great deal by working closely with the US in mounting counter-terrorism operations in Yemen, and has developed a network of bases and facilities in Yemen and around the Arabian Peninsula which it will be able to exploit for the foreseeable future. Many believe that Emirati forces have been learning much more than the Saudi military at the tactical, operational and strategic levels.[48]

Despite these real successes, the UAE's leadership determined that the war was a quagmire with no prospect for a military victory. Not only was it costly financially and diplomatically,[49] but it was also raising internal risks for the UAE, a federation where the balance among the seven emirates is fragile. Hundreds of Emiratis have died in Yemen, with a large proportion of casualties hailing from poorer northern emirates, exposing fragile internal dynamics. Knowing this, MbZ started looking for an off-ramp. Still, he did not want to fully abandon Saudi Arabia by suddenly and completely withdrawing, which is why, for example, he supports the Stockholm process and other efforts to find a political solution, and has been pushing Saudi Arabia in this direction.[50]

Heavy UAE involvement in Yemen, moreover, was creating increasing uncertainty in Emirati–Saudi relations. Despite successful efforts to manage these differences at the political level, in Yemen itself Saudi Arabia and the UAE had often been working at cross purposes. Most obviously, the UAE supports southern groups, many of which are separatist, while Riyadh supports Yemeni unity and has tied its fortunes to the Hadi government. Diverging interests have led to clashes between Saudi- and Emirati-backed groups on multiple occasions.

By 2019, it was clear that the UAE had entangled itself in a situation in which its two most important foreign-policy priorities – maintaining good relations with the US and with Saudi Arabia – were being damaged. Saudi Arabia and the UAE had mostly been able to manage these tensions because MbS and MbZ agree on a broad vision for the region (one that involves opposing Iran, boxing in Qatar, relying less on the US, opposing democratic uprisings and behaving more assertively in general) and did not wish to allow lower priorities to interfere with these larger objectives. Yet it was clear that, in the absence of some form of change, disagreements would continue and very likely intensify.

In the US, the UAE saw, with growing anxiety, mounting opposition to the war outside the White House and increasingly loud calls not just for an end to American support for the Saudi-led coalition but, more broadly, for a re-evaluation of the United States' long-standing partnership with Saudi Arabia and the UAE. The UAE viewed its standing among the American political establishment, which it had so carefully cultivated at great expense, as suffering because of its association with Saudi Arabia – especially in the wake of the Khashoggi assassination in October 2018 – and its highly visible involvement in Yemen. The March 2019 vote in the US Senate to end US support for the war in Yemen was symbolic, but it confirmed to the UAE that its anxiety was justified. The prospect of a Democrat winning the White House in 2020, after a campaign in which most candidates, to various degrees, have criticised Saudi Arabia and the war in Yemen, only compounded these fears.

The UAE's active involvement in Yemen had also jeopardised its policy towards Iran. The UAE opposes the Islamic Republic and wants to keep it isolated and weak, but does not want tensions to escalate into a direct military confrontation. It judges, correctly, that because it is on the front line and its economy is dependent on stable maritime trade, war would be highly damaging. It therefore grew increasingly anxious between 2018 and 2019 as tensions between the US and Iran deepened. It also became concerned that the Houthis, who had been launching more and more missile and drone attacks against Saudi Arabia, would eventually also target the Emirates, which they could now do, in large part thanks to Iranian assistance. Diminishing UAE confidence in the reliability of the US as the extra-regional guarantor of its security further contributed to its changing approach towards Iran.

The UAE became more conciliatory towards Iran

The UAE thus became more conciliatory towards Iran throughout the first half of 2019. Abu Dhabi, in particular, did not specifically accuse Iran of being responsible for the attack on four tankers off its coast in May, unlike Saudi Arabia and the US. Emirati and Iranian officials also held rare high-level talks on maritime security, another signal from Abu Dhabi that it seeks to avoid military confrontation and to manage tensions through diplomatic means. This is not a rapprochement, but an effort by Abu Dhabi to reduce and better manage tension with Iran, and to protect its image as a safe and stable destination for investment.

The growing assertiveness of Emirati foreign policy was also raising the risk of overstretch.[51] Notwithstanding its ambitious goals of projecting power in Yemen (and in East and North Africa), the UAE remains a wealthy but mid-sized regional power with a small population. It maintains a deployable ground force of fewer than 20,000 troops.[52] Its deployment of about 3,500 troops in Yemen, alongside its other deployments, exposed it to the risks of biting off more than it could chew.

These risks are best illustrated in south Yemen. UAE actions in the first four years of the war allowed it to position itself as an indispensable power broker, as explained above. These actions were not cost-free, however. Firstly, in part thanks to Emirati assistance, southern separatist forces are now stronger militarily and better organised politically than they have been since unification in 1990. Aspirations for self-rule and independence have grown.[53] The UAE, in other words, has helped unleash forces that will be difficult to contain in the future. This has led to some disagreement with Saudi Arabia, which can probably be managed as long as attention is focused on the Houthis, but will be a major problem in the future. Even though it has steadily developed closer and more or less cordial relations with the STC, Riyadh is still unlikely to accede to southern demands for independence, if only because the north would be dominated by the Houthis.

In some cases, UAE forces and their partners paid AQAP to withdraw from cities and villages and allowed them to keep their weapons and cash.[54] This is reportedly what happened, for example, when the UAE and local partners seized Mukalla from AQAP, with little fighting, in 2016.[55] UAE-backed forces also reportedly agreed to absorb defecting AQAP fighters.[56] Moreover, some local partners who received weapons from the UAE and Saudi Arabia resold them to AQAP and other extremists. In many cases, these weapons had initially been sold to the UAE and Saudi Arabia by the US.[57] Thus, the UAE's approach, instead of decisively damaging AQAP, actually boosted the group by allowing it to keep resources, pay its members, gain experience and receive training as part of pro-UAE militias. It also raises the risk that UAE-backed militias could include sleeper cells, and makes it more difficult to clearly identify who belongs to AQAP. STC officials have complained to the UAE about these dangers.[58]

Some UAE-backed militias are also highly sectarian. In particular, the UAE supports a Salafi militia led by Abu al-Abbas, largely because he vehemently opposes Islah and leads a group of capable fighters. In 2017, the US imposed sanctions on him for being an instructor and fundraiser for AQAP. The coalition nevertheless merged his militia into the national army's 35th Brigade, responsible for the Ta'izz governorate and itself supported by the UAE. In practice, however, the militia still follows Abbas's orders. He subsequently admitted that he continued to receive financial assistance and weapons from the UAE.[59] As with other UAE policies, this support could become costly. Backing militias that reject government authority positions them to play a prominent long-term role. There is also a strong likelihood that, as elsewhere in the country, groups supported by the UAE will continue fighting against Islah.

Many of the militias the UAE supports or supported have been credibly associated with human-rights abuses. Amnesty International has reported that UAE-backed armed groups operate 'a shadowy network of secret prisons' in which Amnesty has documented 'torture with electric shocks, waterboarding, hanging from the ceiling, sexual humiliation, prolonged solitary confinement, squalid conditions and inadequate food and water'.[60]

The Emirati, and Saudi, presence in Yemen is also generating a growing backlash, with many locals resentful at what they perceive as foreign occupation. In the north, many perceive the Emirati presence with mistrust because of its ties to southern groups. Throughout the south, in addition to growing frustration with continued poverty and insecurity, there is mounting resentment at the UAE's heavy-handed tactics. As a result, from Soqotra to Shabwa and Aden, there have been increasingly frequent popular protests against the UAE's presence.[61]

The risk of conflict between UAE-backed groups and other members of the anti-Houthi coalition, and among groups the UAE supports, will remain high. For now, the war between the Hadi government and the Houthis is serving to keep a very fragile lid on the country's multiple fault lines, but there is every reason to expect that other simmering disputes will re-emerge. The situation in Ta'izz, the country's third-largest city and historically an important cultural and political hub, may be seen as a warning of what is to come. By late 2016, the Houthis had been pushed out of parts of Ta'izz, with the front lines not moving much since. But anti-Houthi groups include the pro-UAE Abbas Salafi militia, units loyal to Islah, local militias and others; little unites them beyond their opposition to the Houthis.[62] Tension has steadily grown, with violence flaring occasionally, notably between UAE-backed groups and Islah-affiliated ones.[63] Similar dynamics are likely to replicate themselves elsewhere (notably between the Giants Brigade and southern militias, between southern groups and Islah, and between Tareq and Ahmed Ali Saleh and the many who would resist their return). UAE policies have not sowed the seeds for these future conflicts, but they have helped to nurture them.

Looking ahead

The UAE was making important gains in the south, especially by building major influence in a strategic region and by significantly developing its ability to project power. But despite these gains, losses were mounting, and it did not see the cost–benefit ratio improving in the future. It thus recognised that it was overreaching, and chose to recalibrate instead of doubling down.

Despite the UAE's partial drawdown from Yemen, it retains a strong ability to increase its presence there should it deem this necessary. It maintains a network of bases and facilities, albeit staffed by fewer troops, and has strong ties to armed groups throughout the south and west. It has also learned much about the logistics of deploying troops abroad.

Although the UAE has made efforts to minimise and contain its losses in Yemen, the UAE's ongoing commitment to that country remains risky. The situation in the south in particular is highly volatile, with tensions between the STC and other members of the anti-Houthi coalition very high. Illustrating this, STC-backed units attacked pro-government forces in August 2019 and seized territory and bases in Aden and neighbouring governorates. Saudi Arabia then responded with airstrikes against secessionist positions in Aden.

Under Saudi pressure and mediation, the Hadi government and the STC reached the Riyadh Agreement in autumn 2019, which calls for the formation of an Aden-based unity government bringing together equal numbers of southern and northern ministers, and integrating STC-affiliated forces into national structures. The UAE announced that it would withdraw its forces from Aden and allow Yemeni and Saudi forces to fill the void, in support of the implementation of the agreement.[64] The implementation of the loosely worded Riyadh Agreement has since stalled, with tension and violence ebbing and flowing. This means the UAE is highly likely to remain mired in contentious southern politics.

Indeed, even after its recalibration, the UAE continued to support secessionist groups, and shows no sign of planning to stop doing so. STC-backed forces remain in a tense stand-off with pro-government and Saudi-backed units. The partial withdrawal of UAE forces may end up exacerbating instability in the south: UAE troops acted as a lid on fighting between rival groups in the anti-Houthi coalition. A reduction in this constraining factor could thus lead to greater intra-coalition infighting, potentially to the benefit of the Houthis or AQAP.

Any eventual political process in Yemen will see the contradictions between the differing priorities of the UAE and Saudi Arabia play out. In a best-case scenario, the two could find common ground in supporting a federal solution. For the UAE, this would be positive, as it would institutionalise its influence in an autonomous south. The problem for Saudi Arabia, however, is that Iran would also institutionalise its influence in a Houthi-dominated northwest. The death of President Hadi, who is 74 and in poor health, could also bring many of these tensions to a boiling point, as he would possibly be replaced by his vice-president, Ali Mohsen al-Ahmar, who is close to Islah and widely reviled in the south.

In sum, the UAE can plausibly claim to have reaped significant benefits from its intervention in Yemen. It rapidly established an important foothold in the south, where it has positioned itself as the area's key power broker, an unimaginable prospect only a few years ago. It has learned how to project power in a war-torn country with which it shares no land border; and it has, so far, successfully managed its most important bilateral relationships, with Saudi Arabia and the US. At the same time, the Emirati investment in the war in Yemen, even after the mid-2019 recalibration, entails ongoing risks. The UAE has tied its fortunes to southern groups that include Salafis, separatists and human-rights violators, groups that contribute to the destabilisation of Yemen. The UAE's involvement in that country faces a rocky road ahead, as does its most important success: its partnership with Saudi Arabia.

Acknowledgements

I thank Tahleel Al-Dhabbi for her invaluable research assistance, and two former colleagues for their extremely helpful comments on a draft of this article.

Notes

1   For background, see Kristian Ulrichsen, *The United Arab Emirates: Power, Politics, and Policymaking* (London: Routledge, 2017), pp. 137–226; and Khalid Almezaini, *The UAE and Foreign Policy: Foreign Aid, Identities and Interests* (London: Routledge, 2012).

2   See Karen Young, 'The Emerging Interventionists of the GCC', LSE Middle East Centre Paper Series, 2013. More than a decade of high oil prices, ending in 2014, contributed to this growth.

3   'Military Spending and Arms Imports by Iran, Saudi Arabia, Qatar, and the UAE', SIPRI Fact Sheet, May 2019, p. 6, https://www.sipri.org/sites/default/files/2019-05/fs_1905_gulf_milex_and_arms_transfers.pdf.

4   Robert Gilpin, *War and Change in World Politics* (Cambridge: Cambridge University Press, 1981), pp. 94–5.

5   For a detailed profile of MbZ, see David Kirkpatrick, 'The Most Powerful Arab Ruler Isn't M.B.S. It's M.B.Z.', *New York Times*, 2 June 2019, https://www.nytimes.com/2019/06/02/world/middleeast/crown-prince-mohammed-bin-zayed.html.

6   Confirmed by interviews with diplomats in Abu Dhabi in 2019.

7   See Jean-Marc Rickli, 'The Political Rationale and Implications of the United Arab Emirates' Military Involvement in Libya', in Dag Henriksen and Ann Karin Larsen (eds), *Political Rationale and International Consequences of the War in Libya* (Oxford: Oxford University Press, 2016).

8   Interviews with analysts and diplomats in Abu Dhabi, 2019.

9   Ulrichsen, *The United Arab Emirates*, p. 146. The UAE, as Ulrichsen points out, has participated in every American-led intervention in the broader region since the 1991 Gulf War (Somalia, Kosovo, Afghanistan, Libya, Syria) with the exception of the 2003 invasion of Iraq. About 4,000 American troops are permanently stationed in Al-Dhafra Air Base in Abu Dhabi.

10   See Giorgio Cafiero and Kristian Ulrichsen, 'Abu Dhabi's Influential Hand in Libya and Sudan', *Inside Arabia*, 2 May 2019, https://insidearabia.com/abu-dhabis-influential-hand-libya-sudan/.

11   Confirmed by multiple interviews in Riyadh and Abu Dhabi in 2018 and 2019.

12   See Karen Young, *The Political Economy of Energy, Finance and Security in the United Arab Emirates: Between the Majlis and the Market* (New York: Palgrave Macmillan, 2014), p. 107.

13   See Christian Henderson, 'The UAE as a Nexus State', *Journal of Arabian Studies*, vol. 7, no. 1, 2017, pp. 83–93.

14   See Elizabeth Dickinson, 'The United Arab Emirates in the Horn of Africa', International Crisis Group, Middle East & North Africa Briefing no. 65, 6 November 2018.

15   See Ismail Numan Telci and Tuba Öztürk Horoz, 'Military Bases in the Foreign Policy of the United Arab Emirates', *Insight Turkey*, vol. 20, no. 2, 2018, pp. 143–66.

16   Confirmed by multiple interviews with Saudi, Emirati and foreign

analysts and diplomats in Abu Dhabi and Riyadh in 2018 and 2019.

17 This is strongly supported by multiple interviews conducted in 2019 in Abu Dhabi with Emirati and foreign diplomats and analysts.

18 To label Islah as the Yemeni branch of the Brotherhood is an oversimplification – it is, rather, a loose coalition of moderate Islamist, tribal and business elements.

19 See Adam Baron, 'Qatar's Dispute with Neighbors Reverberates in Yemen', Arab Gulf States Institute in Washington, 19 July 2017, https://agsiw.org/qatars-dispute-with-neighbors-reverberates-in-yemen/.

20 See UN Panel of Experts on Yemen, '2019 Report', 25 January 2019, p. 16, https://reliefweb.int/sites/reliefweb.int/files/resources/S_2019_83_E.pdf.

21 Thomas Juneau, 'Iran's Policy Towards the Houthis in Yemen: A Limited Return on a Modest Investment', International Affairs, vol. 92, no. 3, 2016, pp. 647–63.

22 This was clearly demonstrated by multiple interviews in Riyadh and Abu Dhabi in 2018 and 2019. In the words of one interviewee with direct access to the most senior levels of the Emirati government, 'the UAE is in Yemen because of Saudi Arabia, not Iran'.

23 The ISY is relatively weak, especially compared to AQAP, and poses a marginal threat to the UAE. See Elisabeth Kendall, 'The Failing Islamic State Within the Failed State of Yemen', Perspectives on Terrorism, vol. 13, no. 1, 2019, pp. 78–87.

24 See Michael Knights, 'The UAE Approach to Counterinsurgency in Yemen', War on the Rocks, 23 May 2016, https://warontherocks.com/2016/05/the-u-a-e-approach-to-counterinsurgency-in-yemen/.

25 See Nick Turse, 'Despite Denials, Documents Reveal U.S. Training UAE Forces for Combat in Yemen', Yahoo News, 16 January 2019, https://news.yahoo.com/despite-denials-documents-reveal-u-s-training-uae-forces-combat-yemen-171513437.html?soc_src=hl-viewer&soc_trk=tw.

26 For one of many examples of criticism of Hadi in Emirati or Emirati-friendly Yemeni media, see 'Mas'uul Imaaraaty: Al-Ra'ys Hady Sayughaadir Sadat Al-Hakm Al-'aam Al-Muqbil' [Emirati Official: President Hadi Will Leave Office Next Year], Aden Al-Ghad, 22 December 2018, https://adenalgd.net/news/356157/.

27 Interviews in Riyadh and Abu Dhabi in 2018 and 2019.

28 See UN Panel of Experts on Yemen, '2019 Report', p. 17.

29 In the words of one senior southern leader, 'Islah is our real enemy' (interview in Abu Dhabi, 2019). Islah vigorously opposes southern independence and has a history of hostility towards southern groups.

30 See Noel Brehony, Yemen Divided: The Story of a Failed State in South Arabia (London: I.B. Tauris, 2011).

31 Interviews with southern leaders in 2019.

32 Interviews with southern leaders and UAE-based diplomats and analysts in 2019.

33 For one example of how southern Yemeni media perceive Emirati actions in the south, see Muhammad Fahd Al-Junaydi, 'Al-Khaleej ua

Al-Januub: Rihlat Al-Bahth 'an Al-Mafquud' [The Gulf and the South: The Quest for the Lost], *Aden Al-Ghad*, 9 January 2019, http://adenalgd.net/news/359463/.

34 Interviews with southern leaders in 2019.

35 Interviews with analysts and southern leaders in Abu Dhabi in 2019.

36 See 'Al-Hazm Al-Amny Yulqy Al-Qabd 'ala 'asabat Tamtahin Sarqat Al-Daraajaat Al-Naariyyat Bi-'aden' [The Security Belt Arrests a Gang that Has Been Stealing Motor Bikes in Aden], *Aden Al-Ghad*, 20 September 2018, https://adengad.net/news/338032/.

37 See 'Al-Hizb Al-Amny: Lihadithi Al-Asbab I'taqalnaa Qiyaadaat Hizb Al-Islah' [The Security Belt: For These Reasons, We Arrested the Leaders of the Islah Party], *Aden Al-Ghad*, 20 September 2018, https://adengad.net/news/338014/.

38 See 2019 UN Panel of Experts on Yemen, '2019 Report', p. 20.

39 For more detail on this support, including information on the training, infrastructure and vehicles provided, see Yasir Al-Yafa'i, 'Al-Imaaraat Tuass' Da'm Al-Ajhiza Al-Aminiyya Fy Hadramawt' [The Emirates Expand Their Support of Security Devices in Hadhramaut], *Al-Bayan*, 19 January 2019, https://www.albayan.ae/one-world/arabs/2019-01-19-1.3464067.

40 See Eleonora Ardemagni, 'Two Hadramawts Emerge in a Fractured Yemen', Middle East Institute, 22 April 2019, https://www.mei.edu/publications/two-hadramawts-emerge-fractured-yemen.

41 See Yara Bayoumy and Phil Stewart, 'Iran Steps Up Weapons Supply to Yemen's Houthis via Oman – Officials', Reuters, 20 October 2016, https://www.reuters.com/article/us-yemen-security-iran/exclusive-iran-steps-up-weapons-supply-to-yemens-houthis-via-oman-officials-idUSKCN12K0CX.

42 See Brian Perkins, 'Saudi Arabia and the UAE in al-Mahra: Securing Interests, Disrupting Local Order, and Shaping a Southern Military', *Terrorism Monitor*, vol. 17, no. 4, 2019.

43 See 'Muaajihaat Bayna Al-Quwwat Al-Sa'udiyya ua Al-Ahaaly Bil-Mahra' [Confrontations Between Saudi Forces and Families of Mahra], *Aden Al-Ghad*, 12 October 2018, https://adenalgd.net/news/342296/.

44 See, for example, 'Yad Imaaraatiyyah Haaniyah fy Mustashfiyyaat Al-Yaman wa Maraakizha As-Sahiyyah' [A Warm Emirati Hand in Hospitals of Yemen and Their Health Centres], *Al-Bayan*, 9 January 2019, https://www.albayan.ae/one-world/arabs/2019-01-09-1.3455132.

45 Interviews in Abu Dhabi in 2019.

46 See Aziz El Yaakoubi and Lisa Barrington, 'UAE Scales Down Military Presence in Yemen as Gulf Tensions Flare', Reuters, 28 June 2019.

47 See Jonathan Fenton-Harvey, 'The UAE Still Has Military Ambitions in Yemen Despite Withdrawal', *Al-Monitor*, 8 November 2019.

48 Confirmed by multiple interviews with diplomats and analysts in Riyadh and Abu Dhabi in 2018 and 2019. In fact, there is significant frustration among Emirati commanders with the Saudi military performance.

49 Precise figures are unavailable, but the

war in Yemen is likely to have cost the UAE several billion dollars annually.

50 According to interviewees, the UAE told STC members to stop criticising the Stockholm process.

51 In the words of one interviewee: 'This [the intervention in Yemen] is typical UAE foreign policy: it overestimates its own power and underestimates that of others.'

52 Michael Knights, 'Lessons from the UAE War in Yemen', Lawfare, 18 August 2019, https://www.lawfareblog.com/lessons-uae-war-yemen.

53 See Peter Salisbury, 'Yemen's Southern Powder Keg', Chatham House, March 2018.

54 See Maggie Michael, Trish Wilson and Lee Keath, 'AP Investigation: US Allies, Al-Qaida Battle Rebels in Yemen', APNews, 6 August 2018, https://apnews.com/f38788a561d74ca78c77cb43612d50da.

55 Bel Trew, 'Inside the UAE's War on Al-Qaeda in Yemen', Independent, 15 August 2018, https://www.independent.co.uk/news/world/middle-east/uae-yemen-civil-war-al-qaeda-aden-dar-saad-gulf-saudi-arabia-conflict-a8492021.html.

56 See Bel Trew, 'Former Al-Qaeda Footsoldiers Have Been Allowed into Yemen Forces, Admits UAE Military', Independent, 16 August 2018, https://www.independent.co.uk/news/world/middle-east/yemen-civil-war-al-qaeda-soldiers-uae-military-emirati-a8494481.html.

57 As one interviewee pointed out, while it is true that weapons have made their way to extremists, that was not the original Saudi or Emirati intent, but a by-product of the messiness of the war. See also Amnesty International, 'Yemen: UAE Recklessly Supplying Militias with Windfall of Western Arms', 6 February 2019, https://www.amnesty.org/en/latest/news/2019/02/yemen-uae-recklessly-supplying-militias-with-windfall-of-western-arms/.

58 Interviews with southern leaders in Abu Dhabi in 2019.

59 See Sudarsan Raghavan, 'The U.S. Put a Yemeni Warlord on a Terrorist List. One of Its Close Allies Is Still Arming Him', Washington Post, 29 December 2018, https://www.washingtonpost.com/world/middle_east/the-us-put-a-yemeni-warlord-on-a-terrorist-list-one-of-its-close-allies-is-still-arming-him/2018/12/28/f3c4fb5b-f366-4570-b27b-75a3ed0f0f52_story.html?utm_term=.3199484bf633.

60 Amnesty International, 'Yemen: UAE Recklessly Supplying Militias with Windfall of Western Arms'. See also Amnesty International, 'Disappearances and Torture in Southern Yemen Detention Facilities Must Be Investigated as War Crimes', 12 July 2018, https://www.amnesty.org/en/latest/news/2018/07/disappearances-and-torture-in-southern-yemen-detention-facilities-must-be-investigated-as-war-crimes/.

61 See Samuel Ramani, 'UAE Faces Growing Resentment in Southern Yemen', Al-Monitor, 26 July 2019.

62 On the complexity of local dynamics in and around Ta'izz, see Adam Baron and Raiman Al-Hamdani, 'The Proxy War Prism on Yemen: View from the City of Taiz', New America Foundation, December 2019.

[63] See Mustafa Naji, 'Taez, ville martyre et oubliée', *OrientXXI*, 14 May 2019, https://orientxxi.info/magazine/yemen-taez-ville-martyre-et-oubliee,3082.

[64] See International Crisis Group, 'The Beginning of the End of Yemen's Civil War?', 5 November 2019, https://www.crisisgroup.org/middle-east-north-africa/gulf-and-arabian-peninsula/yemen/beginning-end-yemens-civil-war.

Review Essay

A Great and Growing Rift

John A. Gans, Jr

The Great Rift: Dick Cheney, Colin Powell, and the Broken Friendship That Defined an Era
James Mann. New York: Henry Holt & Co., 2020. $32.00. 432 pp.

By the time Colin Powell, 49, and Dick Cheney, 45, met in Germany in autumn 1986, both had already learned the lessons that would shape not just their decades-long relationship but American foreign policy itself. Powell was a three-star general commanding the United States Army's V Corps in Germany after serving as senior aide to the secretary of defense. Cheney, who had been White House chief of staff in the Ford administration, was a long-serving congressman stopping in Wiesbaden on return from a visit to the Middle East (p. 61).

That short visit left an impression, with each man taking note of the other. The meeting also began a remarkable partnership: Powell and Cheney went on to work together at the Department of Defense and to navigate the challenges of the early post-Cold War world. Yet, as James Mann makes clear in his welcome and engaging new dual biography, *The Great Rift*, the world views and weaknesses Powell and Cheney brought to that Wiesbaden meeting eventually undermined not just their relationship, but also American foreign relations.

John A. Gans, Jr, is the director of communications and research at the University of Pennsylvania's Perry World House. He interviewed Colin Powell, Dick Cheney and many of their colleagues for his book *White House Warriors: How the National Security Council Transformed the American Way of War* (Liveright, 2019).

Survival | vol. 62 no. 4 | August–September 2020 | pp. 209–216   DOI 10.1080/00396338.2020.1792140

In the years ahead, historians will try to understand just how in 2020 – 34 years after that meeting – the United States found itself so divided at home and diminished in the world. Few have done more than Mann, whom I worked for as a researcher ten years ago, to understand those governing the nation in that era. In widely respected books, Mann has gotten into the White Houses of presidents Ronald Reagan, George W. Bush and Barack Obama, and into the heads of those working there.

In his new book, Mann subjects Cheney and Powell to the same scrupulous treatment. Along the way, the author reveals new details on their broken relationship and makes a compelling argument for why the United

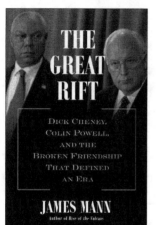

States finds itself mired in such a sorry state today. By disagreeing so viciously over relatively minor policy differences, Powell and Cheney ruined their relationship and made catastrophic misjudgements. They also created an opening for Donald Trump to hijack not only their political party and the US government, but also America's relationship with the world.

'More data than judgement'

Like Trump, Powell grew up in New York; but the Powells, a family of Jamaican immigrants, lived in the South Bronx. Powell, who paid for college through the US Army's Reserve Officers' Training Corps, went on to serve two tours in Vietnam, the first before the United States had taken an active role in combat and again five years later during the worst part of the war. For the latter tour, Powell earned the Soldier's Medal after a helicopter he was riding in crashed and he dragged three wounded servicemen, including his commanding officer, to safety.

Carrying the weight of senior leaders became Powell's speciality. Within two decades of that accident, he served as an aide to the deputy director of the White House's Office of Management and Budget, the deputy secretary of defense and the secretary of defense, then as deputy national security advisor and national security advisor. Powell excelled as a gatekeeper, note-taker, briefer and jacket-carrier in part because, as one former boss said, 'he had the diplomatic finesse to say no without alienating people' (p. 18).

Along the way, Powell often used the word 'no' in policy debates. He distrusted foreign-policy experts, who he believed produced 'more data than judgement' (p. 14). Too often, those experts also produced interventions like the one in Vietnam, which Powell called a 'half-hearted, half-war' (p. 15). As a result, he would spend most of his career pushing against such would-be strategists and such interventions, which Powell believed Americans did not support enough and for which the military was not sufficiently prepared.

One of the most impactful moments of Powell's post-Vietnam career was a job he did not take. The then-colonel was offered a position on Jimmy Carter's National Security Council by national security advisor Zbigniew Brzezinski. But Powell turned down the opportunity to go to the White House. It was not about politics: he had voted for Carter. Instead, Powell wanted to stay with the troops and in military operations, and away from the sort of analytical policy work required of the president's team.

Powell's heart was with the army, an institution he excelled in from the start. It was more than a personal attachment. Powell was a particular type of institutionalist, one who had seen his cherished organisation go bad – in the army's case after Vietnam – and fought to rebuild it. At one point Powell's mantra was 'Save the army', according to his speechwriter (p. 115). More than protecting an institution he helped save, Powell believed the United States would be in trouble without a strong army – whether in the aftermaths of Vietnam, the Cold War or 9/11.

'You're never yourself'

Cheney's father was also an institutionalist, working for more than three decades at the US Soil Conservation Service in Wyoming. The stability of Cheney's upbringing, according to Mann, instilled in him a 'desire for movement, upheaval, and disorder' (p. 15). As a young adult in Wyoming, Cheney found it: drinking, digging up trouble and dropping out of college. He worked a series of odd jobs, including stringing power lines, before getting his life together – finding a forceful wife and pursuing a PhD in political science.

Cheney never finished the doctorate nor went to Vietnam; he was given deferments as a student and then as a parent. But the war also shaped his early career. After a stint on Capitol Hill, Cheney joined Richard Nixon's administration, which struggled to survive the political maelstrom created by crises of its predecessor's making (Vietnam) and its own (Watergate). With the right mentor – former congressman Donald Rumsfeld – and Machiavellian manoeuvres, at age 34 Cheney became chief of staff to Nixon's successor, Gerald Ford.

Though Mann calls Cheney 'lucky' to avoid the political damage of the era, the real gift was a low profile – one of his Secret Service code names was 'Backseat' – and a reputation for achieving results. In the words of one colleague: 'when you gave something to Dick, it happened. It got done' (p. 20). Mann also notes Cheney had a 'distinctive deep voice, the sound of gravitas and self-assurance he would employ in one high-level job after another. It was a voice that seemed to function almost as a seductive gas, soothing and winning over the people who run America from day to day' (pp. 33–4).

That voice sounded reasonable, but it masked a deep conservative streak. After Ford lost the 1976 presidential election, Cheney ran successfully for Congress two years later – despite having had the first of five heart attacks – and some expressed surprise at his less than centrist opinions. But Cheney later said: 'when you're in a staff job, you're never yourself' (p. 49). Under Rumsfeld and Ford, Cheney kept his views hidden; but on his own, the congressman made a point to emphasise how conservative he was.

Cheney did have one un-conservative project, however. Just as Powell's experience in Vietnam shaped his later institutional views, Cheney's experience in the post-Watergate, post-Vietnam White House shaped his. As a member of Congress, Cheney wrote in an academic article that 'the "imperial" presidency is, in my view, a myth' (p. 51). In journal articles, congressional proceedings and positions of influence, Cheney sought to radically rebalance government toward a White House he thought was too weak, and away from long-standing institutions such as Congress and Powell's army. Cheney was an early advocate of what has come to be known as the 'unitary executive theory' – whereby the president holds complete authority over the executive branch under the US Constitution –

advanced in recent decades, including by Attorney General William Barr on behalf of Trump.

'Your buddy, Colin'

For several years after their meeting in Wiesbaden, Powell and Cheney kept in touch. They helped each other when they could and celebrated each other's successes. For example, in December 1988, Powell wrote Cheney a congratulatory note on his promotion into a congressional leadership position. Powell explained that it would 'not only benefit your party but also those committed to good government and to all Americans. Your buddy, Colin' (p. 84).

Despite their rapport, Powell and Cheney only became formal partners in 1989 by coincidence. Newly elected president George H.W. Bush's first pick for defense secretary had to withdraw in scandal, and Cheney's name was next on the list. Powell, then commander of US Army Forces Command, overseeing all army units in the United States and Puerto Rico, was the most junior of all the military's four-star officers, and thus much farther down the list of candidates to be the next chairman of the Joint Chiefs of Staff. Regardless, Cheney pushed the White House to make the historic appointment.

What commenced was a consequential partnership. Together, Powell and Cheney led the US military through several tumultuous years: the end of the Cold War and America's first real hot wars since Vietnam. Powell and Cheney did not always agree on what to do, most famously on the decision to evict Iraq from Kuwait during the 1991 Gulf War. But the two were able to overcome their differences because, as the Pentagon's leaders, their shared interests differentiated them from those seeking a post-Cold War peace dividend and military-funding cuts.

Yet it was only a temporary partnership, and exploring why is this book's real strength. More than just about any other author, Mann appreciates the games played by the powerful and power-hungry. For him, understanding Powell and Cheney requires appreciating where they spent their early careers: as support players inside those games. Each, in the author's words, 'started as an unusually talented staff aide; each proved adept at the basic task of getting things done for his bosses' (p. 11).

Neither Powell nor Cheney was a geopolitical visionary or even an above-average strategist compared to the boldest names in American foreign policy, such as former secretary of state Henry Kissinger or Brzezinski. Powell and Cheney were doers, a label Mann suggests could apply to both, not dreamers. Such a skill was useful after Vietnam when their bosses made the decisions and the Soviet Union kept options limited, and it remained useful even after the Cold War, with George H.W. Bush in charge and the military simply seeking to undermine those who dreamed of defence cuts.

After 9/11, however, when the United States needed big ideas and strategic decisions, Powell and Cheney, as secretary of state and vice president respectively, failed. They fell back on doctrine – Powell's belief in war as an option of last resort and only with overwhelming force, and Cheney's hard-edged hawkishness and heavy-handed treatment of adversaries. When neither approach proved a good fit for the challenges of the so-called 'global war on terror', the two did not go back to the drawing board or try anything new; they just started fighting each other.

'Diminished figures'

In Mann's estimation, Powell and Cheney are 'remembered now as diminished figures'. Their policy missteps – most significantly the 2003 war in Iraq, which Mann deeply analyses and convincingly blames on both – are one reason why. But even more than that disastrous conflict in the Middle East, Powell and Cheney diminished themselves with the depth and pettiness of their fights in Washington, which Mann reveals in new detail.

Why? Powell and Cheney were not, in Mann's view, 'lifelong rivals or enemies' (p. 5). Both were capable of real relationships: both stayed married to their first wives and developed deep and abiding professional and personal friendships. They worked together well during the George H.W. Bush administration, even if it was an alliance of convenience and kind. Yet when the stakes were highest, their relationship fell apart.

In the years since the 2003 war, it has been easy – given the disastrous outcome – to forget how many American policymakers agreed with the need to confront Iraq. Even in the White House Situation Room, where Powell and Cheney were comfortable disagreeing, the conversation around what Mann calls a 'nondecision' had less to do with 'whether' than 'how' (p. 281). Debates about what Mann rightly calls 'secondary' issues of timing and international support grew heated, but the fundamental question never got asked (p. 281). Nor did Powell ever voice outright opposition to the war, or Cheney force the big-picture conversation. Instead, they debated – and broke up over – 'tactics', as Mann makes clear (p. 289).

As in any bad relationship, the Powell–Cheney breakdown was driven by several factors, including respective inadequacies. Mann writes that 'Powell's problem was that he could not find a home or a base in either of America's two political parties', and that Cheney 'could never master the public side of electoral politics' (p. 4). Because neither Powell nor Cheney could develop an enduring bloc of public or political support, their only hope for changing policy was to win Washington's inside game, and the easiest way to do so – as they learned during their earlier careers – was to try to increase bureaucratic resistance to each other's ideas and, if that failed, to try to destroy each other.

While Mann focuses on two decades, 1988–2008, it is impossible not to consider what Cheney and Powell's fights meant for the rise of Trump. Trump's candidacy was another matter on which Powell and Cheney disagreed. Though Powell had his doubts about former secretary of state Hillary Clinton, he voted for her. Meanwhile, Cheney eventually endorsed Trump, though he has criticised some of the president's choices in office.

Trump's appeal has little to do with endorsements and more to do with the great – and growing – rift between the US government and the governed. Since 9/11, Americans' confidence in government has collapsed: last year, only 17% trusted the US government 'to do what is right'.[1] Perhaps more important than the baseline distrust is Americans' belief, as polls suggest, that the collapsing trust in government is one reason why the United States is struggling to solve problems at home and abroad.

Powell and Cheney have not been the only infighters, leakers and log-rollers in Washington over the last 20 years. But their misbehaviour has proved especially costly because, as Mann's book makes clear, their disagreements undermined the usually sacred issue of national security at an unusually critical moment in American history – the aftermath of 9/11. If two national leaders with so much experience and so much on the line could not figure out how to work together, how could the government ever get anything done?

Trump, an amateur in government and statecraft, rode that distrust to Washington, or, as he called it on the campaign trail, the 'swamp'. And he has used the presidency that Cheney helped empower to bludgeon the permanent bureaucracy (including Powell's army), which Trump and his team have called a 'deep state' intent on subverting the will of the people. The resulting breakdown in government could not have come at a more damaging moment than the current one, with the coronavirus pandemic, subsequent economic crisis and domestic unrest over police brutality and ingrained racism.

The US government's present failure reflects not just Trump's mismanagement, but also America's increasing rifts at home and with the world. It is neither right nor fair to put the blame for those breakdowns on the current president alone. For decades, Powell and Cheney were the voices that explained the world to their fellow citizens. Mann's book is a reminder of why Americans stopped listening and why rebuilding Washington's credibility is the only way the United States can narrow those rifts.

Notes

[1] Pew Research Center, 'Public Trust in Government: 1958–2019', 11 April 2019, available at https:// www.people-press.org/2019/04/11/ public-trust-in-government-1958-2019/.

Review Essay

Northern Exposure

Russell Crandall and Frederick Richardson

El Norte: The Epic and Forgotten Story of Hispanic North America
Carrie Gibson. New York: Atlantic Monthly Press, 2019. $30.00.
560 pp.

In 1932, Californian conservationist Christine Sterling commissioned Mexican artist David Alfaro Siqueiros to paint a mural in Los Angeles's El Pueblo neighbourhood as a kind of urban-revival project cum tourist attraction. Sterling was expecting a piece that romanticised the Mexican past, but when the painting was unveiled to a sizeable crowd in October 1932, it quickly became clear that the communist-leaning Siqueiros, a contemporary of celebrated muralists Diego Rivera and José Clemente Orozco, had different thematic priorities. Painted on an 18-by-80-foot (5.5-by-24-metre) wall, *América Tropical*, which drew a startled response from onlookers, depicted a crucified indigenous man surrounded by images that included Mayan motifs and armed revolutionaries, prompting Sterling to label it 'anti-American' (p. 349). Shortly thereafter it was summarily painted over, and was only returned to public display in 2012, after intensive restoration efforts.[1]

Russell Crandall is a professor of American foreign policy and international politics at Davidson College in North Carolina, and a contributing editor to *Survival*. His new book, *Drugs and Thugs: The History and Future of America's War on Drugs*, is forthcoming from Yale University Press in autumn 2020. **Frederick Richardson** graduated from Bowdoin College in 2019 and is a master's student at Johns Hopkins University's School of Advanced International Studies (SAIS).

Survival | vol. 62 no. 4 | August–September 2020 | pp. 217–224   DOI 10.1080/00396338.2020.1792141

As historian and journalist Carrie Gibson makes clear in *El Norte: The Epic and Forgotten Story of Hispanic North America*, the story of *América Tropical* speaks to larger themes in North America's Hispanic history: for centuries, that history has been both romanticised and obfuscated. This can be seen in the revelry of Cinco de Mayo and Columbus Day, depictions of Hispanic culture in the media and modern political discourse surrounding Mexico, all of which paint an uneven, misleading account of Hispanic contributions to North America's past and present.[2] Through her impressive research and enthralling prose, Gibson combats this simplification and presents a rich history that has too often been left untold.

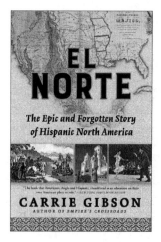

Continental claims

Naturally, *El Norte* begins by exploring the colonisation of North (and South) America by conquistadors and the empires they represented. The New World, viewed by the European empires as a potentially lucrative source of wealth, engendered fierce competition, even within individual nations' own colonial missions. Spanish colonists, for instance, were often rewarded for carrying out expeditions by being granted an *encomendero*, allowing them to collect tribute from native populations. However, this placed the colonists in conflict with Catholic missionaries, who believed, rightly, that their work to convert Native Americans was being hampered by their maltreatment at the hands of the colonists. The Spanish Crown, seeking to curtail these abuses, passed the Laws of Burgos in 1512, which put restrictions on the *encomienda* system. In response, some colonies chose to adopt a policy of *obedezco pero no cumplo*, according to which Spanish mandates were obeyed with a certain degree of latitude.

Gibson makes clear from the outset that colonial borders in the New World (and later in the American West) were ever shifting. A territory such as the Fort Mose area in Florida could, at the beginning of the eighteenth century, be claimed by the Spanish, the French and Native American tribes. Recognising that such a dynamic, complicated history could easily span multiple volumes, Gibson tethers each chapter to a specific location, using the place to reveal broader developments during a given time period. For instance, chapter six, 'Nootka Sound, Canada, ca. 1760s–1789', details Spanish efforts to curtail British and Russian incursions on what would eventually become Canadian territory. However, the focus is more broadly on increased European interest in North America's west coast, as the chapter also describes the construction of the California mission system and the resulting effects on the native population. Thus, Nootka is not the sole focus of the chapter, but rather a launch point for a larger exposition of European ambitions in the Pacific. Another outstanding chapter, 'New Orleans, Louisiana, ca. 1790–1804', showcases how the French Revolution, slavery and the 1803 Louisiana Purchase harmed Spanish interests in the vast, largely unknown region. A chapter on 'San Antonio de Béxar, Texas, ca. 1820–48' depicts the Texas independence movement and the conflicts that it engendered with Spain (and later Mexico), while subsequent chapters on Miami, Florida, from 1960–80 and Tucson, Arizona, from 1994–2018 reveal the Cuban exodus to Florida and the beginnings of the cocaine era (Miami), and the present-day US border crisis (Tucson). This method of sketching broad historical developments by detailing their effects in a concentrated area helps keep *El Norte* to a refreshingly lean 450 pages. It allows Gibson to strike a remarkable balance between breadth and depth that allows her to cover an incredible amount of material without overwhelming the reader.

Focus on the individual

As much as the exploration and subsequent white settlement of the American West was driven by political, economic and social forces, it was also catalysed by individuals. Thus, *El Norte* underscores the influence of individuals who were integral in shaping the history of Hispanic America. Some of the names – Hernán Cortés, Juan Ponce de León, Bartolomé de Las Casas – will probably strike most readers as at least vaguely familiar. But Gibson also lavishes attention on figures who may be less well known, such as Álvar Núñez Cabeza de Vaca, whose epic eight-year journey began in 1528 and took him from Florida to the Gulf of California, and Juan de Oñate, a Creole born to Spanish colonists, who in 1598 led an expedition from Santa

Bárbara, Mexico, into the modern-day US state of New Mexico. Searching for a passageway to the Pacific, and no doubt motivated by the prospect of establishing his own *encomienda*, Oñate and his men pushed north while contacting numerous Indian tribes. Due to abuses that included the systematic amputation of the right feet of survivors of the Acoma Massacre, Oñate was forced by the Spanish to return to Mexico City to answer for his actions. Nevertheless, the Spanish mission in New Mexico continued, albeit with significant infighting between colonial authorities and Franciscan friars.

Another figure profiled by Gibson is James Long, who, in 1819, led a force originally from Mississippi across the Louisiana border into the Spanish territory of Texas. Although this operation had not been sanctioned by the US government, its aim was to free Texas from Spanish control, clearing the way for greater Anglo settlement. While this particular incursion was promptly defeated, Moses Austin arrived in 1820 to petition the Spanish government to allow him to build a settlement. He died soon after, but his son, Stephen, established a colony in what was now Mexican territory, Mexico having won its independence in 1821. Stephen would help lead another independence movement, this time against Mexico. After being routed by the forces of Sam Houston in 1836, the Mexican leader Santa Anna was forced to recognise Texan independence, and in 1845 Texas was admitted to the United States.

While Houston, Austin and Oñate were clearly influential in the development of their respective regions, Gibson discusses how their complicated legacies have been reinterpreted by subsequent generations, noting, for example, that in 1998 a statue of Oñate near Alcalde, New Mexico, was vandalised by members of the Acoma people, who cut off the statue's right foot as a reminder of Oñate's abuses against their ancestors (an incident that presaged the current controversy surrounding the toppling of statues[3]). More recently there has been debate over whether the capital city of Texas, named for Stephen Austin, should be renamed given his advocacy of slavery.[4] Indeed, many of the protagonists in *El Norte* – not least Christopher Columbus himself – have come under contemporary scrutiny for actions that in the past may have been overlooked, if not celebrated. Nevertheless, their contributions to the development of Hispanic North

America are an essential part of the story, and Gibson skilfully weaves them into her larger narrative.

Gibson likewise devotes attention to the ways in which Dutch, English, French, Portuguese and Russian colonial efforts influenced the rise and fall of the Spanish presence in North America, noting, for example, that the English Reformation encouraged many Protestants to make the trip to the New World in search of opportunities that were unavailable back in Europe. As Gibson points out, Spain could not match the flood of Protestant settlers. Britain's victory in the Seven Years War brought with it territorial gains that allowed for an even greater expansion of its population. Thus, other European actors would have as much of a say in determining the outcome of the Spanish colonial project as the Spanish themselves.

Enter the United States

By the second half of the book, the European powers recede as the United States emerges as 'a more confident and stable nation' (p. 179). However, growing American confidence was to bring it into conflict with its neighbour to the south: Mexico. As noted, Gibson discusses the gradual erosion of Mexican control over Texas and New Mexico in the nineteenth century. Of course, the United States had imperial ambitions beyond Mexico, as demonstrated by its 1898 war with Spain that resulted in American acquisition of Guam, the Philippines and Puerto Rico. Incorporating these new lands into the United States raised heated debates about which groups were deserving of citizenship and which were not, debates that highlighted the inadequacies of the United States' racial system. Ambiguity surrounding the idea of 'whiteness' led 1850s Tejano Mexicans to assert their Spanish origins in a bid to be classified as white, an assertion which was contested by nativist groups well into the twentieth century. Cubans fleeing the conflict against the Spanish in the late nineteenth century (100 years before a new wave of Cuban exiles would flee the rule of Fidel Castro) found themselves trapped in similarly complicated racial dynamics. In the Jim Crow South, light-skinned Cubans enjoyed similar privileges to Italians and other Mediterranean immigrants, while darker-skinned Cubans were classified as black, severely limiting their opportunities in their adopted country. Indeed,

Gibson's book continually demonstrates that throughout North American history, 'belonging' often had ethnic, geographical and racial requirements.

Gibson continues to raise questions of race and acceptance in her discussion of a variety of locales in the early to mid-twentieth century, including places in California, Texas and New York where Hispanic populations – some new, others older than the states themselves – carved out a distinct, if uneasy, existence. She notes that Mexican Americans returning from the battlefields of the Second World War had to forgo their enjoyment of post-war life to take up the fight against 'Jaime Crow', a set of informal rules meant to deny Mexicans and Mexican Americans an equal place in society. Discriminatory housing laws, in tandem with segregated schools, ensured that Mexican Americans were denied the same privileges as white Americans, touching off a prolonged struggle for equal treatment. Later discussion of contemporary problems along the US–Mexico border, including illegal immigration, drug trafficking and vigilante justice, serves as a powerful reminder that long-standing questions of ownership and exclusion are as relevant today as ever.

Indeed, as Gibson notes in her compelling discussion of transplanted Hispanic culture, 'in a shared Anglo-Hispanic popular culture, who or what is "Hispanic" remains unresolved. A commoditized Hispanic culture can only give a veneer of cohesion' (p. 401). She demonstrates that there is a long tradition of appropriating Hispanic culture in the United States. Record labels, for instance, were quick to capitalise on the popularity of the rumba and the mambo between the First World War and the mid-1950s, adding English lyrics to Latin motifs and conjuring up songs with Latin labels but few other Hispanic credentials ('Mambo Italiano' and the like). Similarly, Hollywood became enamoured of Mexico in the 1930s, introducing American viewers to characters such as Zorro. Contemporary consumer culture has taken this trend to an extreme, as Americans have embraced a watered-down Hispanic culture – Taco Bell restaurants, margaritas, songs by performers such as Jennifer Lopez – which often propagates distorted stereotypes of Hispanics and allows Americans to separate Hispanic culture (at least their version of it) from complicated issues such as the United States' immigration policies and US–Mexico relations. It is perhaps telling that President Donald Trump, a vocal critic of Mexicans, touted his eating of a taco bowl on Cinco de Mayo in 2016 as evidence that he 'love[s] Hispanics'.[5] American adoption of Hispanic culture, no matter how superficial, is used to conceal the profound difficulties faced by the United States in grappling with its Hispanic history and its current relationship with the Hispanic world.

El Norte proves that the territory, population and culture of the United States would not be what it is today without the Hispanic elements of the North American story. The version of history taught in most American high schools would have us believe that European expansion in North America began in New England and that the push west, as described by Frederick Jackson Turner (father of the influential 'Frontier Thesis'), was driven solely by the United States. Gibson complicates this history by unequivocally showing that the Anglo history of North America is inseparable from its Hispanic history. *El Norte* is an ambitious work that covers a tremendous amount of material. Yet Gibson maintains clarity and readability throughout, even while achieving a quick narrative pace. Ultimately, she delivers a book of impressive breadth and meticulous detail that adds necessary and enlightening context to an underappreciated aspect of North American history.

Notes

1   See Christopher Knight, 'Two Murals, Two Histories', *Los Angeles Times*, 20 February 1994, https://www.latimes.com/archives/la-xpm-1994-02-20-ca-25050-story.html.

2   See, for example, Lulu Garcia-Navarro, 'The Real History of Cinco de Mayo', National Public Radio, 5 May 2019, https://www.npr.org/2019/05/05/720376183/the-real-history-of-cinco-de-mayo; and Katie Reilly, 'Here Are All the Times Donald Trump Insulted Mexico', *Time*, 31 August 2016, https://time.com/4473972/donald-trump-mexico-meeting-insult/.

3   See Andrew Restuccia and Paul Kiernan, 'Toppling of Statues Triggers Reckoning over Nation's History', *Wall Street Journal*, 23 June 2020, https://www.wsj.com/articles/trump-seeks-to-protect-monuments-from-vandals-with-tougher-sentences-11592922449.

4   See Mathew Haag, 'Stephen F. Austin Defended Slavery. Should the Texas Capital Be Renamed?', *New York Times*, 31 July 2018, https://www.

nytimes.com/2018/07/31/us/stephen-f-austin-renaming.html.

5 Ashley Parker, 'Donald Trump's "Taco Bowl" Message: "I Love Hispanics"', *New York Times*, 5 May 2016, https://www.nytimes.com/politics/first-draft/2016/05/05/donald-trump-taco-bowl.

Book Reviews

Asia-Pacific
Lanxin Xiang

Has China Won? The Chinese Challenge to American Primacy
Kishore Mahbubani. New York: PublicAffairs, 2020. $30.00.
320 pp.

With his usual lucidity and provocativeness, Kishore Mahbubani has written yet another cool-headed analysis of a subject of great importance for the world's future: the ominous direction in which US–China relations are moving. He starts with the assumption that the United States lacks a long-term strategic vision, while China is always in possession of one, an assumption he says is shared by Henry Kissinger (p. 2). For Mahbubani, the model for long-term thinking is George F. Kennan, the father of the Cold War containment strategy, who served as the first director of the Policy Planning Staff at the US State Department. According to the author, there is no equivalent of Kennan in Washington today, even as the US seems to be stumbling into a new cold war with China. The only 'long view' coming from President Donald Trump's Policy Planning Staff characterises the rivalry with China as a contest with a 'non-Caucasian' power, reflecting nothing but a deep fear of the 'Yellow Peril' (p. 7).

The author raises ten questions for policymakers in Washington, the main thrust of which is that, firstly, the US cannot win a cold war with China without allies, and will need not only Western democracies but also a majority of UN member states to take its side. But the US has lost much of the soft power it accumulated in the decades following the Second World War, and it is unclear that it can win an ideological war with China as Beijing gains more and more goodwill from the large number of countries that are part of its Belt and Road Initiative.

Survival | vol. 62 no. 4 | August–September 2020 | pp. 225–230   DOI 10.1080/00396338.2020.1792142

Secondly, the US strategy during the original Cold War was to force the Soviet Union into bankruptcy by vastly outspending it in the military domain. This approach may not work with China, not only because Chinese economic strength is steadily catching up with that of the US, but also because China possesses formidable financial power. The Achilles heel of the US economy is the unique position of the dollar, which may be vulnerable.

Thirdly, the respective temperaments of Beijing and Washington are totally different. Whereas the US is driven by 'emotions' and displays a 'loss of temper and self-control', Beijing remains calm and stable. In a major geopolitical competition, 'the advantage always goes to the party that remains cool-headed and rational' (p. 8). There is therefore reason to doubt that the US can prevail against its communist rival this time.

Mahbubani also offers some advice to Chinese leader Xi Jinping, urging him not to underestimate the US. This is indeed sound advice, given that the Chinese leadership became dismissive of US power in the wake of the 2008 economic crisis. This has led a hot-headed Xi to make strategic mistakes as he has pushed a more assertive agenda. But Mahbubani seems to have underestimated the strength of the nationalism unleashed by Xi's Middle Kingdom hubris and its dire consequences. The author's most dubious argument is his claim that Xi's move to concentrate power in his own hands provides a 'global public good' by containing nationalism within China (p. 138). Despite this overly optimistic assessment of Xi's behaviour and abilities, this is a timely book that should be read by anyone puzzled by the rapid deterioration of the relationship between what are arguably the world's two most important nations.

Becoming Kim Jong Un: A Former CIA Officer's Insights into North Korea's Enigmatic Young Dictator
Jung H. Pak. New York: Ballantine Books, 2020. $28.00. 336 pp.

In this fascinating book, a former top analyst at the CIA provides a multidimensional portrait of the mysterious young dictator of North Korea. The most interesting part of the book is the author's detailed analysis of the reasons why Kim Jong-un has not only survived as top leader despite his relatively tender age, but seems to have rapidly strengthened his position. Brutality and decisiveness are winning traits for a dictator, but Kim is also highly skilful at using the powerful mysticism surrounding the Kim dynasty that has been developing for more than 70 years.

Kim's grandfather, Kim Il-sung, was a national hero in the fight against the Japanese. The North Koreans worshipped him like a god. Consequently, 'the spirit of Kim Il Sung seeped into every aspect of a North Korean's life', says author Jung Pak (p. 11). Kim Il-sung's son, Kim Jong-il, held the status of demigod, his official biography reading 'like the Book of Genesis' with its plethora of 'begats' highlighting the genealogies of important individuals (p. 30). It was always going to be difficult for Kim 3.0 to match his father's, not to mention his grandfather's, mystic power. Thus, at the beginning of his leadership, he decided to evoke the spiritual power of reincarnation by obtaining a 1950s-style haircut to emphasise his resemblance to his grandfather.

Kim certainly inherited his forebears' brutal methods in dealing with real or potential rivals. His appalling treatment of his uncle Jang Song-thaek, once North Korea's number-two man, is a case in point. After his sentencing for 'counter-revolutionary' activities, Jang was reportedly taken to the Kanggon Military Training Area on the outskirts of Pyongyang and executed by anti-aircraft guns (p. 106).

The most interesting dimension of Kim 3.0's character is how it was influenced by Western culture when he was a high-school student in Switzerland. He is a millennial, and North Koreans of the same age group belong to what is called *jangmadang*, or the 'market generation'. They are said to be obsessed with consumerism and digital culture, which Kim is actively encouraging, rather than seeking to turn back the clock by restoring the country's previous economic austerity and anti-consumerism. The result is a unique version of reform featuring market relaxation (informal markets) and impressive economic growth (p. 99). For those who have underestimated Kim from the start, it now appears that the man dismissed as 'short and fat' by Donald Trump is adept both in domestic control and geopolitical manoeuvres. Certainly, he has played Trump like a fiddle. Pak's analysis is balanced and penetrating, and her informative book deserves a wide readership.

The Hermit King: The Dangerous Game of Kim Jong Un
Chung Min Lee. New York: All Points Books, 2019. $28.99. 290 pp.

Chung Min Lee, a South Korean diplomat and scholar, considers Kim Jong-un to be a clever and calculating man who intends to lead the hermit kingdom for at least 40 years. His talent and capability seem to have been underestimated by many outsiders, perhaps including Chinese leader Xi Jinping. Kim became leader of North Korea in 2011, while Xi became China's top leader in 2012. But Xi refused to meet Kim until March 2018. In the United States, Kim has also been belittled and mocked by politicians and the media alike as a 'little rocket man' and a 'crazy fat kid', implying that this spoiled offspring of a dictator cannot be taken seriously.

According to Lee, however, Kim's 'concerted psychological operation against South Korea and the United States' has worked (p. 235). He played the nationalism card with leftist South Korean President Moon Jae-in, encouraging him to focus on the path for peaceful unification. His grand strategy lies in convincing the United States that he is willing to dismantle his nuclear weapons and intercontinental ballistic missiles over the longer term, while simultaneously achieving inter-Korean detente to ensure a steady increase in South Korean investment and a political 'disarmament in South Korea' (p. 65). Luckily for Kim, the current US president has a penchant for bonding with dictators. Styling himself the 'Great Negotiator', Trump thinks a nuclear deal is just like a real-estate deal. But despite the symbolic thaw in US–North Korean relations after the Trump–Kim summits, no real progress has been made toward denuclearisation in North Korea.

The author firmly refutes the idea prevalent in both the West and South Korea that North Korea's nuclear weapons were developed as a bargaining chip for obtaining other benefits. On the contrary, Pyongyang 'never had any intentions of giving up its nuclear arsenal', says Lee (p. 188). He concludes that Kim is playing a dangerous game. On the one hand, he is tempting Trump with the prospect of denuclearisation, a goal which has eluded every US president since Bill Clinton. Kim can never deliver it, but he believes even an empty promise will serve the political interests of the US president. If a second Trump administration increases the pressure, however, this may lead to a breaking point. On the other hand, Kim is risking his family's dynasty as the North Korean people gain more access to the outside world. Kim may not be able to 'stem the tide of two potent forces: information seeping into North Korea ... and the awakening of the North Korean people' (p. 238). This thoughtful book should be read by anyone with an interest in recent developments on the Korean Peninsula.

Special Duty: A History of the Japanese Intelligence Community
Richard J. Samuels. Ithaca, NY: Cornell University Press, 2019.
£27.99/$32.95. 355 pp.

Richard Samuels has produced an informative book about the evolution and current state of the Japanese intelligence community. He notes that the phrase 'intelligence community' glosses over the many weaknesses of Japan's intelligence system, including stovepiping and a lack of coordination, turf wars and political tribalism. As one Japanese historian aptly put it, 'many observers simply throw up their hands and declare "Japan has no intelligence community"' (p. xiv).

The author traces the root of the problem to Meiji-era Japan, when the extraordinary success of the country's modernisation and industrialisation failed to produce an equally modern intelligence system. Japan's leaders knew their aim was the domination of continental Asia and the Western Pacific, 'but knowing and learning were not always in sync' (p. 242). Japan's main interest was China, but Tokyo's human intelligence heavily relied on disreputable and self-serving ruffians known as 'continental adventurers' (*tairiku ronin*). Civil–military coordination was minimal, to the detriment of Japanese decision-making.

After the military takeover of the Japanese government in the 1930s, Japan's overconfident generals ignored intelligence analysis that argued for caution based on intelligence reports indicating that the United States' industrial capacity was 10–20 times larger than that of Japan. The surprise attack on Pearl Harbor was a tactical success that further convinced the military leadership of its invincibility. Subsequent 'intelligence failures in counterintelligence as well as at the strategic level' contributed a great deal to Japan's defeat (pp. 55–6). The Soviet spymaster Richard Sorge, for example, was able to pass sensitive information to Moscow for years.

In the post-war period, from 1945 to 1991, the Japanese government had little incentive to reform or improve its intelligence system, because Japan's national security now depended on the United States. Intelligence activities focused on internal security, making spies of the police force. Inter-agency coordination remained weak.

The sudden end of the Cold War 'left the underdeveloped Japanese intelligence community clueless about what was in store' (p. 248). After a few years of tinkering, Japanese leaders started building a centralised intelligence system. The rationale was that, to become a 'normal state', Japan needed an efficient intelligence machine. The establishment of a national security council on the US model in 2013 symbolised the change. The idea was to concentrate power in the prime minister's office over key intelligence functions including collection, analysis, communication, covert operations and oversight. The ambitions of Japanese intelligence reformers are far from fulfilled, however, because old habits die hard and institutional change in Japan has never been easy. As the author concludes: 'The failure to strike an effective balance between power and insight has come at great cost to Japan and to its neighbors' (p. 262). This is a historical lesson Japan has yet to learn.

Chinese Communist Espionage: An Intelligence Primer
Peter Mattis and Matthew Brazil. Annapolis, MD: Naval
Institute Press, 2019. $45.00. 359 pp.

The authors claim in their preface that Chinese communist espionage has been neglected by China watchers for the sake of commercial relations, and that most recent books on the subject fail to 'pierce the veil' because so few consult Chinese sources (p. vii). This seems like a promising beginning, arousing readers' curiosity and interest in what could be new ground. Sadly, the rest of the book is rather disappointing. For one thing, it is not a work of scholarly analysis, but merely a 'primer' or reference work. Since there is little analysis, readers gain no insight into the methodology, institutional character or unique features of the Chinese intelligence system as compared with other intelligence organisations such as the KGB, the CIA or Mossad.

After a brief survey of the history of Chinese communist espionage, the authors present an alphabetical who's who of Chinese intelligence leaders and top spies, as well as detailing important operations. Since this list makes up the bulk of the book, it seems reasonable to expect that the factual accuracy of these profiles would stand the test. Moreover, the authors boast a bibliography of hundreds of Chinese sources. Nevertheless, the book's mistakes are too numerous to be counted. In a key chapter entitled 'Chinese Communist Intelligence Leaders', for example, the descriptions of the career paths of several key figures are plainly wrong. Wu Xiuquan, head of China's military-intelligence department (known as '2PLA') in the late 1970s, is described as having worked directly under Deng Xiaoping in his Second Field Army (p. 11). But Wu was the deputy chief of staff of Marshal Lin Biao's Fourth Field Army. He never worked for Deng. The authors also refer to Wu as a 'lieutenant general' (p. 51), but formal military ranks had been abolished by Mao Zedong and were not used at that time. They were not restored until 1988, after Wu had already retired, as he complained bitterly in his autobiography (a book that is not listed in the bibliography of *Chinese Communist Espionage*).

Another notable mistake can be found in the profile of Li Zhen, the powerful minister of public security during the Cultural Revolution. Li is described as a subordinate to Marshal Chen Yi (p. 89), but the latter commanded a different field army. Ironically, Li's real boss was actually the former spymaster General Chen Geng, who is prominently profiled in the book.

Last but not least, Luo Ruiqing, China's first minister of public security, is said to have joined Mao's guerrilla troops at Jinggang Mountain in late 1920 (p. 95), but Luo never had the chance to be a 'Jinggang Mountain Hero'. By the time he joined the Red Army, Mao had already abandoned the mountain base. These are just a few examples of the kind of errors that undermine the value of this book as a reference work.

Russia and Eurasia
Angela Stent

The Firebird: The Elusive Fate of Russian Democracy
Andrei Kozyrev. Pittsburgh, PA: University of Pittsburgh Press,
2019. $35.00. 352 pp.

Andrei Kozyrev, Russian foreign minister from 1991 to 1996, begins his inform-ative and sobering memoir recalling how, in December 1991, he called president George H.W. Bush from a Belarusian hunting lodge to inform him that the Soviet Union had ceased to exist. He hoped for a democratic Russia and a bright new future for relations with the West. His book recounts in vivid detail how and why that dream remains unfulfilled.

The fate of Russian democracy lay in the hands of Boris Yeltsin, a decid-edly imperfect democrat. Kozyrev paints a complex portrait of a man whom he admired but was frustrated by. He describes Yeltsin's 'deep-seated and overwhelming lust for power' (p. 56) and his erratic behaviour, exacerbated by medical problems and excessive drinking. Yeltsin was nevertheless a charis-matic personality and, when he focused, a promoter of reforms.

When Kozyrev asked Yeltsin why he had not followed the example of other ex-communist countries in dismantling the Soviet-era secret police and banning their future participation in public life, Yeltsin replied: 'The KGB is the only organized state structure left by the old regime that works. Of course, it was criminal like everything else, but if we destroyed it, we would have risked unleashing total chaos' (p. 34). That decision facilitated Vladimir Putin's rise to power and his creation of a political system dominated by men from the intel-ligence services.

Kozyrev set out to radically alter Russian foreign policy, seeking good rela-tions with Russia's neighbours, integrating Russia into the West and developing cooperative ties with other countries. Almost from the beginning, the career diplomats in the foreign ministry and many in the parliament opposed him, criticising his pro-Western stance and calling for Crimea's return to Russia. The Bosnian War was particularly contentious. In recounting the difficult nego-tiations that ultimately led the Kremlin to cooperate with NATO, Kozyrev highlights a major Russian grievance: the United States and its allies in the 1990s failed to treat Russia as an equal. NATO began its bombing campaign without informing Russia beforehand, as Kozyrev believes it should have.

Today, many in Russia and the West blame NATO enlargement for the dete-rioration in Russia's relations with the West. Kozyrev rejects that view, but he believes that president Bill Clinton and secretary of state Warren Christopher

Survival | vol. 62 no. 4 | August–September 2020 | pp. 231–237   DOI 10.1080/00396338.2020.1792143

deceived Yeltsin by persuading him to sign on to the Partnership for Peace pro-gramme without telling him that, shortly thereafter, NATO would admit new Central European members. Kozyrev himself wanted Russia to join NATO and was assured that this was possible. He emphasises that Yeltsin's invitation to join the G7 was an important step toward Russia's search for equal treatment.

By 1995, Kozyrev realised that both domestic- and foreign-policy reforms were being undermined, and that his own position was becoming increasingly tenuous. He successfully ran for a Duma seat in Murmansk, only for Yeltsin to replace him as foreign minister with the more nationalistic Yevgeny Primakov. Yet Kozyrev remains a long-run optimist: 'Sooner or later, the Russian people will rise up again and reclaim the Russia they deserve' (p. 339).

The Compatriots: The Brutal and Chaotic History of Russia's Exiles, Émigrés, and Agents Abroad
Andrei Soldatov and Irina Borogan. New York: PublicAffairs, 2019. $30.00. 384 pp.

Russia has the third-largest diaspora in the world, and these 'compatriots' have for over a century had a complicated and contradictory relationship with the motherland they abandoned. Moreover, argue Andrei Soldatov and Irina Borogan in this gripping book, 'the Kremlin has considered the presence of Russians in Western countries – particularly the United States – both its biggest threat and its biggest opportunity' (pp. 6–7). In recounting the story of the Russian émigré community since 1917, the authors describe how the Soviet and Russian intelligence services have targeted their opponents abroad, seeking both to neutralise them and, when possible, to recruit them.

The Soviets early on began to use 'illegals' – agents with no diplomatic cover who assumed non-Russian identities – to pursue real or imagined oppo-nents abroad. In recounting the details of the meticulously planned operation that led to Leon Trotsky's assassination in Mexico, the authors detail the role of the Communist Party of the United States of America (CPUSA) in imple-menting orders from Joseph Stalin's secret police. Indeed, CPUSA leader Earl Browder and his deputy, Russian émigré Jacob Golos, worked for and were funded by Stalin's intelligence services, rather than representing the interests of the American working class. Even after Trotsky was dead, the New York Residentura told Browder to keep spying on suspected Trotskyites.

For Soldatov and Borogan, the history of Soviet émigrés is one of failure. Successive waves of émigrés – White aristocrats, social democrats, Ukrainians, Jews – disliked each other, and were unwilling and unable during the Cold War to organise themselves into a united front to oppose the USSR. In the post-Soviet era, these divisions persisted among a new wave of émigrés, which partially explains why there is no effective Russian lobby in the United States similar to those of other ethnic and national groups.

During Russia's brief period of openness in the 1990s, political emigration ended. Instead, compatriots began to return to Russia, to make money and to try to unify Russians who had remained and Russians who had left. Boris Jordan, scion of an aristocratic family, was instrumental in reconciling the two estranged branches of the Orthodox Church, one headquartered in Moscow and the other in New York. For a few years, it was possible to be a 'Global Russian' living in the West but maintaining close ties to Russia.

The Putin restoration slowly put an end to that. Once again, there are political émigrés, but Putin views the large Russian diaspora as something the Kremlin can use to advance its own interests: 'A strong diaspora can only exist if there is a strong state' (p. 176). Russia actively recruits members of its diaspora to serve its needs, but also seeks to neutralise those who criticise the Putin regime, including by resorting to traditional KGB poisoning techniques.

Soldatov and Borogan conclude that the collapse of the Soviet Union changed very little for Russia's intelligence services. Yeltsin failed to reform the KGB, and its successor agencies largely inherited its world view and modus operandi, including its suspicion and manipulation of a sometimes nostalgic Russian diaspora.

The Return of the Russian Leviathan
Sergei Medvedev. Stephen Dalziel, trans. Cambridge: Polity Press, 2019. £17.99. 286 pp.

Why did Russia, after a brief period of post-Soviet experimentation with pluralism, freedom of expression, competitive elections and cooperation with the West, return so quickly to the traditional Russia of the past – an authoritarian and nationalistic Russia in which the Kremlin uses fear to control its population while also threatening the outside world? In this wide-ranging and trenchant collection of essays reviewing Russia's last 30 years, Sergei Medvedev focuses on four drivers of the Putin regime: the war for space, the war for symbols, the war for the body and the war for memory.

Medvedev's starting point is the 2014 annexation of Crimea, when Russia ended 'the twenty-five year project of normalization and adaptation to the global world that had been going on since 1989' (p. 14). Russia has always been contemptuous of Ukrainian independence and does not consider Ukraine a state, but rather a 'lesser Russia' (p. 37). The vilification of Ukraine and its leadership, says Medvedev, is an integral part of the restoration of the traditional Russian invader-state. Yet aggression against Ukraine has been counterproductive, driving the country closer to the West.

In the twenty-first century, oil and gas have been replaced by fear as Russia's principal export: 'Putin's Russia is one of the producers and beneficiaries of [today's] Hobbesian world, in which its main resource – fear – and its main services – security measures – are in great demand' (p. 91). Russia cannot solve the world's problems, but it can make them worse.

Medvedev chronicles the rise of 'biopolitics' – the attempt by the state and its nationalist supporters to use eugenics and demography as a means of intruding into and controlling people's private lives. This includes the promotion of 'traditional family values', laws against 'homosexual propaganda', pro-natalist policies, the decriminalisation of domestic violence and the ban on Americans adopting Russian children.

According to the old Soviet adage, 'the past is always changing'. Whereas Mikhail Gorbachev and Boris Yeltsin attempted to confront the dark pages in Russia's past, historical revisionism has now returned with a vengeance. Medvedev praises both leaders: Gorbachev, he says, has 'remained a democrat to the end' (p. 188.) Yeltsin, despite his shortcomings, had two redeeming qualities: 'his ability to ask for our pardon, and his ability to leave on time' (p. 192). The current leadership, he reminds us, has neither.

Medvedev praises the Boris Yeltsin Presidential Center in Ekaterinburg, which has generated controversy because of its positive portrayal of the 1990s, a decade seen as the 'original sin' (p. 243) by the current occupants of the Kremlin. The museum presents an alternate view of post-Soviet Russia, one that is not authoritarian, imperial or Moscow-centred, but non-imperial, federal and free. This was the promise of the 1990s that ended after Putin came to power.

Why has post-Soviet Russia, unlike post-war Germany, been unable to confront its past and move on to a better future? One reason is the difficulty of comprehending the sheer horror and multitude of Stalinist repressions. But there is another reason: unlike post-war Germany, post-Soviet Russia was not occupied by foreign democracies demanding a reckoning with the past.

Ukraine and Russia: From Civilized Divorce to Uncivil War
Paul D'Anieri. Cambridge: Cambridge University Press, 2019.
£22.99/$29.99. 282 pp.

Why have Ukraine and Russia been unable to develop a workable relationship since 1991? Paul D'Anieri answers this question by examining the development of ties between Kyiv and Moscow since the Soviet collapse, and placing them in the broader context of Ukraine's and Russia's relations with the United States and the European Union. His analysis highlights how intractable the problems, which led the two countries from civilised divorce to war, really are.

The end of the Cold War, argues D'Anieri, set in motion two forces that were bound to clash: democratisation in Eastern Europe and Russia's insistence that it retain its great-power status and continue to dominate its immediate neighbourhood. Ukraine was the country where independence and a commitment to democracy most challenged Russia's definition of its national interest.

These tensions were clear even as the USSR dissolved. Yeltsin had two major motives when he met with the leaders of Ukraine and Belarus at that hunting lodge outside Minsk to dissolve the Soviet Union. He wanted to get rid of Gorbachev and the Soviet Union, but he also wanted to retain a 'centre' dominated by Russia that would control the Soviet nuclear arsenal and coordinate economic activity. Ukraine's Leonid Kravchuk, however, opposed any idea of central control.

Ukrainian–Russian relations have alternated between cooperation and antagonism since 1991, and D'Anieri links these cycles to Ukraine's domestic developments. Kyiv's failure under successive governments to undertake reforms gave Russia more leverage as the West grew increasingly sceptical about its commitment to fight corruption.

The Russian–Ukrainian energy relationship symbolises the dilemma that Kyiv faces as it confronts Moscow. Ukraine's need for Russian gas – at subsidised prices – and its role as a gas-transit corridor have perpetuated a dependence that is counterproductive to the consolidation of Ukrainian independence. Gazprom may depend on Ukraine for gas revenues, but energy remains a major source of leverage for Russia. What has been lost in the debates over the Nord Stream II pipeline is that it would be preferable for Ukraine to wean itself from dependence on Russian gas if it wants to strengthen its own sovereignty.

In discussing the events that led to Russia's annexation of Crimea in February 2014, D'Anieri suggests that Moscow may have decided to annex Crimea before Victor Yanukovych fled to Russia, and that his ouster did not cause Crimea's seizure. The operation was clearly not spontaneous, but well planned. Similarly, the launch of the conflict in the Donbas region was a product of both local separatist forces and direct Russian intervention.

D'Anieri reviews how the Ukraine crisis might be resolved, detailing the various suggestions for a 'grand bargain' in which Ukraine eschews any quest for NATO membership and accepts the loss of Crimea, in return for Russia removing its troops from Ukraine and its support for the separatists in the Donbas region. But the author is sceptical about whether Russia would be satisfied with this new status quo.

Understanding Russia: The Challenges of Transformation
Marlene Laruelle and Jean Radvanyi. Lanham, MD: Rowman & Littlefield, 2019. £24.95/$39.00. 171 pp.

In this succinct exposition of Russia's domestic developments and foreign policy, Marlene Laruelle and Jean Radvanyi de-emphasise the uniqueness of Russia's path, comparing it to the stresses of transformation that many states confront. Thirty years after the Soviet collapse, they write, 'multiple ghosts haunt both the Russian elites and the society, from concerns about demographic and economic decline to worries about the country's vulnerability to external intervention' (p. 1). In their view, Russia is a work in progress, dealing with a multitude of simultaneous challenges.

The authors reject depictions of Russia as a kleptocracy or accounts that focus on nationalist, neo-imperial ideology. Claiming that it is simplistic to characterise Russia as authoritarian, they focus on the implicit social contract between the regime and society, which, they argue, is working. In their view, Russia is more pluralistic than many outside analysts realise.

The country is still coming to terms with the territorial losses it suffered when the USSR collapsed, say the authors, and Russia's leaders have yet to reconcile themselves to their new borders. Russia's war with Georgia in 2008 and with Ukraine in 2014, its recognition of two breakaway Georgian enclaves and its annexation of Crimea make clear that it has reneged on its commitment in 1991 to respect the territorial integrity of the post-Soviet states.

The authors argue that Russia's policy in the 'near abroad' has been a failure. The Kremlin focused too much on relations with the West, neglected Russia's neighbours and assumed that ties with them were a given requiring little special effort. Hence, although the world was impressed by the peaceful break-up of the USSR, Russia's wars with Georgia and Ukraine remind us that the break-up is still in process.

Russia has yet to develop a consensus on national identity. For a large, multi-ethnic state with vast regional differences, the struggle between accepting a civic, as opposed to an ethnic, identity continues. For Putin, the reality of demographic decline, especially among Slavs, threatens the survival of the state and colours the debate about identity.

Russia's economy has proven more resilient to Western sanctions than the EU and United States initially calculated. 'Sanctions', the authors argue, 'appear to have proved the value of the Russian leaders' autarkic strategy amid a world in economic turmoil' (p. 88). Nevertheless, the Russian economy is overly dependent on exports of raw materials, and the Kremlin has not invested enough in the manufacturing sector, nor are property rights protected. Meanwhile, the country's brain drain continues.

The authors reject the premise that Russia acts as a spoiler globally. Rather, they describe it as a country trying to manage rapid change as it continues to seek a new global role and advocate for a new international order. To bring some perspective to the discussion, they remind us that Russia represents less than 2% of world GDP. It will soon face a choice between being a junior partner to the West, or to China.

Politics and International Relations
Steven Simon

Shields of the Republic: The Triumph and Peril of America's Alliances
Mira Rapp-Hooper. Cambridge, MA: Harvard University Press, 2020. £22.95/$27.95. 272 pp.

The title of this book is a distinctly unironic appropriation of Walter Lippmann's mid-Second World War classic, *Shield of the Republic*. One can't help but appreciate the self-confidence of a contemporary political scientist who self-consciously associates herself with Lippmann, the avatar of modern American foreign policy, as a kind of New Testament evangelist to his Old Testament prophet. In 1943, Lippmann had descended from Sinai holding aloft the tablets of the law, on which were inscribed:

> Without the controlling principle that the nation must maintain its objectives and its power in equilibrium, its purposes within its means and its means equal to its purposes, its commitments related to its resources and its resources adequate to its commitments, it is impossible to think at all about foreign affairs. (*Shield of the Republic*, 1943)

As the chosen people entered into battle against the communist bloc in 1948, he declared:

> One world we shall not see in our time. But what we may see, if we have the vision and the energy, is the formation of a great western community, at least a confederation of federations of European and American nations, determined to give the lie to those who say that our civilization is doomed and to give back faith and will to those who fear that freedom is perishing where it originated. (*Boston Globe*, 13 April 1948)

Mira Rapp-Hooper has taken up the cause at a moment when the value of alliances in US security strategy has come under withering attack from both the right and left. President Donald Trump has expressed contempt for the transatlantic Alliance, mocked it, accused it of theft and rejected the logic of collective security that underpins it in favour of a fee-for-service arrangement. In his case this is part of a larger pattern of distrust of the sly peasant for city slickers, combined with a deeper conviction that the world sees him as a mark. Since he does not distinguish between himself and the country he allegedly governs, he

 DOI 10.1080/00396338.2020.1792144

takes international transactions of any kind as a manoeuvre to pick his pockets and make him look like a fool. He displaces his own psychopathology onto governments whose operations are more likely to be based on interests of state and rules of the road. Rapp-Hooper does acknowledge, rather charitably, that there is a kernel of truth to Trump's view of the NATO Alliance insofar as the allies do not spend as much on defence as they really should, behaving more like free-riders. On the other side, new voices in the Washington debate about the purpose of American power in a changing world, embodied by emerging or evolving think tanks that incubate future foreign-policy officials, have called into question the utility of alliance commitments that no longer correspond to core US interests (as narrowly defined), and in the absence of existential geo-strategic threats, as against, say, climate change or pandemic waves. This debate is, in a sense, a signifier of the post-post-Cold War world. It is spearheaded by a handful of prominent established academics and a cohort of millennial activists who came of age decades after the collapse of the Berlin Wall and whose frame of reference is more 9/11 than the colossal struggles of the twentieth century.

Perhaps it is for the benefit of this cohort that Rapp-Hooper rehearses the history of the transatlantic Alliance championed in a bygone epoch by Lippmann. Her crisp, lucid account is worth reading even for those who are familiar with the US foreign policy of that era. Memories do need to be refreshed from time to time. The author argues counterfactually that the risks to the United States – and likelihood of war with the Soviet Union – would have been significantly greater in the absence of the Alliance, which she argues did not cost the US very much. She notes as well that NATO allies did not drag the US into wars, or even invoke Article V of the Washington Treaty.

Her segue from the golden age to the present is somewhat less convincing. Alliances need enemies, threat perception being the great aggregator of sovereign cooperation and commitment. Rapp-Hooper acknowledges this, at least implicitly, by characterising Russia and China as potentially hostile powers against which the US and other like-minded states must balance. The argument could be seen as circular. The new school of restraint – which should probably be registered as a trademark – is unlikely to be impressed by the author's case. For restrainers, strategic alliances constitute a slippery slope to intervention. One might argue that the states most likely to pull the US down the slope are not treaty allies, and that it would therefore be unfair to tar them with the brush of, for example, the informal US–Saudi security relationship. Regardless, those interested in the development of US foreign policy over the next decade will find this informed polemic a useful key.

Holding the Line: Inside Trump's Pentagon with Secretary Mattis
Guy M. Snodgrass. New York: Sentinel, 2019. $27.00. 352 pp.

James N. Mattis, former defense secretary and commander-in-chief of US forces in the Middle East and South Asia, dominated the news cycle in Washington recently by issuing a statement that lashed Donald Trump as unfit for office. As defense secretary, Mattis had been knowingly referred to by the president's critics as the 'adult in the room' where the president and his aides screamed and blubbered in their playpen. There was no doubt that Mattis carried himself with a dignity and seriousness of purpose that was noticeably absent from the administration. He was reported to have stymied, or at least tried to, the president's impulsive moves to undermine key alliances, exclude transgender soldiers from the military, redeploy US forces to the border with Mexico, withdraw from the multilateral nuclear agreement with Iran signed by Barack Obama in 2015, and remove US forces from northeastern Syria, where they helped largely Kurdish forces fight the Islamic State and acted as a bodyguard for Kurds threatened by Turkish aggression. Mattis was something of an outlier under Obama, whose advisers thought he was trying to box the White House into a confrontational posture toward Iran. He was in fact outspoken regarding his perception of the Iranian threat, but did not seem likely to engineer a war in the Persian Gulf.

Given his prominence and his role in legitimating criticism of a generally bulletproof but controversial president, his co-authored autobiography, *Call Sign Chaos: Learning to Lead*, published last year, had been slated for this slot among the other reviews. That book, however, is generally silent on larger policy issues and, regarding the Trump administration, deafeningly so. The book is valuable nonetheless for readers interested in the kind of military career that culminates in four-star rank. In armed forces as large as those of the United States, there are only 11 four-star generals in the US Army, nine admirals (equivalent to four-star general) in the Navy, four in the Marine Corps and 14 in the Air Force. In contrast, there are 141 lieutenant-generals, 310 major-generals and 420 brigadier-generals. Mattis was clearly one of the elect, and how he got there would be of intrinsic interest to those who study the workings of large organisations and the nature of leadership.

Fortunately, former Navy commander Guy 'Bus' Snodgrass, who spent 17 months as Mattis's chief speechwriter and communications director at the Pentagon, has written the book one wishes Mattis had. Although the account treats Mattis quite favourably, one can see why he was ultimately forced out by reading between the lines. Firstly, Trump really is a formidable character, who early on lambasted the military's top leaders for what he saw as their consistent failures on the battlefield. This frontal assault put the Pentagon in an impossible position from the very outset of the new administration. Mattis, unable at that point to shed the mentality of a career officer in favour of a cabinet secretary with considerable political capital, did not push back. Secondly, Mattis shunned alliances that could have worked in his favour, particularly with the national security advisor, Lieutenant-General H.R. McMaster, given that their views largely coincided. But the difference in their ranks made the idea of partnership unacceptable to Mattis, for whom McMaster seemed to have been regarded as a junior staffer. In Snodgrass's view, Mattis could also have made better use of the media, which was already on his side, to the point of discounting Mattis's scandalous involvement with Theranos, a fraudulent company whose products proved dangerous to users. But Mattis thought of reporters as the enemy and made it clear that they were off limits to his department. Snodgrass also observes that Mattis preferred military over civilian staff, which engendered groupthink in a way that hobbled informed decision-making. Finally, Mattis seems to have regarded Congress as an adversary as well, and passed up opportunities for collaboration that might have hemmed in the White House and produced better policy outcomes.

A State at Any Cost: The Life of David Ben-Gurion
Tom Segev. Haim Watzman, trans. New York: Farrar, Straus and Giroux, 2019. £30.00/$40.00. 816 pp.

Tom Segev, an academic with a journalist's eye for telling detail, has covered Israeli society in and around the 1967 war, and Palestine under the British Mandate. His book *One Palestine, Complete* made brilliant use of letters and diaries to convey ground truths about the evolution of the Jewish and Arab communities in Palestine during this crucial period, when the *Yishuv* – the Zionist population – consolidated its institutional dimension and Palestinian Arabs waged war against the unwilling British sponsors of Jewish immigration. The British Army crushed their resistance with indiscriminate violence. In *A State at Any Cost*, Segev examines the life of David Ben-Gurion, one of three individuals inarguably responsible for the success of the Zionist project, the other two being Theodor Herzl, the itinerant, driven journalist who gave the Zionist impulse a platform and structure in the 1880s; and Chaim Weizmann, the British chemist who leveraged his access to Britain's political leaders during the First World War to press the Zionist cause and encourage British backing in the form of the Balfour Declaration. Herzl demonstrated that ideas matter to great causes; Weizmann, that powerful allies are essential to weak clients; and Ben-Gurion, that a powerful, unscrupulous and determined politician is essential to seeing a project through, in this case in the face of armed opposition from within and without, and on behalf of a traumatised, dislocated Jewish population.

Segev's biography of Ben-Gurion is the first in a long while and makes effective use of archival material that became available in the interim. Segev himself is counted among the so-called new historians in Israeli academe who were once considered revisionists with a leftist tinge who used government archives to highlight Israeli deliberations that undermined the prevailing narrative, especially regarding official disregard for opportunities to stabilise relations with Arab states in the 1950s and, of course, Israeli operations during the war of independence that triggered the outmigration of Palestinian Arabs in 1948. As a practical matter, most Israeli historians are 'new' given the transformation of revisionism into academic conventional wisdom that tends to occur in any research field. This biography, therefore, does not so much break new ground as present Ben-Gurion as a more fully fleshed-out figure. It offers detail on his ample eccentricities and political ruthlessness, as well as on the central paradox of his career, which was that he was both the linchpin of a newly sovereign state and a reflexive outsider. And not just in life: Ben-Gurion refused to be buried alongside the other giants of Zionism on Mount Herzl in Jerusalem, preferring instead to be interred at Sde Boker, the desert kibbutz where he made his home after his ejection from Israeli politics.

Ben-Gurion was right about the big things, from a Zionist perspective, all of which are still in the headlines: the question of restraint in claiming territory as against exploiting opportunities as they arise; the imperative of great-power sponsorship; and the fact that it would take a century before Arabs would accommodate to a Jewish state. The image of the ambassador of the United Arab Emirates to the United States, Yousef Al Otaiba, addressing himself directly to an Israeli audience in 2020 as a prospective ally suggests that Ben-Gurion was prescient indeed. That a halt to annexation was Otaiba's condition for progress was equally a reminder that sometimes restraint can be useful.

How the West Stole Democracy from the Arabs: The Syrian Arab Congress of 1920 and the Destruction of Its Historic Liberal–Islamic Alliance
Elizabeth F. Thompson. New York: Atlantic Monthly Press, 2020. $30.00. 496 pp.

This detailed account of Syria's fate in the wake of the First World War is timely in several ways. Most obviously, because a century later Syria's fate remains undecided, largely owing to the intervention of outside powers pursuing their own objectives. *Plus ça change.*

Less obviously, author Elizabeth Thompson persuasively traces the familiar split between Islamism and secular authoritarianism to French colonial interference in a post-war Arab effort to create an independent state that would have accommodated both Islamists and liberals. Thompson constructs her argument systematically by providing a lively account of the wartime context. The British enlisted Hejazi Arabs in a guerrilla campaign intended to complement the main thrust of an assault launched from Egypt through Palestine to dislodge Ottoman forces and threaten Turkey from the south. To secure Arab cooperation, Britain pledged to support a post-war sovereign Arab state ruled by a Hashemite king, Faisal bin Hussein bin Ali. The general outline of ensuing events is widely understood, and Thompson's book does not challenge it. The British reneged on their promise and transferred control of Syria to the French in return for French acquiescence in British control over Palestine and northern Iraq.

The author's contribution, rather, is to reveal the extent to which the Arabs under Faisal had embraced constitutionalism, the idea of citizenship and inclusive political participation. She does this primarily through meticulous analysis of Arabic primary sources. Of particular interest is the role played by Rashid Rida as a key adviser to Faisal. Rida is well known as a public intellectual and theorist of political Islam based in Cairo, out of reach of Ottoman enemies. He probed the weakness of the Arabs in the face of Western imperialism and explored remedial actions Arabs might embrace to restore an equilibrium with European power. His hands-on involvement in the creation of a new independent state amid the wreckage of the Ottoman Empire turns out to have been vital. As an Islamist, he nonetheless worked toward what could have been a state that incorporated both Salafism and liberalism. This bold experiment was throttled by French determination to control greater Syria, Britain's calculation that its own strategic interests necessitated its support for a French imperial fantasy and the US concession to both countries' wishes. We will never know if the experiment would have succeeded; the factionalised politics at the time and the geographic scope of the notional state suggest that its prospects were poor.

Thompson focuses usefully on the American role, which initially stoked Syrian nationalist sentiment through the King–Crane Commission, an exploratory body that interviewed many Syrian intellectuals and reported sympathetically on their case for independence. But with president Woodrow Wilson's death and Washington's prioritisation of its interest in maintaining wartime ties with Britain and France, the US abandoned the nationalists it had inspired.

The Inevitability of Tragedy: Henry Kissinger and His World
Barry Gewen. New York: W. W. Norton, 2020. $30.00. 480 pp.

Every generation gets its own Henry Kissinger – Machiavellian dissembler, pre-ternaturally shrewd strategist, unscrupulous courtier and now the apostle of *Weltschmerz*. It's hard to believe that Kissinger left office in 1977 and never again served in government. There have been two recent biographies of Kissinger, both released in 2015: the first volume of Niall Ferguson's authorised account, which recounts Kissinger's life at 60-second intervals, and Greg Grandin's more conceptual assault from the progressive left. These were preceded by Walter Isaacson's 1992 account, which weighed in at 892 pages – serious avoirdupois. That work shredded Kissinger's legacy under a veneer of ambivalence and, like Ferguson's, was obsessive in its granularity. In 2007, Jeremi Suri wrote *Henry Kissinger and the American Century*, an academic study that makes up in insight what it lacks in page length. Barry Gewen, an editor for the *New York Times Book Review*, has now provided a palate cleanser in advance of Ferguson's Volume Two. The book does not recap Kissinger's life story in its 97-year span (to this point), but rather concentrates on key episodes in Kissinger's experience to capture the essence of the man and his world view.

Rather than replough these fields, Gewen's book is more of a meditation on American foreign policy, especially the perennial tension between moral values and strategic interest. Kissinger's career is a useful way of addressing the subject, since Kissinger's quasi-academic writing and his approach to foreign policy as national security advisor and secretary of state reflected on the rightful priority of these factors in decisions about matters of state. To frame his argument, Gewen situates Kissinger in the mental world of a handful of thinkers, all Jewish, who had witnessed the collapse of the Weimar Republic and the rise of Nazism. This group included Hans Morgenthau, one of the founders of foreign policy as an academic discipline; Hannah Arendt, a disciple of Martin Heidegger's before and after the war, and a distinguished philosopher in her own right who coined the controversial phrase 'banality of evil' to describe Adolf Eichmann at his trial in Jerusalem; and Leo Strauss, the political philosopher who, among other things, pointed to the dangers of relativism. Gewen also assigns a prominent role in the shaping of Kissinger's outlook to his mentor in the US Army, a German émigré named Fritz Kraemer, who had opposed National Socialism, but from the right. The implosion of the Weimar Republic engendered a bleak pessimism among the intellectuals who lived through it, a tragic view embraced by Kissinger. Gewen does not dwell in equal measure on all of the momentous issues on which Kissinger placed his stamp. There is a great deal, for example, on the overthrow of Salvador Allende in Chile, but relatively little on Kissinger's Middle East diplomacy. But you can't have it all.

Closing Argument

Notes from a Pandemic: Bologna, Rome, Nanjing, Vienna and San Jose

Emma Mika Riley, Christopher Olivares, Laura Rong, Niklas Hintermayer and Zoe Mize

I

Emma Mika Riley

18 March, Bologna to Rome

Two weeks ago, Bologna had only two confirmed cases of coronavirus. Now there are over 100,000 cases nationwide, the second-largest number of cases in the world, and the largest number of deaths. In the second week of March, 20 fellow students who didn't evacuate to their home countries were arrested during a birthday party because groups of more than six people had been made illegal. Since then, almost every night has brought a new decree from the Italian government imposing harsher restrictions. In the first wave, all schools were closed. Then concert halls, church services, museums and sports stadiums. Finally, the entire country was put under lockdown. I could not leave the house without proper documentation unless I was going to the grocery store or pharmacy. The medieval city I called home was unrecognisable.

This is not Italy's first plague, of course. In the *proemio* (prologue) of *The Decameron*, completed in 1353, Giovanni Boccaccio portrayed a society ravaged by a disease so terrible that people responded in unpredictable ways:

The authors are graduate students at Johns Hopkins University's School of Advanced International Studies (SAIS Europe) in Bologna, Italy.

Survival | vol. 62 no. 4 | August–September 2020 | pp. 245–260   DOI 10.1080/00396338.2020.1792145

> Then some there were who thought that a sober way of life was a good
> method of avoiding infection. So they gathered into groups and kept
> clear of everyone else, shutting themselves up in houses where no one
> was sick and where they could live comfortably, consuming choice food
> and wine in moderation, avoiding all excess, not speaking to anyone
> outside or hearing any news of the dead or sick, but enjoying music and
> what other pleasures they could muster. Others, drawn into a contrary
> opinion, declared that heavy drinking, pleasure-seeking, and going
> round singing and enjoying themselves, gratifying every urge and
> making mock of what was going on was the best medicine for such a
> serious disease.

As the events of the past weeks unfolded and the Associated Press alerts
on my phone became more frequent, I witnessed both of these reactions.
The Decameron as a whole, however, is not a book about the plague or
society's reaction to a rampant infectious disease. It is a collection of 100
stories told over the course of ten days by a *brigata* of ten narrators united
by friendship: seven women and three men who fled the plague with their
servants to the Florentine hills. The scene Boccaccio presents in the *proemio*
of survivors who 'took a single and very inhuman precaution, namely to
avoid or run away from the sick', is at odds with the common theme of
pity and friendship woven into the 100 stories they tell each other.

In 2020 too, there are conflicting stories ranging from the cavalier to the
panicked as both ideas and the disease spread around the world. As cases
increase, the laws change and the narrative shifts. This sequence repeats
itself in stages within different countries. In a time of crisis, it's important
to tell the right stories.

Initially, European leaders of the far right blamed migrants for the
spread of coronavirus. Fortunately, this wasn't a convincing story. Public-
health officials were not much more persuasive in claiming that a global
crisis required a global solution and cooperation to find a vaccine, or at
least an agreement to all wash our hands more frequently. At first, scientists
warned that the panic going viral online was a bigger threat than the actual
virus. As cases multiply, however, the virus itself feels pretty scary.

The same day as the lockdown in Italy and the day before the World Health Organization (WHO) officially declared a pandemic, the United States was telling a different story. President Donald Trump tweeted: 'The Fake News Media and their partner, the Democrat Party, is doing everything within its semi-considerable power … to inflame the CoronaVirus situation.' Within two weeks, even public-health experts were caught by surprise, as an increasingly fatal disease overwhelmed countries' health-care systems.

Now Italy is suffering for not acting sooner. This grave error is not lost on the Italians who have used their time in isolation to create YouTube videos talking to themselves of ten days past, warning of the disaster that is yet to come for other countries that make the same mistakes. Other countries have started to adopt stricter regulations. I watch the progression of stories cascade from denial to urgency through strings of tweets and hackneyed memes of the soaring cost of hand sanitiser and toilet-paper shortages on my social-media pages. Most conversations now are competitions over who was inconvenienced more by the pandemic. Yet, the medical workers in New York City know very well the true horrors of trying to treat an uncontainable disease with dwindling supplies.

Boccaccio wasn't too concerned about telling the truth in his stories. Instead, his stories were for the amusement of medieval women who

> restricted by the wishes, whim, and commands of fathers, mothers, brothers, and husbands remain … most of the time limited to the narrow confines of their bedrooms, where they sit in apparent idleness, now wishing one thing and now wishing another, turning over in their minds a number of thoughts.

I now appreciate this sentiment. The police stand outside on every corner of Piazza Maggiore. They are polite, but they are omnipresent. The only traffic on the streets is a truck that circles the neighbourhood with the megaphoned command of 'stai a casa' (stay at home).

One night, my friend Sam and I made an elaborate plan to see each other. We would meet in one of the pharmacy lines that snaked between the columns of the porticoes to stand two metres apart and wave to each other. We would carry a grocery item or medicine in our tote bags for the walk in case the police asked where we were going. Finally, despite our desperation, even this seemed too risky and we stayed home. I capitulated to the reality that Boccaccio described, where the only solace I found during a time of social isolation was in a good story.

Many of the 100 stories that make up *The Decameron* are funny, moralistic or scandalous, and almost all are about a time before an invisible disease devastated the narrators' worlds. Now the stories I sought as a distraction from reality featured characters living in a world that I already missed, in which people met at bars, went to concerts and studied at school. That world existed just a few weeks ago.

Frantic texts from Sam shattered the temporary comfort I felt from my stories. His messages alerted me about the US State Department advisory to return to the US or 'prepare to shelter in place indefinitely'. I was already resolved to stay, but the word 'indefinitely' was unsettling.

Within 12 hours, on the 13th day of quarantine, I had packed all of my belongings and stuffed them into a rental car, with Sam driving down an empty highway under a grey sky towards Rome's Leonardo Da Vinci–Fiumicino – the last operating airport in Italy. We joked about the absurdity of the situation and the resemblance of the outside world to a scene from *Zombieland* to mask our overwhelming sadness. There was a long silence. I concentrated on not being crushed by a wall of suitcases. 'You know', said Sam, 'I've never been to Rome before'.

II

Christopher Olivares
15 April, Bologna

As home confinement has gone from days to weeks, a broad sweep of commentary foretells 'rebirth' in any number of areas – market capitalism, attitudes about climate change, national security. With so many predictions of a paradigm shift, this coronavirus moment has the feeling of moving from one world to another. I fear what this will mean for education, one of the few traditions of human society that cuts across time and cultures.

The transition from campus to Zoom hasn't prevented me from watching other people's reactions to the professor. Direct messaging has replaced whispering to a neighbour. But what I have missed is the ability to find someone after class, invite them for a beer and let what we have learned filter into our daily conversations that try to make sense of the world around us. I have taken to calling people on the phone after class, grasping for a way to replace the bar-shaped hole in what remains of my graduate-school experience. As I resign myself to what might be a lost semester, I'm encouraged that I will be able to advocate against the expansion of online education from a first-person perspective.

There will be a post-coronavirus world. My fear is what that world will be. I can't help but think of Ray Bradbury's 'All Summer in a Day'. Margot, an Earth-born child moved to Venus at age four, swaps sun for sunlamps, as I have replaced being outside with the sunlit window in the room of my repatriated Spanish flatmate. I long for the world where I was able to leave my house. Like the children in the story, we are all faced with doubt and a lack of information. All the children except Margot can only speculate how sunshine feels when it emerges from the clouds once every seven years. Like them, we can only imagine what 'normal' will emerge when this crisis is over.

III

Laura Rong

27 April, Bologna to Nanjing

From late January to mid-March, I had trouble sleeping. At the beginning of the year, I was worried about my parents in China. A month later, the virus reached Italy. For two months, I have been reading news articles, interviews and diaries written by people in this pandemic.

One of these people was Chinese writer Fang Fang, who documented her experience of living in Wuhan from late January to early March in a book, *Wuhan Diary*, about to be published in the United States and in Germany. Fang Fang wrote in Chinese about her daily life in Wuhan using simple language reflecting how normal people endured the crisis. Reading her diary, I realised how isolated and helpless Wuhan was in late January. So when Italian Prime Minister Giuseppe Conte announced the first 11 towns under lockdown in Lombardy, I was heartbroken to see Italy on its way to becoming a second Wuhan.

According to Fang Fang's diary, from late January to February there was a shortage of medical supplies for everyone in Wuhan. Ordinary people were forced to live at home without masks. Since mail and food deliveries were halted or seriously delayed, Wuhan's inhabitants had to survive on their storage for the Chinese New Year, during which Chinese people normally prepare a great amount of food for family gatherings. This year, it became essential for survival. Meanwhile, doctors and nurses staffing intensive-care units (ICUs) were exhausted and running out of medical supplies. The situation improved only after China constructed two large ICU hospitals in early February, and transformed stadiums and conference centres into temporary isolation locations for people who couldn't quarantine at home in February. By late January, however, many had already died.

Fang Fang wrote about her experience as a middle-class woman who did not have to worry about life under the lockdown. In contrast, other diaries, interviews and online posts expressed the desperation of people who lost their businesses or risked their lives.

Many doctors were on the verge of mental breakdown. 'I was giving water to a patient and she said the water is too hot, so she'll drink later. Then she died', said a doctor in Wuhan. 'I wanted to do things for them yet there was so little I could do to save their lives.' More than 10,000 kilometres away, a doctor in Milan said something similar.

Tragedy often resonates beyond the boundaries of time, and evokes shared empathy across different historical periods. As the first country to experience the virus, China had a difficult period controlling it. Wuhan and other cities in China are re-emerging with shared traumatic memories that will become part of the Chinese identity. The same will apply to Italians, Brits and Americans. The world will be different after COVID-19 because of their memories.

There were also diaries and audio recordings of people who continued to work during the lockdown. 'I am afraid of the virus, but I had to survive', said a delivery man in February. Working for one of the biggest delivery platforms in China, he barely makes ends meet during normal times. At the time of the crisis, he risked his life by delivering food to hospitals in Wuhan. 'Hospitals are the last place healthy people would want to visit right now, but if I don't go, doctors at the front line will starve.' Another delivery man helped carry a patient to the nearby hospital with his e-bike. The patient was diagnosed with coronavirus later that day. 'Even if it is a job for survival, at least I could do something for the city.'

There were also people who had to shut down their businesses. While I was complaining about not being able to go out with my friends anymore, musicians and bars in Wuhan were declaring bankruptcy. Wuhan is an important music city in central China, famous for its Strawberry Music Festival every spring. Many artists who perform in music festivals and bars have lost their main source of income. Thousands of people live-streamed the virtual Strawberry Music Festival in late February to support Wuhan's artists.

8 April 2020 was a day of deliverance for Wuhan. The number of existing cases in the city declined to fewer than 100, and the city decided to finally reopen airports and train stations. In January, many people had travelled to Wuhan from other places in China. When the lockdown started, some of them rushed to catch the last train or last flight to leave the city, but most were stranded in the epicentre, unable to return home. Now, after three months, they were finally able to go home. On 8 April, the owner of a hot-dry noodle shop was interviewed by China Central Television (CCTV). Like pasta for Italians, hot-dry noodles play an essential part in the lives of Wuhan people, who eat them for breakfast every morning in local restaurants. 'After closing down our restaurant and surviving on limited food for more than 70 days, I woke up at 3am to cook the noodles and prepare for the day.' In the early morning, people were already lining up outside her shop, waiting for their first bowl of hot-dry noodles since late January. As the first customer received his noodles, the streets became busy again. A taxi driver posted on social media about his experience of going back to work. 'Normally I hate the traffic in Wuhan, but when I was stuck in a traffic jam for the first time in 3 months this morning, I cried.' With the number of new cases declining in Italy, I am expecting people in Milan to have their first espresso under the Mediterranean sunlight again.

As China gained control of the outbreak in March, the battle was just beginning in Italy, Iran and South Korea. As the country with the largest number of citizens residing overseas, China has faced pressure from abroad. Thousands of Chinese citizens returned to China, and many brought the virus back. In retrospect, the country appeared to effectively manage the coronavirus because of its stringent quarantine policy, effective allocation of resources and funding for the construction of hospitals to save its healthcare system from collapsing. Without these measures, many places in China would have suffered the same fate as Wuhan. China could not afford another round of nationwide outbreaks.

In response to the growing cases from overseas, China has taken stringent measures to control the influx of people and has suspended regular visas for foreigners. These measures have proven effective. When I returned to China in mid-March, the Chinese government had listed more than 20 countries as 'red-zone' countries. In Frankfurt Airport, Air China measured the temperature of every passenger five times to make sure no one had a fever before they boarded the flight. Those who had a temperature higher than normal were left in the airport, unable to go home until their temperature went down. After I landed in Beijing, people in thick protective gear transferred me to a hotel in my hometown where I was quarantined for 14 days. A few days after I returned home, new rules came into effect. People from abroad were temporarily prevented from returning to their home cities: all had to quarantine in the city where their flights landed to avoid infecting others on domestic flights or trains. Several days ago, some provinces in China announced that they had decided to extend quarantine policy to 28 days for people from abroad – four times the length of the American quarantine. I was lucky to be able to purchase a ticket to go back in March. However, a few days after I ended my quarantine, China decided to cut the frequency of incoming international flights from daily to weekly. The high cost of tickets and long periods of quarantine barred many Chinese students from returning home. As European countries gradually slow the spread of the virus, some companies are resuming flights to and from China. As of early July, the European Union had been negotiating with China to lift their mutual travel ban, but tickets for international flights were still expensive.

Dedicated doctors, nurses and ordinary people who continue to work during the lockdown have enabled China to manage its coronavirus outbreak effectively. With stringent quarantine policies and technology to track everyone's travel history, China has controlled the regional spread of COVID-19 around Beijing and is gradually emerging from the pandemic. The cost has been high, but probably worth it.

IV

Niklas Hintermayer

28 April, Bologna to Vienna

There was great surprise and some ridicule in the media when Sebastian Kurz, at the age of 24, was appointed the new Austrian People's Party (ÖVP) integration state secretary in 2011. The press quickly rendered its judgement: too young, too inexperienced and perhaps too arrogant to take on the difficult matter of integration. What qualified Kurz, who until then had only been a member of the Wiener Landtag (the Vienna state parliament) and federal chairman of the Young ÖVP (the party's youth organisation)? In the latter position, he had attracted attention with some embarrassing remarks, touring Vienna with the slogan 'Schwarz macht geil' (black makes you horny) in a black SUV called 'Geilomobil'. (Black is the conservative People's Party colour, in distinction to the Social Democratic Party's red.) But Kurz was convinced from the start that he was up to the task. By 2017, Kurz was the youngest chancellor in Austrian history.

On 25 February, the first two coronavirus cases in Austria emerged: two Italians working in Tyrol. Two days later, three cases of coronavirus infection were reported in Vienna. On 5 March, Tyrolean authorities were informed that 14 Icelanders had tested positive for coronavirus after returning home from the ski resort of Ischgl. On 7 March, a German bartender at the après-ski bar Kitzloch (where the Icelanders had been drinking) also tested positive. The bar was not closed until 9 March. 'A transmission of the Corona virus to guests of the bar is rather unlikely from a medical point of view', the provincial sanitary directorate announced on 8 March. The Tyrolean authorities reacted too late: thousands of infected ski tourists took the coronavirus home with them.

The first major restrictions on public life in Austria occurred on 10 March, 12 days ahead of Germany. Indoor events of over 100 people and outdoor events of over 500 people were prohibited, and universities were closed. The federal government was asking the population to reduce social contacts to a minimum and to observe hygiene regulations. Schools would also close a few days thereafter. Entering and leaving Austria was prohibited in principle.

I returned home on 15 March from Bologna via Munich to Vienna. The last days in Bologna were emotional: little by little bars and restaurants closed, there were fewer people on the streets, even during the day, and soon the parks closed. One had the feeling that the city's cultural core was breaking away. In Vienna, I spent a fortnight in quarantine. But I quickly felt that even though officially the measures did not differ substantially from those of Italy, the situation here was different. Since 15 March, Austrian residents have been allowed to leave their homes only to go to work, buy food, help other people or go for a walk – all with a minimum distance of one metre. In mid-March, some people were also jogging during the day along the Danube Canal or enjoying the first rays of sunshine, even in pairs. The streets were by no means completely empty. This was not disobedience or defiance. In a city of millions, social contacts are simply difficult to prevent, even outdoors. I heard more and more voices saying that Austria had the matter well in hand: 'The Federal Chancellor is doing quite well.' At that time, Austria had 800 infections and one death. 'We are aware that these are massive restrictions', Kurz explained, 'but they are necessary to defend the health of the Austrian population, to starve Covid-19 and to protect especially the older generation in our country'.

On 16 March, Chancellor Kurz said that only professional work that could not be postponed, urgent errands and helping other people were reasons to leave home. Everyone who could work from home should do so. Since then, Kurz has repeated himself like a prayer wheel: he thanked the Austrian population for their help, saying that together, as 'Team Austria', we would overcome the crisis, that the whole thing was a way to a 'new normality'.

I am not a supporter of his politics at all, but I have to concede that Kurz has not managed things badly at the peak of the coronavirus crisis.

He does what he does best: standing confidently in front of the camera, in a perfectly fitting suit, and answering press questions with deft rhetorical flourish. That, for now, is most of what is needed to make a good impression on a frightened population.

V

Zoe Mize

22 May, Bologna to San Jose

I was a graduate student in Bologna when Italy announced the lockdown of a handful of its northern cities. Then, overnight, nearly all of the north, including part of Emilia-Romagna, was placed under a red-zone travel ban. Two friends and I were on a weekend getaway at a Tuscan farmhouse while we prepared for an economics final, and I worried about returning to Bologna. A 70-minute delay on our first train to Florence felt portentous, though my friends and I were able to sit in adjoining seats, next to strangers, even. We stopped for sandwiches near the Uffizi Gallery, where an employee patrolled the line, ensuring sufficient distance between groups. The man making my sandwich wore sky-blue gloves, and no mask.

Too many had fled the northern regions, as it turned out, packing midnight trains headed towards houses in the south, and Prime Minister Conte announced only two days later that the entirety of the country would now fall under the *zona protetta*, the protected zone. At first restaurants stayed open and police only patrolled after six in the evening. My roommate and I celebrated her birthday by lunching in a park and getting gelato at Cremeria Santo Stefano. Only two patrons were allowed in the gelateria at a time. As we left, we must have lingered too long by the case of gelato cakes and were promptly scolded by a woman whose curses were muffled by her N95 mask. After the restaurants closed, I found myself thinking of her black eyes squinting above the fabric.

A day or two later, I joined my friends in the local park for a run. We ran in opposite directions to avoid any accusation of group exercise. Individuals lay scattered, sunbathing in the grass, and I wondered idly about tan lines from their masks. Some wore athletic wear like a disguise, a costume conveying purpose. I did three laps on the outermost path, one mile each, and promised myself six for tomorrow. At 9:30 that night, Bologna's mayor announced that all parks would now be closed.

I still ran, but I now paced back and forth on the outer ring road where the ancient walls once stood to insulate central Bologna from the surrounding countryside. Others walked and ran and biked, all of us avoiding eye contact in passing. I carried a piece of paper in the waistline of my shorts, the auto-certification form vowing to the *carabinieri* that I had a reason to be outdoors; I was not sure exercise would count as a necessity but it felt very necessary to me. Bells usually tolled at noon on Sundays, and hearing them as I lapped Porta San Mamolo, I knew they sounded over empty chapels. By midweek they rang daily for the dead.

When the first ten Italian cities had gone under lockdown, only 150 cases had been confirmed. Not two weeks later, twice as many were dying per day. I refreshed and refreshed Johns Hopkins University's COVID-19 map, watching the tally of infected tick upwards with each click. I read that the ill were spirited away to hospitals, where they often died alone, isolated from their families in an effort to spare lives, and to save precious space in hospitals and in mortuaries, and in the ever-expanding pages of local obituaries. Overwhelmed doctors were beginning to face impossible decisions over which lives could be most conceivably saved, while elsewhere bodies awaited collection by funeral parlours well over their capacity. And the bells rang daily.

My roommate and I were asked to pack up a friend's apartment. She lived on the floor below us and left with only a duffel bag, six days before the *zona protetta* swallowed Bologna. We rolled her clothing, sorted her non-essential medications, took down her decorations and filled two large suitcases, leaving them propped against a wall for whenever she'd be able to arrange shipping. She told us to take all her food, so we did. I felt like a looter. We had so many bags of rice and pasta that we created a stockpile in an absent roommate's bedroom.

After another week, outdoor exercise became the target of new restrictions. No movement outside one's neighbourhood. But I had no neighbourhood. I had one block of houses and shops linked by portico. I was still determined to stay, to measure my block in laps if I must. I pre-empted my family's concerns about the situation by sending a 1,000-word email to my grandparents explaining that I felt safe in Italy, secure that any mitigating effect on the virus's spread was worth the restrictions to my own liberties. 'This is a bold and honourable attempt on the part of the government to save Italy and to save other countries from further contamination', I wrote.

Then the US State Department released an advisory recommending that Americans abroad either return immediately or prepare to shelter in place for 'an indefinite period'. Indefinite is a scary word. Italian quarantine, on the other hand, was measurable and had an end date: 3 April – or at least a point at which the measures might be re-evaluated. I had assumed that if the quarantine ended, if the pandemic should improve in any way, I might be able to return home. I also realised that I had been operating on a rather silly assumption: if the situation did not improve, or if it got much worse, perhaps persisting beyond the end of my school term, US authorities would come collect me. Now I knew they would not.

My roommate was the first to sound the alarm to leave. She asked me to come with her, and I told her we should wait. I was adjusting to life in quarantine under a government that had itself adjusted – I knew the rules, the expectations, the boundaries because little else by then could feasibly change or be taken away. To travel to the US would throw me back into a situation deeply and discomfitingly unknowable. Few lockdowns had been imposed, few attempts made to limit the spread of the virus. While I spent my spring break within the confines of my small Italian apartment, my sister spent hers travelling to Nashville from Seattle, where she hopped between friends' houses before returning to our home in San Jose. The US seemed dangerous; if I did not fall ill in Italy, I most certainly would in the US.

But then another friend called to tell me she wanted out. And then another. So I joined them, not wanting to be left indefinitely alone. We called airlines to ensure flights were running, and were given vexing answers; flight cancellations were now the standard. I rang the embassy and was redirected to a call centre, where a warm and anonymous voice assured me only that it was not the government dictating cancellations. She advised we book a flight but plan to stay put. Angry, I hung up and bought us six tickets for that Sunday out of Rome.

We booked rental cars, afraid of exposure on the train. After taking the last automatic transmission car from the rental agency at the train station, we drove to Bologna airport to hunt down one more. As we waited for the Hertz attendant to process my friend's passport, a new-wave soundscape played for an arrivals lobby empty except for the six of us and a person buried deep in a sleeping bag propped against the opposite wall. I glanced at the departures board and saw only two flights, both to Rome, both cancelled.

On Sunday morning, we drove to Rome buried in luggage piled high enough to block my rear-view mirror. I could only look forward onto the vacant highway, naked under the grey sky. Unfamiliar with the metric system, and with no other cars against which to match my speed, I drove too slowly. All external sound seemed to melt right into the blacktop, leaving the road quiet and our words hanging thick in the car. We imbued fresh and painful meaning into our last meals, last espressos, last trips to the corner store.

We stopped once, at a roadside rest area, and again at a gas station 20 minutes from the airport. The map guided us through a strip mall, which we agreed felt not only empty but also abandoned, apocalyptic. As I stood alone on the gas station's concrete forecourt, I found myself surprised that the diesel flowed readily from the pump. The world was not ending.

At the airport, the six of us checked in our baggage and handed over auto-certification forms to the masked guards, promising with our shaky signatures that we were heading home, out of Italy. Maybe there were other flights that day, other passengers waiting at other gates, but I remember now only the sensation of gliding over white flooring past the hollow black of darkened storefronts to our own gate in the farthest corner, where we queued a metre apart, not yet convinced that we were allowed to leave.

But we were. As I sat on the plane waiting to taxi, I hoped for another moment of relief. Instead, during the pre-flight safety demonstration, I worried that passengers would neglect or not be allowed to remove their surgical masks should oxygen from the drop-down masks in the overhead compartment be required in an emergency. Crises could compound.

We stayed one night in a New York hotel and left early the next morning for two weeks in Chicago. My friend's parents were vacating their apartment for three of us to self-isolate, the recommendation for all those travelling from Italy. By the time we arrived at O'Hare, we were again advised to self-isolate, as New York City was now considered by nervous governors to be a 'hot zone' for the virus. Yet a customs agent there had laughed at my friend for wearing latex gloves. In the apartment, we Lysol-wiped our luggage and stripped our travel clothes off to wash.

My friends and I took our temperatures daily on the advice of the WHO, and we recorded the fluctuations using a pink ballpoint pen and a handcrafted chart. We had groceries delivered by persons instructed to leave them at the door and wore masks to do our laundry. Our lives in Chicago were not as restricted as they were in Italy, and we were relieved. I could run again, and I did. I wore gloves and often ran in the grass rather than share the narrow footpaths of Legion Park. I was the infected now, or might be. I feared for the unmasked neighbour who tried to introduce me to her boxer, Porkchop, as she headed to the park, but I was angry when I had to run in the street to avoid three elderly men chatting on the sidewalk. An emergency alert on my phone during my first few days in Chicago informed me that Mayor Lori Lightfoot had closed all lakefront parks and greenways to encourage social distancing. But on the way to the airport from my friend's apartment, the same day President Trump proposed that Americans might be able to gather for Easter services, I saw pedestrians and runners crawling through the parks.

Now I am settled into my third quarantine, in San Jose. There are no bells that toll while I run through our neighbourhood. Snails crawl across the sidewalks on cloudy days, and I run in the empty roads so I might not crush them. I jaywalk six-lane avenues with two-minute walk timers and admire the hills peering over the Santa Clara Valley; my last visit home, they were brown with summer, but are now a vibrant green.

California began its own shelter-in-place order within days of the extension of Italy's *zona protetta*, and as other states were only beginning to contemplate similar measures. The result has been a slowing of the contagion, a promotion of California from its status as the early US epicentre. While I shelter here, I've spoken to a handful of friends who chose to stay behind in Bologna, and who remain hopeful that our school building will reopen, that access to the library, the study lounge, the cafe will be restored by the close of term in May. 3 April has come and gone, and Italy has extended its quarantine for at least another month, though with some easing of restrictions. Italy's outbreak has faded from the front pages of the newspapers here as the infection rate steadily declines.

The US has found no consensus on the length of shelter-in-place orders; the longest is Virginia's, expiring 10 June. Eight states, meanwhile, have refused any type of stay-at-home order, and President Trump has commended their strategies of ignorance as models for launching the rest of the nation back into the workforce. News sites now publish articles on the phased reopening of states such as Tennessee alongside reports of record-breaking daily death tolls. The number of infected continues to balloon despite a national shortage of tests; my family debates over dinner whether the death rate can be considered accurate when patients are most often tested from their deathbeds.

I am here, now, and intend to be for an indefinite time, a concept I am coming to accept. My family has developed our own hobbies, our means of building a tiny future within the confines of our quarantine. Every morning my father plays Animal Crossing, the game recently popular for its soothing qualities; I glance up from my morning crossword to see his avatar catch fish or plant a peach tree. My mother has taken to feeding the crows in our neighbourhood with peanuts hoarded in her jacket pockets. (I've found unshelled peanuts in the washing machine, the dog's bowl, the couch cushions.) The birds have come to anticipate her daily walk by flocking ominously outside our house. I sit in our garden and hear my sister practising scales on the piano. Waiting here, I have learned to temper my optimism, to lean into the endlessness, to not predict.